Respectable Mothers, Tough Men and Good Daughters:
Producing persons in Manenberg township South Africa

Elaine R. Salo

Langaa Research & Publishing CIG
Mankon, Bamenda

Publisher:
Langaa RPCIG
Langaa Research & Publishing Common Initiative Group
P.O. Box 902 Mankon
Bamenda
North West Region
Cameroon
Langaagrp@gmail.com
www.langaa-rpcig.net

Distributed in and outside N. America by African Books Collective
orders@africanbookscollective.com
www.africanbookscollective.com

ISBN-10: 9956-550-26-4

ISBN-13: 978-9956-550-26-5

Praise for Elain Salo and for this Book

'To say that Elaine Salo's *Respectable Mothers, Tough Men and Good Daughters* has been long-awaited is to signal both its importance and the conditions of its writing. Published posthumously, Salo's book puts in print the culmination of a lifelong commitment to a profoundly intersectional black feminist praxis and the most ethical conduct in the writing of other people's lives: in theorizing the processes of the making of persons and in the recognition of the constraints as well as the freedoms afforded people for self-authorship in the time of postapartheid. *Respectable Mothers, Tough Men and Good Daughters* is not only long-awaited for the way it compels anthropology to rethink its method as theory and theory as ethics, but in the ways in which that very practice of living fieldwork—"in which the field is home"—defines Salo's work not only on the printed page, but in a decades-long commitment to mentorship, care, and advocacy of "Others" that has reshaped the discipline. Such commitments emerge very clearly in the pages of this ethnography, which at one level simply describes the often brutal lives of women, men, and children living in Manenberg, Cape Town; and on the other, meticulously outlines the contradictions of their proximity to violence, dignity, and respectability.'

Anne-Maria Makhulu, Duke University, USA

'If I was asked to use one word to describe Salo's intersectional portrayal of personhood, alienation and hope in Rio Street, Manenberg it would be, compassionate. Through an intimate understanding of men and women, young and old, living in Rio Street, Salo coaxes the reader into her ethnographic account of deprivation, loss, creativity and respectability. The first to use the lens of respectability (*ordentlikheid*) in South African anthropology, she introduces us to the minutiae of quotidian life for those who self-define as unemployed and/or working class coloured men and women. Robbed of the identities vested in locality or place, Manenberg residents are compelled to create new forms of belonging and social networks when they are forcibly removed from their homes during apartheid, to a barren, windswept outpost. These networks, organized and led by older women (*moeders*), are invested with communal power to 'make persons'; to make those who were normally invisible to the apartheid state, and arguably continue to be invisible to the current democratic South African government, visible. Detailing the moral economy created by the *moeders* Salo weaves locality, personhood (identity), respectability politics, hegemonic masculinity and intersectionality into an evocative text that resonates with authenticity and lucidity. In Salo we had a compassionate, endearing, and humane feminist anthropologist whose keen intellect and gift for story-telling are on show here.'

Joy Owen, University of the Free State, South Africa

'Elaine Salo's compelling case study of Manenberg township in Cape Town brings to life the residents of Rio Street in the 1990s, examining how they negotiated the multiple systems of inequality – defined by gender, race, age, class, and history – that shaped their daily lives and social practice. Her subtle analysis shows how changing South African social policies created the economic and spatial environments in which Manenberg residents live and how residents have formulated notions of community, morality, and identity within those environments. Salo shows how differentiated notions of personhood are formed through daily interactions, social relations, and decisions made in real life contexts and constraints, and how mothers, men, and young women understand and shape their life opportunities through concepts of respectability, motherhood, toughness, and sexuality. Salo's powerful analysis of personhood in Manenberg is important and long overdue -- *Respectable Mothers, Tough Men and Good Daughters* will be a highly influential book.'

Corinne Kratz, Emory University, USA

Table of Contents

Acknowledgements ix

Preface x

Sophie Oldfield, African Centre for Cities,
University of Cape Town x
Desiree Lewis, Women and Gender Studies,
University of the Western Cape xiii

Chapter 1: Manenberg - An In-between
Place with In-between People 1

A. Introduction.. 1
B. Autobiography and the research context:
On being the "native" anthropologist................................. 7
C. Negotiating access to Manenberg.................................. 11
D. Learning about mothering in Manenberg 13
E. Theoretical debates about structure
and agency in contemporary anthropology........................ 15
F. Power, agency and structure....................................... 15
G. Personhood, agency and power.................................... 18
H. Personhood and agency in the
context of a South African township 25

Chapter 2: Making Race,
Making Space: Locating Coloureds
in South African History and Urban Planning............ 31

A. Discourse and debate about race on the margins 32
B. Coloured in relation to which other?
Depends on where you're coming from 39
C. Segregation and apartheid –
the makings of the racially exclusive nation..................... 45
D. Unifying white identity –
the era of segregation 46
E. Making nations: apartheid's
imagined communities 53
F. Racial stratification and urban space

in Cape Town, 1800s – 1980s..57

G. Manenberg and the racial ideology
of apartheid after 1950...60

Chapter 3: Clearing the Wilderness: Defining Identity from Within 65

A. Coming to Manenberg: erased histories
and displaced persons 71

B. The loss of personhood and identity............................79

C. Peopling Manenberg: Stories of arrival........................82

D. Clearing the social and natural wilderness:
Defining colouredness in the new place 85

E. Defining identity from within local spaces:
A view from the periphery within....................................93

F. Thirty years after the move: The economic
and cultural aspects of identity.......................................96

G. The economic capital of local identity.........................97

H. The spatial and temporal capital of identity:
defining local communities 100

Chapter 4: Making Mothers, Producing Persons: The Gendered Ideology of Orality and Space in the Local Community... 111

A. Gendering housing and welfare access,
gendering household formation 112

B. Making *moeders:* A daughter's rite of
passage into adult womanhood 119

C. Policing the moral career:
Maintaining respectable mothers 128

D. *Ordentlikheid:* the ideological
scaffolding of the moral economy.....................................139

E. Graciousness under fire: Stoic mothers
encounter the state 144

F. The masks of respectability:
Managing the suffering from within..................................147

G. Judging and mothering persons

in the community 150

H. Conclusion 158

Chapter 5: *Mans is ma soe*: Men, *Moeders* and Ideologies of Masculinity 161

A. Strong Bones: Making a coloured man 162

B. Teaching Toughness: preparing boys
for manhood 168

C. Becoming men through the *moeders* 170

D. Gendering boundaries, gendering persons:
lesson in defining community 171

E. Making *'n Ou*: Gangs' rites of passage 178

F. *Ouens en Skollies*: Respectable men and thugs 183

G. Claiming women, making fathers 193

H. Conclusion 209

Chapter 6: Good Daughters: Incorporating young women into respectable personhood 211

A. Good daughters: Incorporating adolescent
women into *ordentlikheid* 213

B. Respectable adolescent women in time and place 216

C. Becoming a working woman 223

D. Beyond the errand run and behind
closed doors: Agency through the values
and practices of respectability 232

E. *Onnosel en onbeskof*: Young rebels
challenging the boundaries of *ordentlikhied* 236

F. Conclusion 241

Chapter 7: Taxi queens and glamorous gangsters: Emerging changes in Rio Street 245

A. Taxi queens and glamorous gangsters:
Emerging changes in Rio Street 245

B. Unravelling the economic scaffolding
of local personhood 249

C. Television programmes:
Remaking race, remaking the nation 251

D. Imagining the new femininity 257

E. Reconfiguring the masculine meanings
of space in the local context 261

F. Conclusion.. 263

Bibliography 275

Epilogue: A Tribute: Elaine
Rosa Salo (1962-2016) 283

Kelly Gillespie, Department of Anthropology and Sociology,
University of the Western Cape

Acknowledgements

This book is published in memory of Elaine Rosa Salo.

It is dedicated to Jessica Salo and Miles Miller, who live Elaine's legacy in so many beautiful ways, and to the women and men of Manenberg, who inspired Elaine's life with wisdom and humour.

Thank you to Colin Miller, Elaine's partner, for his love and dedication and for his commitment, along with Elaine's brothers, Ken and Bertram Salo, and sister-in-law Faranak Miraftab, to ensure the posthumous publication of this book.

This book is based on Elaine's doctoral thesis, completed in the Department of Anthropology at Emory University in the USA. Thank you to Corinne Kratz for her supportive, rigorous and always caring advising and to Ivan Karp, Randy Packard and Don Donham, members of Elaine's dissertation committee. Thank you as well to the Department of Anthropology at Emory University for their financial support towards the editing of the book.

The publication of *Respectable Mothers, Tough Men, and Good Daughters* is the product of many caring hands. Thanks in particular to Zaide Harneker, who carefully read and copy-edited every word; to Francis Nyamnjoh, who wholeheartedly encouraged its publication and helped broker a relationship with Langaa Press; to Sophie Oldfield, who edited and helped shepard the manuscript to publication; to Desiree Lewis and Kelly Gillespie whose insights in the preface and epilogue, respectively, reflect in such meaningful ways on Elaine's words, work and worlds. Thank you too to Koni Benson, Kelly Gillespie, Al Kagen, Corinne Kratz, Anne-Maria Makhulu, Francis Nyamnjoh and Joy Owen, dear colleagues and friends who participated in the initial planning of ways to publish this book following Elaine's passing. And, lastly, thank you to many friends, students and colleagues at the Universities of the Western Cape, Cape Town, Pretoria, and Delaware, as well as elsewhere in the world, who inspired and were inspired by Elaine.

Preface

Sophie Oldfield,
African Centre for Cities
University of Cape Town

Tragically Elaine Salo passed away from cancer in August 2016, prior to completing the reworking and publishing of this book. To honour her and this work, her family, friends and close colleagues committed to publishing this work posthumously. In publishing *Respectable Mothers, Tough Men and Good Daughters: producing persons in Manenberg township South Africa,* we hope Elaine's work can be used in full, in its nuance, in its narratives, and in its method and theorizing.

Elaine described *Respectable Mothers, Tough Men and Good Daughters: producing persons in Manenberg township South Africa* as the interplay between two tales:

> [O]ne is the tale of my own biography as a coloured woman, as I make a subjective journey from non-reflective insider to the self reflexive privileged outsider in the process of becoming the native anthropologist. The other tale is that of gendered relationships in a fragment of a community located at the socio-economic and social margins of a city embroiled in the structural conflicts of race, space and class divisions. (2013: 1)

These dual tales, and her interweaving of them inspire us to think critically about ethnography, moral economies and the politics of personhood, and their embedding in the political work of anthropology and critical scholarship. We can build on the precision and richness of the ethnography found in this book.

Elaine had a critical capacity to ask important questions, such as '*Who speaks? Who writes? Who acts? Who mediates? Who analyzes, who is the native informant? Who theorizes? How is knowledge produced and from what 'location'?* She argued, 'These questions are so implicitly imbricated with epistemologies of power, they thread through the core aspects of the power of knowledge production in higher education, and in wider social hierarchies.' (Salo 2016: 4) In remembering Elaine, and in taking her legacy forward, we can find inspiration in her suspicion of powerful givens, in her questioning of "the credibility of Grand Theory, theory emanating from the space of academic legitimacy, the university – as the master means to render visible, interpolate, modularize and mediate the voices, experiences, the very lives of ordinary people, subjected to the scrutiny of the researcher's gaze" (2016: 2).

But, Elaine's contribution far exceeded her published work and writing, the basis on which we conventionally judge the authority of scholars. Her contributions were manifold. Elaine shaped worlds through generous conversations, rigorous, engaging seminars and teaching, and caring and inspiring work with colleagues and students in and outside of the classroom. She welcomed and nurtured into the university a generation of fantastic scholars. She invested in conversations in and beyond South Africa, across the African Continent and Global South, in Europe and the United States, and beyond. She welcomed so many of us into her field, into her home and heart, into her family. She led us, inspired us, chastised and loved us. Her sass and humour, her care and energy helped us write more boldly, think more creatively, act more incisively. She not only kept us going, she inspired us to imagine a more just world.

We hope this book offers the opportunity to carry forward Elaine's work. We hope that it is a foundation to think with her into the future, to build on her passion and care, her capacity and passion to speak truth to power in research and in life.

References

Salo, E. (2013) 'Book Proposal', unpublished paper, Feminist Writing Workshop, 9-11 September, Cape Town.

Salo, E. (2016) 'Memories from an awkward place – Sociology Conference on Gender and Power, University of Pretoria, 2010', unpublished workshop paper, Radicalising Collaborations Through Academic Research, 23-24 June, African Centre for Cities, University of Cape Town.

Desiree Lewis
Women's and Gender Studies
University of the Western Cape

Two months before her death, at a workshop titled "Radicalising Collaborations through Academic Research", Elaine Salo spoke retrospectively about her work on moral economies in Manenberg. Her candid reflections echoed the tone of the event, conceived not as a platform for showcasing academic accomplishment, but as a forum for intellectually and emotionally demanding conversations about how knowledge-making (and its associated rituals and institution) respond to the manifold struggles of our world. In the words of the workshop brief, the objective was to "push [participants] to collectively wrestle with the hard questions and challenges that we encounter through our academic work and practice beyond academia".

Salo's ethnographic study of Manenberg as well as her work as a public intellectual, versatile writer and educator, grapple with these questions in ways that have been varied and profound. In the case of her Manenberg study, however, it is useful to identify three linked areas. One is her acute awareness of the situatedness of knowledge-production, her belief that particular vantage points shape all forms of knowing and, for her, are enmeshed with classed, racialised and gendered experiences and locations. A second is her use of theoretically eclectic and grounded analysis for unraveling meaning-making and identity formation among the subjects about whom she wrote. As the title of her study clearly signals, her work focuses on the productive resources of South African township residents who are rendered invisible not only in globalised academic practices, but also in seemingly "progressive" South African scholarship and political thought. A third is the power of her storytelling. By narrating people's daily responses and the textures of their day-to-day lives, the ethnographer explores a subject about which she was especially passionate: the unseen aesthetics, values and practices of a community's ethical system which has a logic independent of more easily identifiable worlds of poverty, political oppression and organised resistance.

On being a "native anthropologist": situating knowledge

Salo's ethnography foregrounds the conditions under which different knowledges are produced and legitimated. She reflects on her multiple locations in global, national and local relations of power at the very start by testifying to the embodied status of her academic endeavor. In the face of the claims to "truth" within canonical scholarly traditions, right-wing and leftist political doctrine, as well as popular beliefs and stereotypes, she insists that all knowledge-production is produced from particular social perspectives. Her own, she shows, is shaped by class (the relative privilege of being middle-class), racial designation (an ascribed identity as "coloured", despite her discomfort with the ascription) and gender (in influencing her practical and cognitive engagement with her world). The effect of this authorial positioning - alongside an understanding that others have situated knowledge - is not simply to recognise that marginalised groups have different experiences and perspectives, but to centre their logic.

The self-reflexive turn in social science research may appear to confront the epistemological issues that Salo addresses here: the researcher's social investment in what and how she writes, as well as how others produce knowledge in relation to their socially determined locations. As Richa Nagar cautions, however, this sometimes leads to a fixation with "examining the identities of the researchers" (2014: 19). Nagar writes:

> Despite the proliferation of self-reflexivity in feminist ethnography, much feminist scholarship has tended to avoid some

of the most vexing political questions…How do we interrogate the structure of the academy and the constraints and values embedded therein, as well as our desire and ability (or lack thereof) to challenge and reshape those structures and values? (2014: 18)

Instead of asserting her self-reflexivity, (a term her study actually avoids), Salo engages with the politics of interpretation in ways that substantively destabilise her position of interpretive authority. As a "native anthropologist", a term she invokes with considerable irony, she avoids an authentic "insider" record of the people of Manenberg. Instead, she painstakingly disentangles her multiple investments and relationships to her subjects. The discussion of networks and power broking especially confront the challenges of encountering "difference" outside of hierarchies that usually fix the authority of researchers in relation to researched, or scholarship vis-à-vis local knowledge. In a discussion of critical ethnography elsewhere, she has written

> Ultimately, we must insist that as we produce knowledge, we acknowledge its partiality, and take account of this process as always relational. At the same time as ethnographers we need to reflect upon the grounded character of knowledge production, whilst also taking into account that, as we work across diverse temporal, institutional and geo-spatial contexts, we influence the different registers of and recipients of this knowledge (2010: 93).

Such work revolves around the author's difficult affiliations and disconnections: as a "coloured" South African with experiences of racialised socialisation and struggle that are similar to those of her subjects; as a woman with distinctively gendered forms of access; as the inheritor of classed entitlements that influence her worldview and encounters with others. The methodological and interpretive labour associated with this does not lead to formulaic condescension towards vulnerable groups.

With certain kinds of "ethically accountable" research, the academic's complete power is assumed; "sensitive" research seeks to defend the voiceless from any infringement of their rights, even though a fundamental right – for their voices to be heard and understood - may be entirely ignored. Salo perceives the women and men among whom she works as having complex and passionate sense-making impulses. At one level, then, her analysis is inflected by insight and empathy. At another, her research describes a journey of partial, hesitant and receptive efforts to understand others. A striking example of this is her account of the beginning of her understanding of the ethical standards that women in Manenberg live by when she is taught to question the normativity of her own behavioural codes. She describes how her key informant's "gentle but determined efforts to reshape my behavior…were one of the means through which I came to recognize the importance of the "ordentlike ma" as a concept that defined both a central type of personhood in Manenberg and a set of values that were key to the moral economy" (20). The ethnographer's journey of "learning others' cultures" might seem to be central to several traditions of anthropology. Rarely, however, is the process of "learning" linked to the daunting challenge of unlearning what is not simply already known, but also embedded and difficult to surrender.

Informally and among friends, Elaine Salo often reflected on the tremendous insularity of many middle-class coloured people both in Kimberley, the city in which she grew up, and in South Africa at large. She described their parochialism, anglophile leanings and class anxieties in similar ways to the fiction writer, Richard Rive (1981) and, more recently the sociologist, Zimitri Erasmus (2017). Her mischievous descriptions often invoked the term *colouredes capensis* to reveal the way this group configured itself almost as a genus – different from working-class coloureds and somehow "special" in their intellectual sophistication and left-leaning politics. Like Rive and Erasmus, however, Salo appraised this group as someone ambivalently imbibing many of its suburban and middle-class beliefs. These beliefs found a focus in the stereotyping of township life such as Manenberg's. It is the tremendous effort to question or surrender the known and embedded that Salo's subject-matter and fieldwork often describes. The result is an interpretive scaffolding that is unable to pathologise, patronise, instruct or "correct" the coloured working-class people who are her research participants. The epistemological breakthrough that is therefore made possible is an engagement with others dialogically, rather than writing about others monologically.

Representing "agency"

If the starting point of Salo's ethnogaphy is a willingness to engage in conversations with her participants, it is by assuming a community's agency that she analyses its meaning-making world and ethical universe. Salo homes in on communal understandings of respectability in shaping peoples' sense of shared values and individual self-worth. For women, respectability is rooted in service and loyalty towards others, obedience to authority, sobriety, modesty, and religious adherence, and it is shown that these values are measures of being a good woman either as mother or daughter. Among men, endurance, loyalty to and support for women, families, like-minded men and the community at large become criteria for earning respect, and distinguish *ordentlike ouens* from *skollies*.

Producing Persons in Manenberg Township comprehensively examines the signifiers and codes that create subject positions and ethical values around *ordenlikheid*. Showing how ethical landscapes are crafted through behaviour, dress, language and silences, the author traces changing ways in which individuals acquire or reclaim validating senses of self in the face of circumstances that threaten to dehumanise them. At the same time that she carefully analyses these details, she draws attention to oppressive legacies in the community's notions of respectability. In this sense, her understanding of agency refuses the dualisms of resistance and compliance, categories through which much South African political and academic thought has made sense of social behaviour. Instead, she focuses on provisional, incomplete and contradictory processes of what Stuart Hall conceptualises as "identification" (1996: 2-3). This "always-in-process" construction of the self is realised through legacies that are never wholly new (as proponents of the view that subjects are able to claim authentic identities would argue), yet never simply tools of oppression.

Salo's attention to the women among whom she worked is particularly noteworthy. As she shows, ennobling assertions of personhood transcend identities bequeathed by apartheid authoritarianism, Christian dogma, or gendered obedience even when women seem wholly complicit with these. One way in which this is demonstrated is the argument that agency cannot be discovered in any single or de-contextualised response; it is always manifested within the complexities of specific situations. For example, when women in Manenberg protect gangsters from the police, they may appear to be deviating from *ordentlikheid*, but this situational moral "digression" (failure to respect the law) marks respectability in the form of loyalty towards men who, in turn, have the community's respect because of their own (contextualised) moral virtues. Another example is when women face the humiliation of being interviewed about painful details in their private lives by social workers. Their silence might appear to be abjection. But when taking into account their animated mockery of authority figures once they are free to speak to one another, or even when they draw strength from one another's physical presence within official spaces, their apparent debasement should be read as a dignified stoicism, a recovery of self-respect in the conviction that they are in fact not who others define them as: lacking in morality, motivation, political insight, or the ability to exercise control over their lives.

This example exemplifies what is to me the most innovative intervention in Salo's study of agency: its abiding preoccupation with meaning-making and self-affirmation among non-metropolitan subjects whose sense of personhood is threatened by apartheid, the ongoing oppression of poor South Africans in the country's neo-liberal democracy, as well as popular media and academic scrutiny that denies their dignity and defines them only as statistics of violence or depravation. Salo's work shows, especially in the case of women in Manenberg, how details such as behaviour, dress, speech, everyday exchanges, networking and interpersonal relationships function as a cultural matrix for crafting and reproducing humanising and dignifying identity formation.

Telling stories

In most forms of social science and humanities research, storytelling continues to be disparaged as - at most - a lesser form of analysis, and often as preceding analysis, as not being "knowledge" at all. In the "mirage of merit" (Thornton 2013) that universities set in place, academics are often persuaded that the value of their work must depend on their demonstrating exhaustive "theoretical rigour": the interpreter's performance of authoritative mastery by making a subject submit to his or her explanatory skill. This performance is usually accompanied by the frequent (and often irrelevant) invocation of metropolitan theorists, so that their insertion into the writing automatically establishes its gravitas. In such knowledge, it is as though the writer were trying to ward off any evidence of uncertainty, vulnerability or "ignorance" by leveling out complexity and depth in the name of definitive "understanding". Paradoxically, the ostensible aim of critical social science research – to explore the complexity of human, cultural and social experiences - is often buried beneath the dead weight of academics' ritualistic performance of mastery.

Among a minority of academics, feminist ethnographers have grown increasingly alert to the value of narrative as a form for conveying the complexity of others' worlds. Like them, Salo often relies on thoughtfully crafted and compelling stories about events, people and places. Her concern here is with the "finely grained ethnographic details about the tensions, silences, fractures represented in everyday relations and quotidian activities in local places" (Salo, 2010: 96).

This work intricately engages with the politics of representation and imagination. It is also extremely courageous. This is because any feminist effort to make visible the lives and worldview of socially marginalised communities, and especially the women in those communities, needs to navigate the pitfalls of "giving voice" to subordinate others. One way in which Salo's study confronts this is by integrating verbatim dialogue and speech - both in the speakers' language and translated into English - into her narrative. This allows readers to engage directly with the register of her subjects, rather than to have this mediated by the author. While the study does not pretend to be a collaborative storytelling project, its frequent use of conversational narrative foregrounds peoples' personalities, consciousness and roles in the form of their own voices. One striking example is the account of Liesl a young unmarried woman who, after she bears a child, is obliged to redefine her social identity and role in relation to her mother and the community. At the same time, her mother, who speaks proudly about her obedient daughters before discovering Liesl's pregnancy, struggles to reclaim her threatened status as a good mother. The complex shifts around emotion, interaction, motivation, self-definition and belief in this account are achieved through the author's capturing her subjects' dialogue and speech at different stages and among diverse interlocutors. The reader is therefore made privy to multiple familial, emotional and psychological dynamics as these surface at different moments and over a longer period. Such thick description conveys the ways in which young and older women intricately ratify and define their ethics and identities in relation to one another, and in relation to the moral codes of the community at large. Salo's research and writing also strive to give equal weight to both Liesl's and her mother's points of view. The empathic view of the author therefore ensures that the storytelling becomes multivocal, even though the study does not make claims to be the product of co-authorship.

Another reason why the storytelling avoids appropriating others' stories is the author's transparency about her role in the events and actions she recounts. Far from being a detached or omniscient narrator, she frequently testifies to her active participation, feelings and responses. Salo is in many ways a highly visible and human protagonist in the stories she narrates. The ethnographer is "present" not only as a mediator who explains and contextualises, but also as a protagonist who actively participates in others' lives, learns, struggles to understand and misunderstands.

Yet she also avoids the cynicism that has led to the post-qualitative questioning of empathy or subjects who speak for themselves (see Lather, 2008). Prompted by the conviction that critical ethnography can work in emancipatory ways, her study refuses to give up on the belief that ethnography should seriously engage with the complexities of subject-formation and representation, while also working in politically emancipatory ways. Her political optimism surfaces clearly in this conclusion to her article on critical ethnography in Africa:

> We need to reflect upon the position and identities from which we write. We also need to engage in a relational model of knowledge production across the boundaries of the academy, civil society and the state that recuperates and celebrates marginalised knowledges. These…relational means of knowledge formation will assist us in producing socially relevant knowledge that

constantly interrogate the representation of African societies....
Africans deserve nothing less. (2010: 102)

References

Erasmus, Z. (2017) *Race Otherwise: Forging a New Humanism for South Africa*, Cape Town: David Philip.

Hall, S. (1996) 'Introduction: who needs identity?'. In: S. Hall and P. Du Gay (eds.) *Questions of Cultural Identity*, London: Sage.

Lather, P. (2008) 'Against empathy, voice and authenticity'. In: A. Jackson and L. Mazzei (eds.) *Voice in Qualitative Research: Challenging Conventional, Interpretive, and Critical Conceptions in Qualitative Research*, London: Routledge.

Nagar, R. (2014) *Muddying the Waters: Co-authoring Feminisms Across Scholarship and Activism*, Urbana: University of Illinois Press.

Rive, R. (1981) *Writing Black*, Cape Town: David Philip.

Salo, E. (2010) 'Men, women, temporality and critical ethnography in Africa - the imperative for a transdisciplinary conversation', *Anthropology Southern Africa*, Vol. 33, No. 3&4, pp. 93-102.

Thornton, M. (2013) 'The mirage of merit: reconstituting the 'ideal academic'', *Australian Feminist Studies*, Vol. 27, No. 76, pp. 127-143.

Chapter 1

Manenberg –
An In-between Place with In-between People

A sense of place must also be a sense of people.
Richard Rive 1988

A. Introduction

This book builds an ethnography about personhood in Manenberg, a South African township on the Cape Flats, during a celebrated moment in South African history, namely the transition from apartheid to democracy. Manenberg is situated in metropolitan Cape Town, the city at the southern tip of South Africa. Cape Town is internationally renowned for its physical beauty, its history as a major seaport and colonial centre between the 17th and early 20th centuries, and as the historical site of the South African government. The city has become a major tourist and heritage site, incorporating Table Mountain as its natural lodestone as well as infamous Robben Island, where Nelson Mandela and other leaders were incarcerated for much of their lives.

Manenberg is a dormitory suburb of the city and was established in the late 1960s by the urban planners of the apartheid era. It is situated on the sprawling Cape Flats, on the periphery of the old Cape Town city centre. The old city is nestled in the crook of majestic Table Mountain, overlooking the Atlantic Ocean, whilst Manenberg hugs the grey, windswept sands of the Cape Flats, 15 kilometres away. In order to reach it, from the city one has to travel along the N2, the ribbon of highway that winds its way out of the city, through the narrow green belt of trees that separates middle-class, mainly white neighbourhoods such as Rondebosch and Rosebank from the coloured and African townships, across the Cape Flats hinterland to the east. This journey takes one through the older, respectable middle-class coloured neighbourhoods of Hazendal, Vanguard Estate and Surrey Estate, past the Athlone industrial area into Manenberg.

1

During this 30-minute journey, one is imbued with a growing sense of removal and disconnection from the physical beauty and economic vibrancy of the centre. Yet, despite this sense of removal, Manenberg remains part of the historical and geographic centre of the Cape Flats periphery. The N2 winds its way still further east, past the shantytowns of Joe Slovo, Crossroads and Lost City that were established after the demise of the Influx Control laws in 1985. Historically these laws were used to prevent the permanent settlement of Africans in the urban areas of the old white South Africa. In contrast to Manenberg's concrete and asphalt solidity and its orderly, though dense, residential pattern, the small, haphazardly structured shacks that predominate in these areas, standing cheek-by-jowl, separated here and there by narrow footpaths and balanced precariously on the very edge of a stream or the railway tracks, exude a greater degree of physical and economic fragility and geographic marginality in the city. Further along the N2, approximately 35 kilometres outside the city, and close to the old colonial town Stellenbosch, the new Reconstruction and Development township, Delft, suddenly emerges from amidst the sand dunes and the Port Jackson trees. The tiny houses seemed to have materialised from a child's simple but colourful representation of an urban town. These townships are colloquially referred to as 'Smartie Towns' – in reference to their colourful, miniature character that resembles the tiny, multicoloured chocolate beans popular amongst South African children. This township is typical of the state housing that the new South African state provided between 1995 and 1998 as part of its social delivery program. The bold, new character of the place would be the envy of Manenberg's residents if it were not for the fact that this place is situated far from urban amenities and even further from the Cape Town city centre. Manenberg's location is undeniably preferable, in comparison to the long hours and much money these residents spend commuting to work or places of leisure. The range of residential settlements that was established on this landscape illustrates and represents the historical trajectory of segregationist and apartheid state population and urban policies that, prior to the early 1990s, sought to categorize people according to race, constrain them to live in set geographic locations and determine what housing and services they would receive. The historical perspective is therefore essential if one is to unravel the relationship between state policies, the meanings that peripheral urban space holds for the state as well as for the residents who occupy it, and the contestations over the meanings of personhood that ensue during the contestation over the meaning of place.

Manenberg township is set off further to the east than most other coloured housing estates. The history of settlement in the Manenberg area dates back to the 1600s when successive waves of Dutch, German and Jewish settlers leased the land from the colonial authorities for farming. The land continued to be used for agricultural purposes until the 1930s when the Cape Town City Council earmarked it for mass housing (Koen 1997). Manenberg was one of the last townships to be constructed for the diaspora of the Group Areas Act in the mid-1960s and is located further from the central business district than the older, more spacious low-income coloured townships such as Alicedale, Silvertown and Bridgetown.

Manenberg resonates with deep ambivalence in popular memory. It is associated with the anger and pain that coloured people experienced during the apartheid era, when they, together with Africans and Indians, were forcibly removed from their old homes in and around the city centre after these residences were rezoned as exclusively white areas by racist legislation in the 1960s. The township is home to more than 40,000 people, who were classified coloured under the old racial system of apartheid. Most residents still identify as *bruinmense* (brown people) or coloured. However, they also identify themselves as *Manenberg se mense* (Manenberg's people) to distinguish themselves from the wealthier coloured, Indian and African residents who reside in areas such as Hazendal, Gatesville, Surrey Estate and Nyanga.

The stories that dominate in the media, as well as in most Capetonian citizens' imaginations, about social alienation, violence, poverty and sexual impropriety emanating from the township since its establishment, echo with a deep, abiding sense of shame and inferiority working-class Manenberg residents experience in relation to their identities as impoverished coloureds in the context of white cultural and economic supremacy during the heyday of apartheid. These residents have constructed an alternative moral world with a different set of values and social relations in their efforts to redefine and recuperate a positive sense of identity or personhood. However, their actions in upholding this alternative moral world were further embedded within the wider temporal and spatial processes in South African society. While these residents sought to resist or turn away from the negative definitions of personhood imposed upon them, they were forced to draw upon the resources offered to them through the racial system to build their alternative moral world. In doing so, they assisted partly in reproducing the very same racial system of discrimination. Consequently, I argue that many adult women in their roles as mothers, and unemployed young men in their roles as gangsters or *Ouens*, who occupied the township for most of the day, became the moral police of personhood and the defenders of their communities as a means to redefine and recuperate a positive sense of identity. However, they were only able to do so precisely because the prior spatial and structural location of coloured men and women within the apartheid racial hierarchy provided them with the cultural and material resources to construct an alternative moral economy with a related set of values and persons. In their own efforts to embody this positive sense of identity or personhood, young girls and adolescent women could be seen conscientiously assisting their mothers or other adult women to get through the rounds of domestic chores. And in doing so, as I show in chapter 6, they displayed their adherence to the code of moral respectability, colloquially referred to as *ordentlikheid*.

At the same time, Manenberg is also popularly celebrated as the embodiment of its people's feisty survival in the face of, and in resistance to, the iron laws of apartheid that defined them as a lesser race and sought to keep them apart from other South Africans, white and black. The older men in the community are considered to embody this spirit of survival, colloquially referred to as having *sterk biene* or 'tough bones,' after a lifetime spent enduring long-term unemployment, imprisonment or exercising rigid religious self-discipline. This spirit of survival is memorialized in a song entitled 'Manenberg' by renowned South African jazz musician Abdullah Ibrahim. Yet the crude, racist sentiments expressed by many Manenberg residents about Xhosa-speaking Blacks in the contemporary post-apartheid era, and many residents' decision to vote for the Nationalist Party of the old apartheid-era during the first democratic elections, do not sit easy. Most residents' definition of Xhosa-speaking people as 'the Other' is intimately enmeshed with the definitions of personhood in the local context that have developed in articulation with, partly in resistance to and partly independent of, the official state notions of personhood based upon race. So, as I explore, notions of respectable femininity are primarily tied up with coloured women's racially privileged access to social welfare grants, and, to a lesser extent, with the moral signification of dress, hair type and hairstyles. Good daughters and respectable mothers in the Manenberg context are identified by their ability to provide for their dependents, dress modestly and control their hair by covering it or by wearing severely neat hairstyles that involve complex processes of braiding or chemical straightening. Women who wore their tightly curled hair in its natural state were said to have *boshare* or bushy hair. This was a sign that they were not sufficiently racially mixed but were racially closer to their indigenous African ancestry. In contrast, men take pride in their ability to keep the 'darkies' out of their communities. This apparent racism evokes enormous discomfort and chafes against the desire of other coloured citizens who proudly embrace their identities as new South African citizens in the post-apartheid 'the Rainbow Nation' and who identify with the nonracial, democratic goals of the new South African state under the leadership of the African National Congress.

For people who know the township and its history intimately, such as prominent Cape Town city councilor Faldiela de Vries and community activists Irvin Kinnes and Christine Jansen, who were raised there, Manenberg and its people represent the stoic resilience of a subjugated community to resist and survive in the face of the economic and racial repression of the past. However, they express bewilderment, anger and frustration at residents' inability to rise and seize the opportunities offered now that liberation has come. Christine Jansen referred to many residents' willful choice to acquiesce instead, in a state of demoralized social and economic dependency upon state welfare, while Kinnes expressed anger at some residents' expressions of crude racism against the post-apartheid state, in which Africans dominated. All these perceptions of Manenberg and its residents are shot through with implicit assumptions about the relationship between personhood, race, place, agency and history. These activists defined personhood within the dominated population in the binary terms of victimhood, and agency only in terms of resistance. Furthermore, they assumed that these definitions of personhood were commonplace within the Black population. Their assumptions were widely held within the anti-apartheid movement. The old national state marshalled most of its legislative, economic, judicial and administrative resources to impose an unjust socio-economic system such as apartheid upon all Black South Africans so that the dominant racist ideology appeared to seep into the minute crevices of everyday social interaction. Such triumphalist analyses of resistance imposed their own definitions of personhood and agency upon the populations they studied. In doing so, they failed to ask what meanings the various categories of dominated people themselves imposed upon the everyday apartheid policies and practices and how these meanings assisted them to negotiate their way in and through the warp and weft of daily life under this system. In this study, I examine what meanings Manenberg residents have given to the myriad historical bureaucratic processes through which old apartheid policies and racial categories centre. I ask how these meanings informed the daily interactions between the people who inhabited the spaces of this coloured township, how they actively reconfigured these policies through these interactions so that a particular moral economy was produced within the diverse places within the township, in which specific persons with distinctive agency were identified.

In many ways, Manenberg's residents are not much different than other Black township residents across South Africa who were forcibly removed from their erstwhile homes and made refugees by apartheid. We all share a history of dispossession and exclusion from the country's economic wealth and social and physical resources. At the same time, the laws of separation and exclusion have arrested the processes of hybridization that occurred as people from diverse ethnicities and cultures mingled in the pre-apartheid urban cultural melting pots such as Sophiatown in Johannesburg or Simonstown and District Six in Cape Town. These laws also sowed division amongst Blacks, who were classified into different racial categories such as coloured and African, relocated to homogenous townships on the urban peripheries and fed incipient forms of colourism so that it bloomed into full-blown racism. Despite these divisive processes, we have had to recreate new social and moral worlds within these geographic margins of the country. Created within the racially homogenous townships, this alternative social and moral order reconstructed alternative meanings of race, work and space in the local context of the township in ways that imbued our lives and our sense of personhood with positive meaning in the face of the myriad quotidian forms of belittlement and dehumanization during the apartheid era. This alternative social and moral order itself was constructed through and based upon, the apartheid hierarchies and meanings of race as these inform gender, work and space. Now that South Africa has moved into a democratic era, however, the physical, political, economic and social scaffolding that supported these alternative worlds of meaning are eroding, and with this come transformations in the social construction of personhood, of who society expects us to be as well as who we perceive ourselves to be, in the local context.

In this study, I seek to map out the construction of personhood in relation to race, space and gender, as well as the contestation about the meanings of personhood in the context of Manenberg across the historical transition from apartheid to the post-apartheid, democratic era in the 1990s. This first chapter is divided into two key parts. Having provided a brief description of Manenberg, the township on the Cape Flats where I conducted ethnographic research, I now go on to describe the research methodology employed in this study as well as the debates about the key theoretical concepts, namely personhood and agency, which are central to my analysis. In the second part of the chapter, I discuss the key historical and social processes which constitute the moral economy and which in turn inform personhood in Manenberg. These historical processes include the meanings of the racial category 'coloured,' especially during the apartheid era, and the spatial, economic and social location of people who were classified coloured within the Black hierarchy of deprivation during this period. Finally, I analyse the moral economy of personhood itself and the dominant location of women as mothers in this economy.

B. Autobiography and the research context: On being the 'native' anthropologist

Unlike anthropologists who choose to study societies very different from their own located far away from home, I decided to become the 'native anthropologist.' I turned the anthropological gaze to the place I consider to be home, namely South African society, and onto the coloured people with whom I shared a racial classification under the old apartheid system. In so doing, I sought to understand the social processes from within the cultural and racial community that might be assumed to be my own, in order to interrogate the apparent homogeneity of racial classification from within and to excavate the diversity within this assumed homogenous group. I began my research in Manenberg in November 1997 and continued to work in the area until August 1999. I was motivated to conduct research in the area by three key factors. Firstly, I was interested in documenting Manenberg residents' experiences of a specific history that I shared with them. Like Manenberg residents, I was classified coloured and we shared the apartheid experience of being 'made' into coloured through legislation during this historical period. I show later on in this chapter how the formal South African racial classification rigidly structured our multiple and diverse experiences so that we shared common historical events like forced removals and the subsequent legally enforced physical, social and linguistic separation from South Africans who were differently classified.

Like most of the township's first residents, my extended maternal household was forcibly removed from our ancestral family home in Beaconsfield, Kimberley, in the early 1960s, when I was a year old. We were resettled in a newly legislated coloured residential area on the periphery of the city. I was educated in a racially segregated education system, attending schools for coloureds only. Here we were taught fluency in the two official languages of the time, English and Afrikaans. My leisure hours were similarly structured by my participation in coloured-only sports and other activities, held in separate amenities such as sports fields, public swimming pools and libraries. These experiences were also layered over with those of gender, as parents, teachers and other members in our community socialized us girls into the mores of respectable femininity.

Yet, despite our common racial classification and shared gendered experiences of colouredness, I had to acknowledge that I was different from coloured Manenberg residents. While most of the coloured population were and still are impoverished, I was firmly embedded within the small middle class. My family's class status was entirely due to my parents' careers in building construction and education. The shift in language preference between two generations in our household also marked its social mobility from Afrikaans-speaking coloured working class to English-speaking middle class. My maternal grandparents spoke Afrikaans in the home and used English only in formal contexts such as the church or business environments. My parents, in contrast, preferred to use English as a means to register their opposition to the Afrikaner-dominated apartheid state, and as a signifier of their status as members of the educated class. During this process, I learned that English-speaking communities were considered to be socially and economically superior to Afrikaans-speaking communities. My experiences of racial homogeneity were also coloured over by our privileged class access to privately owned swimming pools in relatives' and neighbours' backyards, my family's ability to purchase books and magazines fairly freely and the economic ability to travel. Young women's education was considered as important as that for men, even while domesticity was still regarded as a core aspect of my own and other girls' upbringing. As a result, my siblings and I only used Afrikaans as a demeaning language and as a means to register contempt or to insult. Furthermore, unlike my less well-off girlfriends, I spent my afternoons reading, playing the piano or completing homework rather than cooking or cleaning house. Later, as I shared these experiences with middle-class white English-speaking or Afrikaner girlfriends, or with middle-class Black, Xhosa-speaking girlfriends, who grew up in the same economic circumstances, albeit on the other side of the walls or the tracks, we discovered that in retrospect, my experiences were no different from their own.

Most Manenberg residents claimed Afrikaans as their preferred language and formed part of the working-class poor in the city. Moreover, they spoke Kaaps, a different, more creolized version of Afrikaans than the version I used, which I had to learn to speak when I moved to Cape Town in the early 1980s. My parents and other family members considered themselves to be coloured. Yet during my student years in Cape Town, they and various friends instructed me to keep my distance from Manenberg residents because they were perceived to be 'rough.' I actively rejected the label 'coloured' as an apartheid construct, having been politicized during the era of Black Consciousness in the early 1980s and during my studies at a liberal, English-speaking white university. I redefined myself as Black, and continue to do so, as I still experience discomfort with the term 'coloured'. Manenberg residents' lives, therefore, represented both a familiar and a different experience of colouredness to my own sensibilities of race and of gender. Secondly, however, whilst defining myself as Black, I had to come to terms with the relatively favourable position coloureds occupied in the Black hierarchy of deprivation vis-à-vis people classified African, and the undeniable fact that many people classified coloured considered themselves to be different than those classified African, and still do so today. Most importantly, I also had an intellectual interest in understanding how diverse communities developed within, and in spite of, apartheid's legislative attempts to create racially homogenous societies within the confines of these segregated townships.

Clearly, these interests developed from the questions about race, gender, personhood and agency that emanated from my personal and political experiences. More importantly, these questions are also of central importance to social theory within anthropology. Anthropologists from diverse historical eras such as the members of the Rhodes-Livingstone Institute in colonial Northern Rhodesia (for example Gluckman,1972) to those from the contemporary postcolonial theoretical school (Spivak 1990), have sought to excavate the meanings of personhood, agency, power and diversity within subordinated populations. Their preoccupation with these issues has informed questions such as: how were the very structures of subordination kept in play over long periods, despite subordinated peoples' resistance? Or how and why do ordinary peoples' daily interactions that appear to be everyday acts of resistance necessarily require a degree of compliance with the very system of domination? Or further, does resistance inherently imply that the dominated and dominators share the same systems of cultural values or meanings? All these questions are shot through with notions of power, structuration, agency and the concept found at the intersection of these three issues, namely personhood. Unfortunately, many have reduced these nuanced, complicated questions of power to those grandiose though blunt binary theoretical concepts, domination and resistance.

I was attempting to understand how the residents in Manenberg negotiated their way through, partially complied with, reproduced, resisted and reconfigured the 'coloured world' that the state had imposed upon them. I recognized that the only meaningful way I could begin to address these issues was to excavate the social and historical processes whereby community, personhood and agency are constructed in a coloured place like Manenberg.

C. Negotiating access to Manenberg

Anthropologists such as Abu-Lughod (1993) and Kondo (1990) have indicated that the role of the ethnographer who embodies the identity of the insider-outsider brings its own set of benefits and trade-offs. Kondo (1990) shows how the insider-outsider anthropologist's apparent common identity with the community in which she works can present a 'conceptual anomaly' (ibid, 11) to its members because she is perceived as being the same as, and yet different to them. My experience conducting research in Manenberg was similar.

My access to Manenberg was facilitated in a number of ways by my familiarity with the language spoken there, as well as my intimate knowledge of the township's history and location in the city. Many residents perceived me to be coloured because I possessed the same cultural and linguistic skills as they did. I did not have to negotiate a linguistic barrier because I am fluent in English, Afrikaans and Kaaps, the creolized form of Afrikaans commonly spoken in the area. In addition, personal relationships became a primary means to obtaining access to the residents and to their dominant concerns. I had worked with anti-apartheid activists there during the 1980s and so I relied on an existing personal network of friends and activists, the public intellectuals who live and work there, to inform me about the current issues that dominated peoples' daily lives.

These networks provided a rich source of knowledge on the historical and social events that shaped and informed residents' everyday experiences in Manenberg. However, as I grew aware of the finer distinctions of power and the layered character of social fields in the township, I learned that these friendships were also limiting. They subtly constrained me to a tightly-knit circle of acquaintances whom the ordinary resident perceived to be insider-outsiders too; 'conceptual anomalies' because they possessed greater cultural capital and wielded enormous authority in the local public sphere. They were referred to as social power brokers because they possessed high levels of formal education, they were able to move across the social and racial boundaries with great ease, and were often exempted from the normative codes of social hierarchy based on generation and gender. I later learned that ordinary residents quickly perceived me to be another power broker because I could switch between different linguistic and social codes with the same ease. Moreover, despite being a woman, I owned a car. In this area where most people relied on public transport such as mini-bus taxis and buses, most residents, especially men, prized cars both as a means of physical mobility and as a signifier of social status. Ultimately I could not rely upon the initial friendships that helped me begin the research to gain access to the ordinary residents. I had to negotiate my relationship with the common people independently, without the mediation of the local power brokers. These ordinary residents would teach me about the dilemmas, the triumphs and the ambivalences that arose as they negotiated and constructed personhood in the daily round of life in Manenberg.

I relied on my eldest brother, Reverend Bertram Salo, who served as the Anglican priest at the Church of Reconciliation in Manenberg at the time of my fieldwork, to introduce me to church members. Through this network, I befriended Vonna, a senior woman head of a household in Rio Street. She welcomed me into her home, and with the passage of time, provided me with numerous insights into the construction of personhood in that community. Initially, I had intended to focus my research on the younger women in Manenberg in an attempt to understand the meanings of female sexuality. Through my friendship with Vonna, I realized that I had to reorient my attention and my behaviour first and foremost to the older women in Rio Street. As I show later, these women embodied an ideal of personhood in the community, making them the arbiters of and gatekeepers to its membership. As I show later, as mothers, these older women were a nexus through which others negotiated and defined their status as persons within a field of relational values that constituted the moral economy in the local context.

D. Learning about mothering in Manenberg

Vonna's home rapidly became my local research base and provided the social space from which I met other residents. Neighbours, friends and acquaintances constantly sought Vonna's advice on one issue or another and clearly, she was regarded as a key advisor and leader in Rio Street. My association with Vonna enabled me to demonstrate my good standing to the local inhabitants. When the women sought her advice on how they could negotiate the daunting bureaucratic labyrinth of the employment market, the social welfare, prison or education system, I was also able to provide additional assistance to them. She often accompanied individual women to the welfare or education offices or the courts, and when I was visiting she requested me to drive them to these locations. In this manner, I rapidly became the unofficial driver for Vonna and the various women whom she accompanied on their missions to seek bail for a son, apply for a social welfare grant for a child or mediate a conflict between their offspring and a teacher. The conversations begun in the living room continued during these car journeys, interspersed by the women's comments about the younger, adolescent women's dress or about the young men's behaviour.

Very soon after our initial meeting, Vonna's remarks about my dress pointed me to the outward signs of respectable, adult femininity in Rio Street. During my first visits to her home, I gradually grew aware of her critical assessment of my dress. I had deliberately chosen to wear blue jeans and simple shirts during my visits so that I could appear youthful enough to the young women whom I had originally intended to befriend. Approximately a week after I had begun visiting her, she drew me aside and instructed me to wear dresses and skirts more often '*want my ma-hulle sê Elaine moet toemaak, sy's 'n ma van 'n kind*' (because my mother and others say that you should cover up, you're the mother of a child). When I began wearing dresses, she admonished me to wear a nylon underwear slip as well, to 'prevent men from seeing everything.' In contrast to my apparently flimsy garb, Vonna always wore modest, knee-length dresses covered by a house-coat and a cotton headscarf. In winter she replaced the headscarf with a woollen hat and added a pair of loose-fitting trousers under the dress. More importantly, she insisted on making me into an *ordentlike ma* (a respectable mother) with persistent encouragement, cajoling and chiding about my dress, and later advising me about my relationships with my husband, my son and other Rio Street residents. In the same manner, she advised a number of younger mothers and other residents in the street about their problems. Vonna's gentle but determined efforts to reshape my behavior and that of the other young women were one of the means through which I came to recognize the importance of the *ordentlike ma* as a concept that defined both a central type of personhood in Manenberg and a set of values that were key to the moral economy. Her persistent interventions pointed to the ways in which personhood and the moral economy were inextricably intertwined.

Young men, whom the Rio Street residents identified as *Ouens* or streetwise men, often sought out Vonna's living room to request that she or her husband pray for them when they were in trouble with the police. Vonna and her husband's actions were unlike those of non-residents, who would have identified these young men as criminals who should be handed over to the police. Vonna also supported the informal system of community justice, in which the male residents beat up young men who deliberately committed crimes against local residents, or vandalized their property. '*Hulle is net 'n klomp skollies, hulle steel van hulle eie mense*' (they're just a bunch of thugs, they steal from their own people), she would say contemptuously. These interactions and relationships enabled me to identify and begin to examine the different kinds of persons that were identified in Manenberg, how they were differentiated by gender and age and the implicit values that informed their interactions.

Clearly, mothers like Vonna were central persons in this community. Her advice, gossip and anger about some individuals' behaviour in the street sketched the central values of the moral economy that shaped the relations between the different persons who were identified in the Rio Street community. Her insights, which were later layered over, countered and nuanced by the social relationships I developed with other men and women, enabled me to distinguish how people demonstrated or negotiated their personhood in Rio Street.

E. The theoretical debates about structure and agency in contemporary anthropology

The issues that I address in this study focus on key theoretical debates in anthropology about the construction of personhood within racially subjugated and impoverished communities in a context of power. Key questions at the heart of the concept 'personhood' are about the relationship between agency and structure. The theoretical relationship between personhood, agency and structure requires us to interrogate the extent to which members of subjugated communities can exercise agency and the processes whereby they assert such agency, and in doing so, possibly reproduce the very structures that assist to subordinate them. This theoretical puzzle also insists that we examine that relationship between the point at which agency fails, at which different persons' freedom to achieve certain goals is denied and resistance may arise, thereby possibly redefining personhood. This ethnographic inquiry is therefore implicitly threaded through with an inquiry about the relationship between history, personhood, agency, and the social processes whereby we make social structure and negotiate power.

Anthropological literature abounds with debates about the relationship between history, social structure, agency, and power (see Abu-Lughod 1993, Donham 1999, Comaroff and Comaroff 1993, Gluckman 1972, Giddens 1984, Karp 1995, Kratz 1994, Rosaldo 1980). In the following discussion, I draw on some key theorists' work to highlight the relevance of these concepts for this study.

F. Power, agency and structure

Anthropologists such as Gluckman (1972), Schapera (1967), Donham (1999) and Murray (1981) have sought to examine the interactions of local communities, whilst embedding them historically and socially within overlapping, intersecting social systems through time and space. The knowledge that the local history of the most isolated village, and the social interaction within it, are rooted within multiple social fields or within overlapping, intersecting local, regional and global systems has led to an awareness of the limitations of as well as the shifts in meanings of agency and power at the local level. It has also highlighted the renewed need to examine the multiple culturally conceived sites of power and the types of persons and agency that are associated with them (Arens and Karp 1989). Similarly, Donham (1999) has also indicated why we need to take account of actors' particular cultural perspective of, and orientation to power as well as the multiple configurations of, and the intersection of, social structures in which our communities are ultimately inserted. In the recent turn to postmodernism, a few anthropologists jettisoned the term 'structure,' and little attempt was made to provide an alternative that still allowed one to remain cognizant of the contingent relationship between history, structure, power and agency. Postmodernist analyses have been produced partly in response to what Giddens has referred to as structuralism's and functionalism's inclination towards objectivism and the 'imperialism of the social object' (Giddens 1984: 2). This approach has also attempted to recover what it considers to be structuralists' and functionalists' inability to explain the processes of change and what was considered to be their woeful neglect of subjects and their agency as well as of the polysemous meanings of action. Innovative postmodernist analyses, such as David Cohen and Atieno Odhiambo's work, 'Burying SM' (1992) paved the way for different registers or interpretations of a single reality to be accepted. However, in the process of centring polysemy and multiple registers of meaning, many postmodernists threw out the structural baby with the false objectivity bathwater. For other cultural theorists, especially those writing from within the broad paradigm of identity politics (see Oyeronke Oyewumi 1997), agency was defined as the ability to consciously focus action so that the original motivation for the action is realized. In such analyses agency is only defined in terms of the actor's ability to consciously resist and transform through action. Here the relationship and the distinction between action, motivation and the recursive ordering of social practices through time and space, namely structuration, are not considered.

In his critique of anthropological work on agency, Ivan Karp (1995) argues that the inability to connect agency to structure and power precludes us from recognizing the limitations of agency and the impact of history and societal structure on our lives.

He indicates that the terms 'power' and 'agency' have become popular buzzwords in anthropology that have come to mean 'what we want it to mean' and so, come to mean nothing at all (p. 1). He also asserts that in our failure to recognize the multiple levels at which power operates, we have lost the ability to explain the relationship between history, structure and agency. Yet if anthropologists are to understand how social processes are 'both given and constructed' (Rosaldo 1980: 14) then we have to remain cognizant of the contingent relationship between these three elements of social life, to apprehend the simultaneous interconnections between them and to illuminate this relationship through ethnography.

In his work on the theory of practice, Bourdieu (1999) uses Mauss's term 'habitus' to describe how social life is both given and reproduced, to replicate the existing unequal social relations. In Bourdieu's terms, the habitus is 'a product of history, (it) produces individual and collective practices – more history – in accordance with the themes generated by history' (Bourdieu 1999: 109). Through habitus, agents refuse to entertain action that 'is any way denied and will the inevitable' (ibid, 109).

Bourdieu's notion of habitus as the practice of structure, like Giddens' (1984) term 'structuration,' enables one to understand how social structure is embodied and lived through personhood. In his analytical schema, however, power resides in the relations of production, which he assumes to be a single set, organized in the interest of the dominant class in society. These relations of production also generate the symbolic order, the doxa that make these power inequities appear to be the natural social order. While the doxa reflects and confirms the objective truth of the dominant class' experience, this symbolic order tricks the subordinate class, through habitus, into misrecognizing their experience of subordination as natural and legitimate. Bourdieu, therefore conceives of the dominant class as being the class who are self-aware and who are fully conscious of how their actions recursively reproduce the structure through time and space to suit their own ends. On the other hand, the subordinate class succeeds only in unwittingly reproducing the very conditions of its subordination. Bourdieu's schema is unable to accommodate the possibility that even though a single system of economic production may dominate within a particular society, different, parallel, or even subordinate systems of production, valorizing moral rather than economic products, may co-exist alongside and articulate with the dominant system of production. Such secondary systems of production would generate a different set of relations of production. Subordinate groups may produce such secondary systems of production and secondary habitus, allowing them different constructions of personhood and therefore different possibilities of agency within intersecting systems of production.

Bourdieu assumes that the habitus within a society, which generates the social conditions within which practice occurs, are mutually shared across the diverse social classes. This explanation fails to accommodate the possibility that dominant and subordinate systems of production, whilst intersecting or articulating with each other, produce heterodox habitus. This heterodox habitus can generate embodied practices of different, hierarchically ordered social classes or genders within a society that recursively reproduces a group's subordination in one sphere, such as the economic sphere, but may well valorize its value system and bring about the intended effects in another spiritual and moral order. Bourdieu's analysis does not accommodate the possibility that agency has both intended and unintended effects within a context of shifting or multiple habitus ordered across time and space. He is ultimately unable to explain how change in social structure is both possible and embodied in individuals' actions, or how new forms of agency and habitus can arise in relation to transformative social processes. I would argue that if one began a social analysis using Fortes' notion of personhood, such an analysis would necessarily expose the intersection of, and the relationship between, multiple systems of production across time and space, because persons and their actions would reflect and embody such intersectionality or articulation. Consequently, it would provide one with the possibility of conceptualizing how subordinate social groups both reproduce the conditions of their subordination and also produce the possibility of social transformation or change in society. At this point, it is necessary to define my own use of 'agency' and 'power.'

G. Personhood, agency and power

I rely primarily upon Anthony Giddens' (1984) definitions of agency and power to inform the ethnographic analysis which follows. Giddens defines agency, in its simplest, most eloquent sense, as people's ability to do things. He indicates that while many have equated agency with intention or motivation, agency or the capability to act can bring about both intended and unintended and often unknowable consequences that are recursive across time and space. Agency produces effect, 'makes a difference in a pre-existing state of affairs' (ibid, 14), and is therefore, transformative and implies power. However, in Giddens' theory, agency produces both intended and unintended consequences. The repetitive, patterned aspect of agency produces unintended, often unknowable, consequences or effects that are recursive in time and space, thereby generating and reproducing structure. Giddens' (1984) theory of agency is similar to that of Reynolds Whyte (1997), who argues that agency is the semantic and bodily means for generating and regenerating the world. Like Giddens, Reynolds Whyte extends the definition of agency to include both the intended and unintended consequences of action and the recursive patterned effects of these consequences through time and space. This recursive effect links agency to social structure and ensures that structure is constantly produced and reproduced. Structure here, unlike its conceptualization in the objectivist social sciences, is therefore not external to human action, but inherently produced and reproduced by it.

Giddens does not define power in terms of the ability to realize intended outcomes, or in terms of ownership of a resource or lack thereof. He considers power as a characteristic of all agency because agency is able to produce intended and unintended effects. His definition of power contrasts with the more popular definition, in which it is considered only as a resource that one possesses together with the ability to dominate, vis-à-vis its lack, which is associated with the vulnerability of being dominated. In his terms,

> we should not conceive of the structures of domination built into social institutions as in some way grinding out 'docile bodies' who behave like the automata suggested by objectivist social science. Power within social systems which enjoy continuity over time and space presumes regularized relations of autonomy and dependence between actors or collectivities in contexts of social interaction... all forms of dependence

offer some resources whereby those who are subordinate can influence the activities of their superiors. (1984: 16)

The simultaneity and the contingent nature of dependence and autonomy between subordinated and dominant groups imply that both possess agency and power. The ability of these two groups to influence each other's actions suggests that there is some measure of compliance and agreement as well as some resistance between them. This situation, which Giddens terms 'the dialectic of control' in social systems, is parallel to Gramsci's (1971) notion of hegemony.

Giddens' definition of agency and power has to be distinguished from other social scientists' definitions, in which agency is equated solely with conscious motivation and intentionality. For example, in his history of the liberation movement, Zimbabwean African National Union (ZANU), Ranger (1985) analyses all ZANU's actions in terms of their desire to end colonial rule in Zimbabwe. In this analysis, he equates agency with intentionality, and in so doing, provides overall justification for all ZANU's actions during the Zimbabwean civil war. Ranger's approach, at least in this historical account, falls into the danger of providing overall justification and self-defence for what Paulin Hountondji (2000) terms 'cultural nationalism.'

The inability to connect agency to structure and power in a more complex, nuanced manner, precludes us from recognizing the limitations of agency and the impact of history and societal structure on our lives. Karp (1995) suggests that we resuscitate Fortes' analytical use of the concept 'personhood' as an eloquent analytical means that not only ties agency to structure, but that captures the duality of social existence, because it distinguishes 'the person who society expects me to be,' which provides us with insight into the structural processes that inform personhood as well as mutually recognized agency, from the individual 'I' who I know myself to be,' that informs the contestations and the conflict about personhood that arise. Anthropologists such as Fortes (1993) have maintained that local ideas of personhood, the locally acceptable means of showing that one is a person, a socially recognized agent-in-society, are what connect one to history, to structural time and therefore to social structure.

Following Fortes, Harris (1989: 608) maintains that 'situated at the intersection of politico-jural, familial, ritual-moral and other domains of social order, the person as a local social and cultural construct also articulates those domains with each other.' In Harris' formulation, personhood is the conceptual fulcrum that allows us theoretical purchase on agency and its efficacy or failure in the various social domains that make up social order. Like Fortes, Harris (1989) also distinguishes personhood from other conceptualizations of human beings, such as the individual or the self. In her view, the concept 'person' 'entails conceptualizing the human or other being as an agent, the author of action purposively directed towards a goal ... to be a person means to have a certain standing in a social order as 'agent-in-society' ... as authors of action affecting human life' (ibid, 602). In short, persons are publicly recognized as having agency and can be distinguished from other individuals whose behaviours or actions are not recognized as having agentive capacities and who are not accorded the standing of personhood. Persons' actions produce mutually recognized effects for and on other individuals and so are implicitly situated within the context of social relationships and an existing socio-moral order. At the same time that these agents are mutually recognized as capable of producing socially identifiable effects, they are also held accountable for their actions. Persons are therefore also liable to sanctions if their actions are mutually defined as damaging or not in keeping with their social standing.

However, Harris argues, not all the person's actions are mutually defined as having efficacy or being purposive and so are recognized as regular behaviour that is not imbued with agentive capacity. Effective action, or agency, is based upon the types of agentive capacities that are assigned to the diverse types of persons in society. These mutually recognized abilities that mark the individual as a person refer to the capacity to make judgements in which mutually acceptable standards of 'logicality, factuality, propriety and morality' (ibid, 605), the capacity to embody the rights, freedoms and duties associated with a particular social role as well as mystical capacities (such as wisdom, charisma, etc.), which, whilst not being visible, are recognized as the legitimate source of action.

In one sense, power is inherent in Harris' and Karp's explanation of agency and personhood. Harris' distinction between behaviour and agentive action is an implicit conceptualization about power; namely about the power of the person to act effectively, as well as the construction of power within a particular social structure that allows for the mutual identification of, or limitations to, diverse persons' agency. The particular social construction of power within a social context defines personhood and agency within this context. The contestation about, and the explication of, agency and its efficacy are also an index of the person's limitations to act effectively within that social context, and of the imposition of structure upon the choices of action available to him or her to act for him- or herself or for the community. We identify agency, Karp argues, 'when it fails – when it has to face its own limits ... agency implies power' (1995: 7-8).

Harris notes that multiple notions of personhood can co-exist. She argues that their co-existence is possible because it is the 'isolation of social contexts from each other (that) facilitates the formation and use of the differing concepts of the person' (Harris 1989: 604). However, while these social contexts may be isolated, she does not entertain the possibility that they may well be generated by different economic and cultural systems of production. Harris fails to expand the concept of multiple personhood to incorporate the possibility that diverse social systems or social structures, with divergent constructs of power, personhood and agency, can intersect, articulate and co-exist in a hierarchical relationship to each other. Fortes' analysis attempts to provide a diachronic as well as a synchronic perspective of personhood as he embeds the concept within structural time. However, he and Harris do not indicate how one might provide an analysis of personhood within multiple, overlapping economic and social systems across space. Their failure to locate the analysis of personhood within social processes both within time and across space has unintentionally created the notion of communities existing within a single cultural and socio-economic context.

Harris, like Fortes, addresses the issue of power, agency and personhood only in relation to the internal dynamics of a single social context. Both these theorists are therefore unable to conceive of the possibility of a heterodox social field, in which multiple socio-cultural worldviews co-exist, in a hierarchical, though dependent, dialectical relationship which may generate different social constructs of personhood. Such a social heterodoxy allows for an individual who is identified as a person in one socio-cultural worldview to be identified simultaneously as a non-person in a co-existing, though opposing socio-cultural worldview. The individual's embodiment of personhood and non-personhood simultaneously implies that the social construction of power and therefore of agency differs within these socio-cultural fields or worldviews.

This scenario allows for the possibility that multiple, distinctive sets of personhood may prevail, which are grounded in multiple, hierarchically ordered, competing or oppositional socio-cultural or economic systems of production, with different socio-cultural worldviews and diverse constructs of agency and power. These different socio-cultural worldviews may each generate a different order of persons, and therefore different social constructs of inequality, of power and of agency. These different constructions of personhood may impinge upon or seep into each other, thereby allowing for the contestation of personhood and agency in social relations (Donham 1999).

Donham (1999) offers one way out of this theoretical entanglement. He argues for the possibility of envisioning diverse constructions of personhood co-existing, albeit in a power hierarchy of dominant, residual and emergent cultural processes. Drawing on the work of Raymond Williams (1977) he argues that

> Residual cultural processes are not just archaic leftovers from previous time periods but are alternative, oppositional ways of living not captured by, or included in the dominant hegemony … Emergent values and relationships … contain genuinely alternative or oppositional ways of living. As new practices are thrown up in any society, there is a continual struggle by the dominant cultural actors to incorporate and to defuse the new. (1999: 140)

Donham draws on the key Marxist concepts of systems and relations of production to indicate how these alternative ways of living and multiple orders of personhood can come about. However, he renovates these concepts by arguing that their cultural content may differ across time and space and draw upon different cultural resources outside the economic sphere. He indicates that many Marxist approaches tend to assume that the processes of inequality only stem from the economic base, within a system in which commodities or goods are fetishized and which generates the primary inequality between classes. According to the classical Marxist analysis of capitalism, world history is only conceived of as the history of class struggle based upon unequal social relations that arise from economic production. In the Marxist schema, power, personhood, and therefore agency are defined primarily in economic terms. However, as Arens and Karp (1989) as well as Donham (1999) suggest, power is a cultural construct, takes varied ideological forms that 'embody … a view of society and (of) human action.' If we examine power as a cultural construct, then 'it also leads to the definition of human social and personal potential' (Arens and Karp 1989: xv), namely personhood and therefore agency.

Donham renovates the Marxist notion of power as productive inequality by examining how such productive inequality is culturally defined within the specific context of Maale society in Ethiopia. He argues that in different historical and cultural contexts, another order of inequality arises from systems of production that are constituted in dissimilar cultural terms or constructs to those of Europe or other dominant Western worldviews. Using field data from the Maale peoples of Ethiopia, Donham then goes on to indicate how Maale patterns of productive inequalities were based upon or located within a system of production that was based upon fetishized fertility, believed to reside in the personhood of the king. Productive inequalities were thus based upon the ideology of the personhood of the king and his agentive powers over fertility. This notion of relational personhood recreated and maintained an order of inequality which was recursive at different levels in the social order. The salient inequality that emerged from this particular cultural system of production delineated the boundaries between prominent social groups and produced the hierarchical distinctions between them. Thus, the salient distinctions within Maale society were those defined between persons of different generations and genders within the household and between lineage heads and junior households within the lineage that distinguished minimal lineage heads from chiefs, and chiefs from the king. So, while an individual could be productive in all social activities, his or her productivity could only gain social recognition if it was constructed as being brought about first and foremost by the king's generative powers.

Donham (1999) then situates the customary Maale notion of personhood within the wider historical as well as the national political and economic processes occurring in Ethiopia at the time, to indicate how the contestations about personhood were instantiated with and informed by them. In so doing he provides us with the view of history and of national politics as viewed through the local lens of Maale personhood situated on the Ethiopian socio-economic and political periphery. Personhood is a central concept in Donham's analysis – but it is further embedded within the long duree of Ethiopian historical, political and social processes. In this manner, personhood is rendered more dynamic as he clarifies the particular tensions about political power and kingship that existed in Maale society at the time of his fieldwork. In addition, he also uses Williams' notions of 'the dominant and the residual' as well as Skinner's and Wallerstein's concepts of space–power to situate the orientation of his analysis from within the particular cultural processes of the marginal Maale society located at the periphery of the Ethiopian state. Donham's ethnographic approach gives voice to local cultural interpretations of history, as they are expressed through the particular contestations about personhood, agency and power.

H. Personhood and agency in the context of a South African township

In this study, I utilize Fortes's and Harris's construct of personhood to excavate the cultural construction of power, personhood and agency within the coloured community of Rio Street in Manenberg. In my analysis, I implicitly assume, like Harris, that the South African cultural construction of personhood is situated at the intersection of its politico-jural, familial, ritual-moral and other domains of social order. I argue that the national South African definition of personhood during apartheid was first informed by British colonial and, later, Afrikaner nationalist conceptions of race. This nationalist formulation of personhood under apartheid led to the formation of a racial and economic hierarchy amongst Black South Africans in which coloured was favourably located. I embed my own study of personhood and agency in Manenberg within the context of coloured people's relatively favourable social and economic location at the centre of the apartheid periphery during the history of racial personhood.

However, I ask how a specific cultural construction of personhood and agency emerges in the local context of Manenberg, which draws upon the historical, political, economic and spatial location of colour in the periods of segregation and apartheid. Like Karp and Arens (1989), I examine how the social construction of persons in Manenberg reveals the specific cultural ideology and contours of power and of agency that exist in this community. Finally, drawing on Donham (1999) and Kratz (2000), I ask how an alternative construction of personhood and of power in the local Manenberg context is informed by the township's marginal location on the periphery of the urban South African landscape.

The meanings and actions of persons in Manenberg are inherently multi-faceted, because they do not only reverberate within the local context but also in the other, wider social and physical contexts that these people must, by necessity, occupy. The meanings of personhood also resonate across time and are embedded within specific historical processes. Personhood is the means that embeds the individual lifecycle or biography within wider historical processes (Rosaldo 1980). Furthermore, the performance of personhood is the means that links individuals across the generations but also the means through which incipient tensions between them are reflected.

This study sets out to examine the historical and social processes that inform the contours of this local moral world, and how they inform the personhood and agency that are identified in this community. I indicate how the Rio Street community draws on the very physical, historical, social and economic processes of apartheid that marginalized it, to create this alternative universe of meaning. I also explore how these aforementioned processes, as well as the alternative moral economy, mould household formation, and shape gender and intergenerational relations, so that a gendered ideology of personhood is produced, with certain persons such as adult mothers identified as having the greatest agency. The women's gendered roles as mothers articulate with and reverberate with men's roles through the lifecycle. Thus women's roles as mothers pivot on, and in turn buttress and uphold, men's roles, first as sons, then as gangsters, *Ouens*, fathers, and finally as ageing ex-prisoners. However, as these gendered roles articulate, adolescent women are straitjacketed into an ideology of femininity in which motherhood is the only role that is celebrated. Finally, I will examine how a new notion of personhood is emerging in the local context, in the post-apartheid era that is finding expression in the lives of the young men and women in Manenberg.

It is important to examine the historical and socio-economic processes that established this specific place Manenberg, classified its residents as members of a specific racial group, namely coloured, and in turn, limited their social and economic opportunities in the South African society. In chapter 2, I explore the historical and the socio-economic processes that inform and shape the racial category coloured. I focus specifically on the legislative processes during the apartheid era, such as the Population Registration Act of 1959 and the Group Areas Act of 1960 that officially constructed Manenberg as a coloured township. In addition, I argue that whilst the apartheid racial legislation defined coloureds as lesser beings than whites, it also located coloureds in a more favourable structural position vis-à-vis those classified African in the Black hierarchy of deprivation.

However, social life does not emerge, willy-nilly, from structural factors. It is constructed through the accretions of social interactions between ordinary people in the everyday context. In chapter 3, I examine the active role that the Manenberg residents play in constructing personhood in the township context. I explore how the residents create an alternative moral world within the township to that imposed upon them by apartheid, through which they recuperate a more positive sense of personhood, agency and community. I argue that through the process of recreating community after resettlement in Manenberg, they draw on coloured women's structural location within the Western Cape economy and the social welfare system as well as the spaces within the township. In this manner, the women's structural location, as well as the township spaces, are reconstituted and given new meaning within a moral economy that upholds the biological and social reproduction of the community. In chapter 4, I examine how the women's identities as mothers or *moeders* emerge as the crux of personhood in Manenberg and are anchored in the moral economy through the ethic of biological and social reproduction. I argue that women's identities as mothers and the ethic of social and biological reproduction effloresce outward from the household, producing an ideology of *ordentlikheid* or respectability, to which all other identities in the community are tied.

Chapter 5 explores how coloured men's structural location as subordinate men within the apartheid racial hierarchy in relation to white men and to coloured women produces an alternative ideology of masculinity in which emotional and physical toughness is valorized. This ideology emerges as men assert their identities as, sons, *Ouens*, gangsters, and fathers through the lifecycle. These identities are subordinate to, yet integrally intertwined with, women's identities as *moeders*. I argue firstly that young men's identities as *Ouens* or gangsters and their associated ganging practices and aesthetics demarcate the boundaries of the moral community in which women assert their power as mothers. At the same time, the young men's simultaneous identities as mothers' sons uphold their personhood in the community, thus rendering the ganging ideology, practices and aesthetics invisible to the ordinary residents.

Finally, in chapter 6, I consider how young women incorporate and are incorporated into the values and practices of *ordentlikheid* or respectability through their public display of sexual modesty and submission to the *moeders'* authority. Their adherence to the ideology of respectability or *ordentlikheid* ensures that they are integrated into the local support networks. However, the current changes in the post-apartheid context have rendered these networks less secure than before, because the old racial economy that buttressed and partly produced the local moral order is declining. The increasingly tentative articulation between the emerging post-apartheid structural processes and the local moral economy has exposed the limits of the *moeders'* power. At the same time, in the wake of the post-apartheid change, new cultural and social processes are emerging that blur racial, gendered and generational boundaries. These cultural processes are evident in the changing racial and moral content of local television soap operas and radio broadcasts, introducing these young adolescent women and men to more cosmopolitan social and cultural worlds that exist beyond the confines of the township.

I indicate that, while the young women and men continue to adhere to the outward forms and practices of respectability, they draw on this new cultural capital to subtly subvert and reconfigure the local meanings of personhood and its associated practices. In doing so, they acquire the new social skills, attitudes and styles that, together with the necessary material resources, may enable them to break free from the boundaries of race and class that have constrained them to living working-class lives in the township. A few courageous young women attempt to acquire the material assets such as transportation or finances that will facilitate their economic and social mobility, thereby introducing new gender identities such as the taxi queens into the local community. However, even as these young women gain access to the more cosmopolitan, cultural and social worlds beyond Manenberg, they may be subordinated within new configurations of gendered power relations.

Chapter 2

Making Race, Making Space:
Locating Coloureds in South African History and
Urban Planning

'He looked at my profile from the right side, then from the left, then he examined
my hair and he has a fine comb there which he runs through the hair of some. He
touched my nose and asked me what my mother's looked like.'
A woman describing being racially classified in the 1950s. Alex la
Guma (1964: iii)

The history of Manenberg and of its residents, and their place in the
social and cultural landscape of Cape Town are deeply embedded in the
historical, socio-economic and political location of coloured people in
the South African nation. Who or what are the 'coloureds'? Are they a
separate race or a separate ethnic group? Do they constitute a historical
fragment of European colonial society? Are they a fictive creation of
racial legislation during the eras of segregation and apartheid? Are they
a part of Black South Africa? What is their place in post-apartheid South
Africa? Questions such as these have occupied a number of scholars
over the years and held the attention of celebrated South African authors
such as Sol Plaatjie, Nadine Gordimer and J.M. Coetzee.

The meanings about being a *bruinmens,* a brown or a coloured person
in Manenberg, and the variations in, and the debates and tensions about
the significance of this identity in this context can only be interpreted in
relation to three key factors. Firstly, the meaning of coloured identity is
informed by the specific historical period and its associated socio-
economic and political processes. Secondly, it is also shaped by the social
science discourse about colouredness and how this discourse itself was
shaped and informed by the political debates about the definition of the
South African nation at the time. Finally, the meanings of coloured
identity emerge from the social relations between South Africans in the
contemporary post-apartheid context and the quotidian processes and

31

discourses that constitute the everyday lives of residents in Manenberg itself.

In this chapter, I provide a sketch of the spatial history of Cape Town to show how the urban planning of the city reflects the national and local debates about race and personhood from the colonial era to the present. I map out the contours of the debates about the meanings of 'coloured' as a racial concept in contemporary South African history and how these meanings are constituted in social science discourse and analysis. This is necessary in order to identify the meanings that colouredness has taken on over time, to explain why the shifts in meaning have occurred, and ultimately how they have informed the establishment of Manenberg and the meanings of personhood in this context. I focus primarily on the discursive construction of colouredness in South African social science to draw attention to the diverse ways in which this category is conceptualized. At the same time, I also trace the trajectory in the development and shifts in the meaning of the term through the history of the Cape Colony and later the Western Cape. These debates about the meanings of race and of colouredness are relevant to the current study on Manenberg because they have shaped and propelled the urban policies that informed the spatial development of Cape Town so that urban location became synonymous with race. And as I argue, later on, the specific location of Manenberg on the city periphery as a coloured township provided its local residents with the resources to build community within the township spaces and to distinguish between the different persons who were an integral part of it. The narrative of race is silhouetted by a related, parallel theme – how social science discourse is so intimately entwined with wider political developments in the South African contexts, and with the debates about personhood and citizenship in the wider national context. This secondary narrative also clarifies why social scientists felt obliged to make moral choices about the representation of race in their work (Saunders 1988).

A. Discourse and debate about race on the margins

Social science writings on South Africa are littered with the primordialist construction of race as a concept that is claimed to be grounded in biological reality and has scientific validity. The 19th-century historian G.M. Theal is probably one of its best-known proponents in the South African context (Saunders 1988). This ideology of race reached its apogee in the policies of the apartheid state. The research and literature on race have long since discredited the scientific validity of the concept (Tobias 1961, Boonzaaier and Sharp 1988). However, the social meaning of race is still a significant factor in many societies and continues to inform debates about nationalism, citizenship and morality – debates that are at the heart of questions about personhood.

In his study of Black citizens of the United Kingdom, Gilroy (1987) argues that precisely because race has no biological basis, the meanings of race as a social category still continue to shape the everyday lives, actions and identities of many people. More importantly, Gilroy indicates that while the meanings that the Black British themselves give to race are often in resistance to those imposed upon them by the British government, these meanings are also formed in dialogue with the wider Black audience both within the United Kingdom and in the diaspora.

The use of race, of terms like 'white,' 'coloured,' 'African' and 'Asian' as social classificatory categories and as a basis of social and legal discrimination, has a long history in South Africa. It is not my intention here to map all the uses of and debates about race and its associated shifts in meanings in South African history. Other, more distinguished social scientists such as Jack Simons and Ray Alexander have already done so, in their seminal work *Class and Colour in South Africa* (1983) for colonial and apartheid South Africa, while Neville Alexander (2002) has written extensively about the debates on race and nationalism in the apartheid and the post-apartheid periods. Suffice it to say that these debates have occupied South African social science because, historically, race and its various configurations with class, space and gender have been key aspects of social stratification in this society. Furthermore, the onset of the apartheid era in 1948 marked the period in which the significance of race increased to become the most salient marker of socio-economic, cultural, spatial, moral and gendered difference. I turn now to the history of the social science literature on race and the debates about colouredness, in order to sketch the historical as well as the conceptual backdrop against which the story of Manenberg and its residents will be told.

The literature which examines the archaeology of the racial designation 'coloured' and its associated meanings can be divided into three broad genres. The first set consists mainly of works by historians who link the origins of the racial category coloured to the social and economic processes within the Cape colony that resulted in the formation of a two-tiered racial society. In these analyses, the meanings of colouredness are considered to emerge from socio-economic processes of the time. These historical analyses highlight the angst of the European colonists as they strove to police the threat of racial pollution posed by the slaves and the indigenous population, at the same time that they depended upon the manual (Simons and Simons 1983) and sexual (Hendricks 2001) labor of the subordinate population in order to sustain the colonial society.

The works by historians such as Vivian Bickford-Smith et al. (1999), Robert Ross (1999), Robert Shell (1994), HJ and RE Simons (1983) and Nigel Worden (1989) are illustrative of this genre. These authors address the political-economic origins of racial stratification in the Cape colony between the 17th and 19th centuries. The history of racial stratification in the Cape is marked by Dutch and later British attempts to create and sustain a colony through the use of slave labour, imported from Dutch colonies in the East and indigenous peoples. Bickford-Smith et al (1999) indicate that the categories 'European' and 'coloured' mirrored the two-tiered racial character of the colonial society, and represented these groups' different economic statuses in this context. They note that the first recorded use of the term 'coloured' as an official racial category occurred in the 1865 population census of the Cape Colony. The category included all Black people in the Cape Colony and reflected their social and economic legacy of slavery and dispossession in this context. Simons and Simons (1983) and Worden (1989) note that despite the legal recognition of the equality of free persons in 1828, and the emancipation of the slaves in 1834, hard labor, the legacy of slavery, the lack of property ownership and harsh ordinances governing the relationship between masters and servants defined the boundaries of race in the colony and dictated the relationship between European and coloured. The common history of slavery and dispossession gave meaning to a category 'coloured' that was imposed upon a diverse group of people by their powerful colonial masters.

Goldin's study *Making Race: The Politics and Economics of Coloured Identity in South Africa* (1987) is one of the few economic history studies that examine the mutations in the official meaning and application of the term 'coloured' since the 1800s. Goldin has argued that a distinct coloured identity emerged by the 1880s in response to the state's introduction of the limited franchise for a few Black non-Bantu-speaking men. This political preference helped initiate the process whereby coloured identity was created. He contends that the battery of racially repressive laws that selectively targeted different Black groups and the numerous bureaucratic institutions set up to implement them further entrenched the reality of separate coloured and African political identities in the Western Cape. The ensuing politics of resistance to these laws led to the establishment of resistance organizations that were racially homogenous, despite the formal rhetoric of non-racialism that they espoused. Goldin contends that only the organization of coloured and African workers by the South African Congress of Trade Unions (SACTU) enabled workers to overcome the racial divide between them.

Like analysts such as Lewis (1987), however, Goldin confines his analysis of the conflict over the meaning of 'coloured' to formal political and trade union organizations. He is unable to excavate the meanings of and contestations about colouredness in local contexts, in relation to the spaces where people classified coloured reside, or in relation to the cultural practices or values that occur in them. Nevertheless, these historians' writings, which map the rise of modern racism in South Africa, do not assume colouredness as a racial given, nor do they assume a pre-existing coherent sense of ethnic identity amongst those included in this category. Instead, they have recorded the political-economic and social processes in the colonial and postcolonial eras in South Africa that gave rise to the use and meanings of 'coloured' as a racial designation, and as a marker of socio-economic and cultural difference (see also Heese 1984).

The second genre is exemplified by the works of social scientists who support the liberal or pluralist definition of the South Africa nation. Most of these works were published between the 1920s and the 1950s, with one publication appearing in 1997. Two key premises inform this perspective. Firstly, it assumes that South Africa is a multiracial society, comprised of four races or ethnic groups, the African majority, and three minorities, white (or European), Indians and coloureds. Secondly, each ethnic group is considered to have 'shared cultural values and practices, religious beliefs, or shared interests' (Pickel 1997: 18). This perspective enjoyed wide support amongst political leaders in government as well as within the Black political movements such as the African People's Organization and the African Nationalist Movement during the period of segregation between 1910 and 1950 (Alexander 2002, Karis and Carter 1972). The Smuts government's segregationist policies were no doubt informed by the liberalist notion of separate race groups or ethnicities in the 1940s. On the other hand, the liberal idea of race and ethnicity, and its associated systems of social organization, cultural values and practices, which informed the work of anthropologists such as Monica Wilson (1936) and historians such as Leonard Thompson (1969), also served to recuperate a positive sense of identity for Black South Africans, especially at a time when the racist apartheid state was in the ascendant and espousing the ideology of white supremacy and Black inferiority.

In the liberal definition, the meanings of ethnicity, race and nationality are accepted as for the most part uncontested and, in the works reviewed here, the three terms are used interchangeably. The authors mentioned here set out to provide social 'flesh' to the given racial category 'coloured.' For example, Macmillan (1968) and Van der Ross (1973) set out to describe the racial and ethnic genealogy of 'the Coloured people'; others such as Theron (1976) and Van der Ross (1973) describe their socio-economic status in South African society during the 1960s, whilst Pickel (1997) examines their social cohesion as an ethnic group in the post-apartheid era. Most of the authors writing on coloured identity acknowledge the heterogeneous origins of the coloured people and admit that this group's physical, socio-economic, cultural and regional boundaries are permeable, fuzzy and difficult to determine. For example, Pickel, drawing on Marais' (1939) explanation of coloured origins, states that

> The origins of 'coloured' people are explained as originating in the 'process of absorption and miscegenation between European colonists,

the indigenous Khoisan peoples of the Cape, imported slaves and the so-called 'Bantu-speaking people', gradually creating a heterogeneous group of 'mixed people' later to be called coloured. (1997: 23)

Her reference to the term 'miscegenation' is instructive and reflects the commonly held negative definition of colouredness as originating in the illicit sexual relations between otherwise pure, bounded ethnic groups.

A palpable sense of profound frustration threads through at least two authors' works as they attempt to mould, by their own admission, the heterogeneous character of this 'racial' group into their implicit theoretical notion of a race or ethnicity as a coherent, unitary group. Pickel's study sets out to investigate whether a coherent coloured identity developed in the Western Cape during the apartheid years, despite noting the multiple and heterogeneous ethnic and linguistic origins of 'the coloureds.' Similarly, in her report on the coloured people's progress, Theron notes the lack of coherence in coloured identity when she states that

Being Coloured is ... not essentially the result of a process of positive self-identification. It is not the expression of a common feeling of being different: it is the result of the reactions or actions of other groups. For these reasons, the Coloured population group does not display the typical characteristics found in a coherent nation or ethnic group in its pattern of behavior. (1976: 463)

Pickel's (1997) study concludes, almost disappointedly, that

it appeared from the historical research that no coherent coloured identity was formed during apartheid. The *absence* of commonly remembered events (amongst the rural, urban and peri-urban respondents) seemed to be the only shared sense of history. All in all, the survey found a variety of micro-identities, rather than a coherent coloured identity. (ibid, 109-110, my emphasis)

Two more recent studies that fall into this genre are the political analyses by Maurice Hommel (1981) and Roy du Pre (1994). Hommel's

(1981) analysis is also intent on recording the history of the numerous formal anti-apartheid organizations that were founded in coloured communities of Cape Town during the era of segregation between 1910 and 1948. His study is descriptive and intent on registering the oppositional political organizations of the coloured people during the eras of segregation and apartheid. While he indicates that political organizations such as the African People's Organization (APO) and the Non-European Unity Movement (NEUM) both espoused non-racial principles, he fails to indicate why the membership of the APO remained confined to the coloured bourgeoisie almost exclusively, whilst the NEUM attracted members from the professional class across the racial spectrum. Hommel's (1981) analysis limits the definition and contestation of coloured identity to the relationship between the state and an undifferentiated coloured population. Accordingly he is unable to explain why the modalities of colouredness were variously expressed in terms of the class experience in workers' support for trade unions under the South African Communist Party (SACP); in terms of racial homogeneity in exclusively coloured support for the APO; or in terms of the support for an incipient notion of unified Africanness that was expressed by the advocates of the NEUM.

Du Pre (1994) prefers to use the term 'culture' rather than 'race' as his central tool of analysis. He argues that the economic, linguistic and cultural similarities between coloureds and whites allowed the former to identify more closely with the latter than with the category 'coloured' itself. Du Pre is intent on showing that coloureds were part of the 'more civilized' white group but were constantly refused equal rights. He claims that 'One cannot blame coloured people for the ambivalence they have shown through the years in their attitude to and relationships with Africans and whites. They sprang out of the European nation and shared its culture, yet were denied membership of it' (1994: 80). Du Pre's analysis does not address the socio-economic differentiation within the coloured group and the impact that class had on individuals' racial identification. He also does not address how the different cultural practices within the group may inform different identities.

While many of these authors admit to the tensions and multiple meanings associated with coloured identity, especially in relation to location, language and class, they fail to utilize this insight in a fruitful manner. The existing ambiguities, ambivalences and tensions in meaning about 'the coloured experience' are either dismissed or invariably used to cast coloured identity in a negative light. Sheila Patterson's study entitled *Colour and Culture in South Africa* (1953) is one of the few works in the liberalist tradition that uses the tension surrounding the definition of colouredness in a productive way. She draws attention to the ambiguous, provisional quality tied to coloured identity, and makes this insight the touchstone of her analysis. She eloquently illustrates how the tensions associated with coloured identity and the debates about its meanings vary across contexts and are shaped by the cultural practices that occur in them.

Despite the apparently different ways in which these two genres of work conceptualize the emergence or existence of colouredness or coloured identity, a common, though implicit, assumption threads through all these works. They all foreground identity formation in a binary relationship to a dominant Other – in this case the colonial or postcolonial state. The meaning of colouredness is only considered to be shaped in complicity with state legislation which defines the boundaries and bodies of 'the coloureds,' or in resistance to it. Consequently, no light is cast upon how the modalities of being coloured are shaped in relation to the actions and discourse within the diverse coloured or the Black populations themselves. This task is left to others, who possibly, by virtue of their embeddedness within and familiarity with the finer aspects of contingent ambiguities, contradictions and complicities of a 'coloured way of being,' are better able to reflect these diverse modalities of colouredness.

B. Coloured in relation to which other? Depends on where you're coming from.

The third genre of work centrally reflects upon the contestation about the meanings of colouredness between the state and the population classified coloured, as well as within the coloured and broader Black population itself. The writings that characterize this genre exist across and are in dialogue with, the state's legislative attempts to impose a restricted, hegemonic meaning on colouredness during the segregationist and apartheid era as well as the democratic transition in

South Africa. Beyond that, they also seek to register the political and cultural agency of people classified as coloured as they assigned their own meanings to a racial category, firstly through the social relations and discourses within their communities, and secondly in resistance to, as well as in complicity with, those that were imposed upon them through administrative fiat. Through these multiple social actions and discourses, they reflect to a greater or lesser extent the diverse interpretations given to the coloured experience by the various professional and working classes who were classified as such, as well as by those who lived in diverse locations within the urban and rural landscapes and also in the different regions of South Africa.

Some authors such as Lewis (1987) and Van der Ross (1973) seek to draw attention to the manner in which the coloured population became victims of state legislation that declared them to be less than equal citizens and that progressively alienated them from the centre of political and economic power from the early 1900s. They note that a number of formal political organizations existed amongst the coloureds between the 1900s and the 1950s; these varied in terms of their members' economic interests, their regional location, and their belief in the numerous socio-political ideologies about race and nation that prevailed at the time. One organization was the African People's Organization (APO), established in 1901, which supported collaboration with the segregationist state to gain coloureds' formal political rights even if this gain was based upon exclusion of the African majority. The Communist Party of South Africa, formed in 1915 as the International Socialist League, was supported by many coloured artisans who rejected the conservative politics of the APO and became members of the open trade unions instead.

The Non-European Unity Movement, in contrast, formed in the late 1930s in response to the removal of Coloureds from the common voters' roll and the establishment of a separate Coloured Affairs Department, rejected collaboration in formal state politics and sought support from members of all the Black groups. These organizations reflected the variety of political responses amongst the coloured population that arose in relation to the legislative processes that imposed a restricted meaning on colouredness. The co-existence of, and tensions between, these three political organizations and the different support they drew on from within the broad Black population at the time point both to the debates about the fundamentally heterogeneous nature of the coloured people and the varied ways in which they prioritized different aspects of their identities. The salience given to these identities differentially informed the opposing political strategies that the oppositional political organizations, as well as the state, adopted during that political period.

As I have indicated earlier, the works by Lewis (1987) and Van der Ross (1973) cited above differ from the previous two genres in that they point to the diverse interpretations of race that were reflected in coloured political organization in relation to the state as well as in relation to the diverse political discourse that emerged within the coloured population itself. However, these works also resemble some of the earlier social inquiries such as Simons and Simons (1983), Goldin (1987), Lewis (1987) or even Worden (1989) in terms of the scale of their analysis. In different ways, they have foregrounded their analysis of colouredness in the context of more extensive geopolitical units such as the South African nation, the Western Cape region or the city of Cape Town. This wide-angle perspective implicitly affords them insights into the impact of wider political, social and historical processes on the emergence or meanings of colouredness. However, the finer subtleties of the cultural politics of race that emerge in the everyday lives and social relations within the local spaces of these larger units and which render the interpretations of colouredness more fluid and more contested are sacrificed.

In contrast, the second set of studies in this genre attempts to capture the cultural politics of race in a dialectical fashion during the apartheid era. Their analyses of race are written both in relation to the restrictive, racist legislation of the apartheid state, as well as in relation to the everyday social relations, actions and discourses of the people who lived in the marginal urban spaces that were socially officially designated as residences for the economically and racially powerless and that were signified as coloured places. The social analyses by authors such as Western (1981), Pinnock (1984), Jeppie (1990) and Constant-Martin (1999); fictive works by Rive (1988), Mattera (1987), Wicomb (1987) and Mda (2007); as well as the documentary *A normal daughter: Kwepie* (1987) by Jack Lewis are noteworthy here. Collectively, their analyses focus on the multiple ways in which these populations create their own ways of being and of personhood through the everyday cultural politics of race expressed in the quotidian processes of their lives. In these studies, the meanings of difference, racial identity and personhood are portrayed as constantly being constructed in a fluid, ever-changing process. These authors focus on the many ways in which coloured identity is essentially an open, contingent and contested category, whose meanings are crafted in part by, and emerging from, apartheid racial definitions and people's reactions to them, and also in the relationships between coloureds themselves, in their discourse and their everyday actions and the popular culture produced in these spaces.

Unlike the first set of studies in this genre, these authors foreground social relations and discourse about colouredness within the more localized context of place in their analysis. In this manner, they indicate how the meanings of, and debates about colouredness emerge from people's myriad interactions themselves, and are informed by the different notions of personhood in the local context, rather than produced only in relation to the hegemonic political and social centre of the old white state. By foregrounding this population's social relations in the urban spaces on the margins, they recuperate their agency to inform the meanings of 'coloured' with multiple, sometimes contradictory, meanings that are often contingent and specific to the local context. At the same time, these authors nest their analysis within the wider view of larger historical and socio-political processes that have shaped the South African nation, and that impinge upon these multiple interpretations of colouredness to a greater or lesser degree.

Jeppie's (1990) study of popular culture and carnival in Cape Town between the 1940s and 1950s exemplifies the aforementioned analysis. He indicates how, through the metaphor and performance of the carnival, and its shifting interpretations within particular local public spaces, various sectors of the coloured working-class population challenged the dominant forms of racial stratification and economic status as well as gender in the Cape Town public sphere. The Cape carnival, which occurs every New Year, consists of troupes of male musicians and dancers (and, in recent years, women) colourfully dressed in satin pyjamas, who parade through Cape Town streets. Each troupe is led by a transvestite, colloquially known as a 'moffie,' dressed in garish women's garments.

Jeppie indicates how the actions of the carnival's participants and its multiply constituted audience reveal the implicit assumptions of colouredness as a marker of gender and class differences that exist within this particular community, as well as its own and the European bourgeoisie's interpretations of the community's social and spatial location in the urban society itself. Furthermore, he argues that the carnival also produced novel, manifold meanings of colouredness that challenged these stereotypes of race, class and gender within the different socio-economic strata of society. In doing so, the carnival created the possibility for subordinate and new coloured identities such as the moffie leader or the bourgeois lady (parodied in the men's dress and parasols) to dominate and to inhabit significant social spaces such as the streets of the central commercial district, without fear of police harassment or disparaging prejudice. Jeppie states

> There was no control over its (carnival's) meaning, the event itself was an interpretation of the community. The occupation of public space by the dispossessed, the control of moment in this commercially hallowed space by the (mainly coloured) crowd, the shift of focus from the powerful onto the powerless ... the overt presence of the ... 'moffie', the uncontrolled mixing of the sexes, generations and also colors, the ... powerlessness of the police all bear testimony to the momentary anarchic character of the festival, to the symbolic inversion of the dominant social and moral order. (1990: 69–7 0)

Jeppie's work ultimately indicates that debates about personhood in relation to race as they are expressed through the carnival are shaped by the particular conjuncture of historical, socio-economic and political processes. In turn, these latter processes are constituted in people's myriad social relations that occur, according to Marx, 'in circumstances not of their own choosing.' In Jeppie's case study, the debates on colouredness during this historical period were shaped by several factors. First, they were informed by the earlier history of the Cape as a European colony, and the location of the Black population within it. Secondly, the debates were informed by the more nuanced social processes of differentiation and stratification that marked the beginnings of an aspirant coloured working class and with it, an ideology of respectability that set it apart from the perceived anarchic socio-economic melange of the inner city. This process itself was shaped by the disputes that raged about the place of coloureds in the wider British Empire, especially after Black servicemen demonstrated their loyalty by serving in the allied forces during World War II (Bickford-Smith 1999). Thirdly, the debate was also shaped by some coloureds' voluntary spatial relocation to the new townships of Athlone and Alicedale on the Cape Flats (ibid).

The removals of migrant African dock workers from Cape Town city centre to Ndabeni on the outskirts in 1902 marked the beginnings of the more rigid spatial separation of race in the semi-independent South African nation, and the growing importance of space as a signifier of race and of class, as the latter increasingly became synonymous with race. This process was deepened when the coloured *petite bourgeoisie* voluntarily relocated to the new townships on the Cape Flats in the 1930s and 1940s (Davenport and Saunders 2000, Bickford-Smith 1999), and reached its zenith during the forced removals during the apartheid era of the 1950s and late 1980s (Wilson and Ramphele 1989, Lemon 1991). These urban relocations reveal the struggles over the physical and social boundaries of the South African nation and how they were (and continue to be) constituted by the dominant legislative processes of the state, as it sought to define and reinforce the dominant ideology of race and nation through control over space and urban planning. More importantly, the hierarchies of race and the social relations between people at the margins of the nation also configure the meanings of space at the margins and the people who occupy them. The review above of the construction of coloured identity in the social science literature indicates how the debates about race were implicitly tied to broader debates about the South African nation. I turn to a brief discussion about the dominant construction of the South African nation through race as it was refracted through class and gender during the period of segregation, and the apartheid and post-apartheid eras.

C. Segregation and apartheid: the makings of the racially exclusive nation

Black South Africans' systematic exclusion from the political and economic rights and privileges of citizenship has been the hallmark of the social and economic processes that forged the modern nation between c. 1910 and 1994. The making of the South African nation is so intimately shaped by the historical relationship between race and class, and shaded with the finer nuances of gender, that, even in the current post-apartheid context, with few exceptions, the meanings of race reverberate powerfully with the local economic, gendered and social signifiers of class, whilst an individual's class position can be accurately inferred from his or her racial classification. The social relations that were shaped by, and in turn shaped, the social structure of race, class, and indeed, gender in modern South African society also moulded the geographical landscape (Lemon 1991). Historians such as Bundy (1986), Simons and Simons (1983), Johnstone (1976), Marks and Trapido (1987) and Wolpe (1988) have indicated how the legal and social exclusion of Blacks, especially Africans, from economic, social and political rights over time was differentially, though tightly, interwoven with three factors, namely the development of South African capitalism, the contradictions between capital and wider race interests as they expressed themselves in poor white workers' economic roles, the struggle between English and Afrikaner nationalisms and the emerging economic and racial differentiation within the Black population.

Firstly, they indicate how the development of the mining, agricultural and other secondary industries in South Africa and their differential needs for a cheap labour force impacted upon Black, especially African, rural-urban and intra-urban spatial distribution and migration and employment status in these industries. Secondly, the struggle between white labour and capital over diverging economic and racial interests helped determine job reservation along racial lines. Finally, the struggles between the more moderate, pro-British segregationists and Afrikaner nationalists for control over the state determined the varying degrees of Black segregation from political, economic and social resources which set up the basis for the differential hierarchy of deprivation that characterized apartheid social engineering and bedevilled liberation struggles during that era.

The development of nationalisms in South Africa after colonialism can be roughly divided into three key periods, namely the formation of the South African Union and the segregation era between 1910 and 1948; the rise of Afrikaner Nationalism and the development of apartheid, between 1948 and the early 1990s; and finally, the transition to democracy and the rule of African Nationalism after 1994. The development of Manenberg, the construction of personhood and the meanings of coloured identity in that local context in the 1990s must be understood in relation to the wider historical developments that mark nationalist formations in South Africa and how they informed coloured identity at the time.

In the following section, I discuss the development of South African nationalisms from segregation to the apartheid era. I show how the meanings of coloured identity shifted from that of being confident Black citizens of the Empire along with the African *petite bourgeoisie* to one of economic and social inferiority, forming the buffer zone between white racial purity and socio-economic superiority, and Black racial impurity, impoverishment and social degeneration. The founding of Manenberg, the social meanings attached to the place in relation to the urban history of Cape Town, and the social meanings embodied by its residents are profoundly marked by the dominant meaning of coloured identity as a racial and territorial buffer zone during the apartheid era.

D. Unifying white identity: the era of segregation

Since the founding of the Union in 1910 until the beginning of the democratic transition in the early 1990s, the debates about the shape and form of the South African nation and the character of its citizens have been dominated by the social and economic relations between the various sectors of the white population. These sectors include the captains of South African capital and the English-speaking settlers who had close ties to the British metropole, the Cape Afrikaner nationalists and the Boers of the erstwhile independent republics. Their debates, actions and struggles over competing political, socio-economic and cultural resources as well as the emergence of mutual interests defined the country's geopolitical boundaries, fixed the limits of its civil society, decided who constituted its citizens, and determined where they would work and live. In many ways, white political and economic domination also moulded the forms of Black political and economic resistance over time.

This does not imply that white interests in the modern South African nation were realized in an over-deterministic, teleological manner. The ideology of European modernization played a major role in facilitating white domination in South Africa. The ideology of European modernization was informed by social Darwinist notions of racial hierarchy in relation to 'civilization' or progress. According to this ideology, European cultural and economic practices, as well as their forms of social organization, occur at the apex of modernization, whilst those of the Black population are located at its base. In the liberal application of this ideology, race may predetermine an individual's location on the modernization scale but it does not necessarily prevent him or her from progressing to, or away from, a more civilized state. Some Blacks may break away from the constraints of race and become more civilized through education, or through socialization in European cultural beliefs and practices, such as conversion to Christianity, practising monogamy and displaying a greater degree of individualism. However, they remain in a state of perpetual development due to the constraining effects of race on ability in the final instance. Europeans, on the other hand, can descend into a state of cultural and economic degeneration but can regain their place at the top of the scale, because of the advantage of race. In the conservative application of the ideology, race is considered to be the only factor that orders the various racial populations differentially on the modernization scale and ultimately fixes their level of civilization, regardless of educational or cultural changes and achievements. Powerful racial stereotypes about the different Black groups abound in South Africa, based upon the social Darwinian principles of race. These stereotypes informed the popular construction of personhood in relation to race in this context.

The formation of a unified white South African identity with mutual interests extending across the class and ethnic fractures was crystallized in the common belief in, and support of, the dominant ideology of European modernization. This ideology found expression in the policies of segregation and glossed over the economic divisions between the English mining industrialists, the Cape Afrikaner intelligentsia, the poor Boer farmers from the old Boer republics and the white working class (Marks and Trapido 1987). However, at times these class differences within the white population became pronounced enough to break through the unifying ideology. Workers' common interests, regardless of race, sometimes emerged as the dominant force that gave impetus to common struggles being waged against employers momentarily during the period of segregation (Simons and Simons 1983). However, these moments of racial border crossings that broke through the hegemonic ideology of modernization were rare and could not be sustained for prolonged periods of time. The political, socio-economic and cultural hegemony of this ideology also held sway amongst the emerging Black *petite bourgeoisie* in the South African context from the late 1800s and informed the idea of the nation. In this way, white interests dominated in the formation of the South African nation.

Before the South African Convention in 1908, the educated Black members who resided within the boundaries of the British colony enjoyed some degree of formal representation in the colonial government and certainly considered themselves to be citizens of the empire. The aspirations of the Black *petite bourgeoisie* to equal status as citizens of the empire were informed by their own belief in the dominant ideology of modernization, and they sought to be a part of this cultural progress through Anglicization and education. The enfranchisement of the Black, propertied, educated class in the colony, the recognition of their property and trade rights (albeit differentially allocated within the British-ruled Cape and Natal provinces as well as within and between the Indian, coloured and African populations), and their access to education through the mission-school system gave impetus to this belief. Many Black men, spurred on by their identities as Black colonial subjects, fought alongside the British troops against the Boers to gain access to the gold fields of the Boer Republics during the Anglo-Boer war. Until the end of the Boer war, educated Blacks living in the British colony looked forward to gaining full citizenship rights. This situation changed when the Union was founded.

The South African Convention, which was held in 1908, set out the formal framework upon which the South African Union was founded.

At the convention, English and Afrikaner participants unequivocally excluded all Black South Africans from participating in the formation of the Union. The convention was primarily concerned with the distribution of power between Afrikaners and the English, and further restricted Blacks' rights in the country. The Black population found themselves on the very margins of the national debate from the time of Union in 1910, despite numerous formal protestations made to the South African state and deputations to the British government about their exclusion (Davenport and Saunders 2000). Black disenfranchisement throughout the period of segregation was accompanied by the formation of the major Black protest movements, among them the South African National Natives Congress (later called the African National Congress), the South African Indian Congress, the African People's Organization and the Non-European Unity Movement, which was mainly supported by coloureds in the Cape. Until the 1960s these political movements had little or no major impact on Black marginalization. This was primarily due to the different class interests that dominated Black politics and that were expressed in the separate agendas of the different political organizations. Black support for any one issue was thus divided across class, racial identity and region. Black political agendas were formulated in opposition to white political exclusionary practices. These exclusionary practices were selectively imposed on coloureds, Africans and Indians and affected the *petit bourgeois* merchants and professionals differently to the workers. Political agendas in the Black political organizations that opposed white political practices of exclusion were necessarily varied. So, for example, African and coloured workers supported the Industrial and Commercial Union in the 1920s. In contrast, the conservative *petit bourgeois* leadership of the African Nationalist Congress were supported by the African intelligentsia, while the similarly led African People's Organization were supported by the coloured intelligentsia in the Cape.

The state legislation which followed during the period between 1910 and 1948 reflected the compromises reached across the major lines of fracture within the white population. One such compromise, reached between capital and white labour, resulted in the Civilized Labor Act in 1922 and the colour bar on jobs, especially in the mining industry (Johnstone 1976). This act protected white skilled and semi-skilled workers from competition with similarly skilled coloured and African workers. A second compromise was reached between the various capitalist sectors about their access to and control over cheap Black labour, especially African labour (Davenport and Saunders 2000). A third compromise was reached between white agriculturalists in Natal, who needed cheap, Indian migrant labour and the Afrikaner nationalists in the Orange Free State and the Transvaal, who felt threatened by the increased presence of Indians, especially as property owners and traders. The segregation of Indians and their repatriation to India were encouraged and Indian property ownership and trade were restricted, especially in Natal, the Transvaal and the Orange Free State. The aspirations of coloured workers were constrained by the job colour bar and their limited access to mineral rights in the diamond fields. However, the coloured *petite bourgeoisie* remained relatively unscathed by more restrictive racial legislation until the late 1940s. This was partly due to the fact that most of the coloured population was concentrated in the more 'liberal' Cape, where they remained a minority until the 1950s. Even though most whites perceived them to be a 'lesser race,' their rights and interests were still administered through the central state until the establishment of the Coloured Affairs Department in 1943, which was set up to administer coloureds separately. They remained on the common voters' roll in the Cape until 1950. Coloureds' exemption from the ever-increasing restrictive laws that prevented African urbanization played a major role in shaping coloured identity as a superior group in relation to Africans. This identity was further reinforced by the Africans' spatial separation from coloureds and whites through the establishment of the separate Native locations in the urban areas from 1923.

The effects of the segregationist laws were reflected in the increasing spatial segregation of racial groups in the country. Whilst coloureds and Indians were encouraged to move voluntarily to the margins of the urban areas, African urbanization was actively restricted. The state control over spatial distribution, migration and segregation of the African population was realized through a plethora of legislation from 1913 onward. The 1913 Glen Grey Act as well as the 1936 Native Trust and Land Act limited African land ownership to the reserve territories in the remote rural areas of the country. In the urban areas, the 1923 Native Urban Areas Act ushered in the creation of African locations as segregated residential areas to be governed separately. African urbanization was further restricted through influx control and the introduction of passes for African men in 1937. The 1945 Urban Areas Amendment Act tightened these controls further. Section 10 of this act required Black men to qualify for rights to remain in the urban area, under a limited set of criteria. Anyone who did not qualify under the terms and conditions spelled out in the act was forcibly removed to the reserve area. These laws set down the legal restrictions on citizenship, but their effects would only be felt during the latter part of the 1950s.

The country's secondary industry emerged and grew during the war years between 1939 and 1945, and required an increased skilled labour force. This need could not be met by the white working class alone. At the same time, the reserve areas were unable to sustain their populations any longer and large numbers of rural Africans migrated to the urban areas, due to the growth of secondary industry (Marks and Trapido 1987). Despite the restrictive racial legislation, this period was marked by increasing racial integration and Black influx into the urban areas. African workers increasingly moved to the urban areas as they were pushed out by poverty in the reserves and attracted by higher wages than those offered by Boer farmers in the agricultural sector. Coloured farm workers were attracted to the urban areas of Cape Town for the same reasons. Afrikaner nationalists, who were resentful about the Smuts government's support for the war, as well as the strict wartime controls over food, became increasingly rancorous about the apparent laxity about racial segregation. Farmers were also resentful about their reduced labour supply, whilst the urban Afrikaner working class felt threatened once again by the growing Black proletariat.

Nationalist intellectuals began working on a social framework for apartheid, which would ratchet up the segregationist policies to a new level. The planned system was based on three key processes of separation. First, the rights of Africans to citizenship would be restricted to the reserves, which would be considered to be their true homelands. Outside the reserves, all aspects of African administration, including housing, employment, health and education, would be administered through the Department of Native Affairs. Secondly, whilst the Indian and coloured populations would be allowed to remain in the white geopolitical territory, they would be governed through separate

Coloured Affairs and Indian Affairs Departments. They would be segregated from white citizens in all aspects of everyday life, such as residence, education, transport, amenities and politics. This segregation would be enacted through territorial and administrative means. Like the preceding segregationist policies, this planned system would be anchored in, and give meaning to, the spatial configuration of the nation. White voters found the simplicity of this plan enormously appealing, especially in a postwar context of uncertainty and the growing presence of Blacks in the urban centres. The Afrikaner Nationalist Party appealed to these racial fears and fought the 1948 elections through the use of slogans such as *swart gevaar* (Black peril) and *oorstroming* (swamping) of the city (Davenport and Saunders 2000, Marks and Trapido 1987). Accordingly, the white population voted the Nationalists into power in 1948 and gave them the mandate to restrict the legal, social and territorial boundaries of the South African nation even further, through their apartheid policies.

After the Afrikaner Nationalists' successful rise to power, they rapidly crafted key laws that would become the collective keystone legislation in the apartheid system. The first of these was the Population Registration Act of 1950, which prescribed the legal definitions of racial groups in the country. This act was set in place to eliminate racial integration, and narrowly defined the individual's lifecycle by constraining social and economic opportunities to those considered most suitable to his or her racial group. The Act was bolstered by the Mixed Marriages Act, which declared interracial marriages illegal, and the Immorality Act, which proclaimed sex across the colour line an offence. These two Acts met the moral fears of those whites who feared that the residential integration between the indigent of all races in the poor urban areas would lead to white moral degeneration. The Group Areas Act of 1950 further restricted coloureds and Indians to their own residential and business areas. White traders and property speculators benefited enormously from the implementation of the Group Areas Act, as 750,000 people were forcibly relocated to newly proclaimed racially homogenous residential and trading areas located on the urban periphery (Western 1981, Wilson and Ramphele 1989). Through the traumas that coloureds, Indians and Africans had experienced as the Population Registration, Mixed Marriages and Group Areas Acts were implemented, they were administratively and physically located as the buffer groups between white and African at the centre of the apartheid periphery.

Africans did not escape the panopticon legislation of the nationalist government, despite having born the brunt of the earlier segregationist policies. Most Africans had already been denied permanent residence in urban South Africa by legislation since 1913. In 1952, the pass laws were extended to women, and they were now expected to meet the same stringent requirements as African men before they were allowed into the urban areas of white South Africa. The further exclusion of African women from urban areas led to a growing concentration of women, along with the unemployed and the aged, in the impoverished reserve areas (Murray 1981, Yawitch 1981). In this manner, the racial segregation of space was even more finely nuanced by gender, so that by the 1980s the spatial distribution of the population on the extreme edges of the national periphery consisted of its most vulnerable sectors, namely poor African women, children and the aged.

E. Making nations: Apartheid's imagined communities

The legislation governing the reserves was expanded through the Bantustan policy of the 1960s, in tandem with the extension of the pass laws, and as a means to further restrict African urbanization. The Bantustan policy emerged from the Afrikaner Nationalist ideology of nationalism. Briefly stated, this ideology promoted the idea that South Africa is divided into 12 different nations, each with its own language, ethnic culture and territory. Echoing European modernization, it stated further that these nations were in different stages of development into mature nations. Whites, Indians and coloureds constituted individual nations, while Africans were subdivided into nine ethnic nations. Indians were considered to be nationals of the Indian sub-continent and had no claim to national territory in South Africa. The Bantustan policy divided Africans into the nine nations by administrative fiat and declared them members of 10 Bantustans. These Bantustans were ideologically defined as nations that would be mentored to independence through the leadership of the independent white Afrikaner nation. At the same time, newly instituted labor bureaus and 'tribal authorities' monitored the labor migration to and from these Bantustans even more closely, to ensure that the various capitalist sectors' labour needs were met (Wolpe 1988, Marks and Trapido 1987). The ethnic fragmentation of Africans on the one hand and the increasing urban marginalization of coloureds and Indians on the other were reflected in further territorial or spatial separation. Platsky and Walker (1985) estimate that approximately 3.5 million people were forcibly removed after the Bantustan policies and the Group Areas Act were implemented. The forced migrations of Black people across the country irrevocably changed the South African landscape. Wilson and Ramphele (1989) illustrate the racial marginalization in South Africa as it was reflected in space.

Coloureds, as well as Chinese and Japanese, posed a greater problem to the Nationalist ideologues. The cultural and linguistic designations that existed within the African population provided them with ready classificatory designations for the nascent African nations, while the history of Indian migration to South Africa provided the nationalists with an identifiable territory of origin for this 'nation.' The numbers of South Africans who were of Chinese and Japanese descent were too small to merit nationhood. The Japanese were arbitrarily designated 'honorary whites' under the Population Registration Act if they resided in a predominantly white community. The Chinese population, who often traded and resided in coloured communities, were classified as such.

However, the hybrid roots of the coloured population, as well as the historical and regional shifts in the meanings of colouredness, presented the Nationalist ideologues with a problem. The origins of coloureds were so diverse that the nationalists were hard pressed to find a unifying ethnic marker that would define them as a nation. Many coloureds shared Afrikaans as a common home language with the white Afrikaners. Historically the use of the term 'coloured' collectively referred to a diverse group of Black people. Marks and Trapido (1987) note that coloured identity emerged as an identity born in resistance to 18th and 19th-century slavery and racial oppression in the Cape Colony. Between that time and the early 20th century, the term 'coloured' was assumed as a collective term for the Black population in the Cape Colony. It included the Khoisan, Xhosas and Mfengus from the Eastern Cape, slaves imported from the various Dutch colonies in the East who were later freed, free Blacks who escaped the North American slave trade and sought refuge in the Cape, the descendants of Indonesian Muslims sent to the Cape as political prisoners as well as the offspring of sexual unions between slave owners and slaves. Historically, the widespread use of Afrikaans as the common communicative form amongst the slaves themselves, and between slaves and the Dutch owners, also marked the slave descendants as Brown Afrikaners.

Later, the term signified relative exemption from restriction and oppression. 'Coloured' was used by the British colonial government to identify Black colonial subjects, whom they claimed had a right to protection from exploitation whilst working on the gold fields of the independent, Afrikaner, South African Republic. During segregation, the term came to signify those who wanted to escape the harsh restrictions that were placed on African urbanization through self-identification as 'more civilized people.' In the words of the African People's Organization, they claimed they were an 'educated class' who should be treated differently from the 'uneducated natives' (quoted in Marks and Trapido 1987: 29). Coloureds were also exempted from restrictive policies such as the Natives Urban Areas Act of 1923 because they resided permanently in the more liberal Cape, where relatively greater freedom of movement for Blacks was tolerated until the 1950s. Finally, the Population Registration Act defined the category 'coloured' as a residual racial category, 'declaring them to be all those who were not defined as white or native' (Goldin in Marks and Trapido 1987: 168). The broad category 'coloured' was then further divided into subcategories that included Cape coloured, Malay, Griqua, Chinese and 'other coloured.'

Despite the ambiguity of the term coloured and the multiple meanings ascribed to it in the official discourse of the state at different times, the Nationalist ideology demanded that a 'coloured nation' be forged. Paul Sauer, a Nationalist minister, noted that a sense of national awareness amongst coloureds was lacking and had to be nurtured to stop the perpetual process of fragmentation that was so characteristic of this group:

> there has been a tendency among coloured people ... for one section
> to do its best to become White, while another section has been engaged in

taking up with the Natives. A sense of national awareness ... has not developed among them ... and if one wants to stop him from splitting up one can only hope to succeed if one develops that sense of national awareness and that sense of pride in himself and his people. (quoted in Goldin 1987: 168)

The challenge was to forge a coloured 'nation' that would be easily identifiable through some homogeneous racial marker. In the absence of a common linguistic or cultural marker, the racial codification of space became the sign for racial homogeneity.

During segregation, many wealthy and skilled members of the coloured *petite bourgeoisie* who sought better economic, educational and other social opportunities changed their identification to white and began mixing exclusively within the better-off social classes. This was common, although disparagingly, referred to as 'passing for white.' Similarly, though less frequently, whites who intermarried adopted a coloured identity. Marriages across the various linguistic and cultural boundaries within the Black population group frequently occurred and couples lived within and between these different forms of Blackness, frequently switching between classifications or selecting one permanently.

The Population Registration, Mixed Marriages and Immorality Acts of 1950 shut down these erstwhile permeable racial boundaries between coloureds and other population groups. The Group Areas Act segregated coloureds into their own residential zones.

However, 'the coloured nation' still lacked a national territory. Accordingly, the apartheid ideologues demarcated the Western Cape as the coloured homeland and the space in which coloured national consciousness would be forged. In 1956, the territory was proclaimed a Coloured Labor Preference area, in which all unskilled jobs would be reserved for coloureds only. The land area was defined by the Eiselen line, which cut across the southwestern part of the country, from the northeastern Namibian border to the southwestern coastal town, George. Africans were expelled in large numbers from the Western Cape and by 1962, more than 30,000 people had been removed from the area. In an effort to escape expulsion and to obtain access to housing and jobs, many Blacks began asserting a coloured identity. Race, bodies and space became even more intimately intertwined through apartheid legislation.

The segregationist and apartheid policies in South Africa have fundamentally transformed the meanings of territory or space over time. Nowhere is this more evident than in the historical organization of space in the urban environment. The historical development of Cape Town is closely intertwined with the ideologies of European modernization and Afrikaner Nationalism. Its spatial design reflects the social relationship between the dominant state and the different sectors of the subordinate Black population, and the manner in which space was used to enforce the beliefs and policies about race and personhood that dominated at the time.

F. Racial stratification and urban space in Cape Town, 1800s–1980s

The construction of Cape Flats townships such as Manenberg reflects a long process of urban ordering, associated with the systematic exclusion of Black South Africans and the racial stratification of space that accompanied this exclusion. Racial stratification has informed urban planning and spatial segregation in Cape Town since the late 1800s. Bickford-Smith (1999) notes that urban segregation of race became a key aspect of early 20th-century town planning in Cape Town, and was considered to be an important characteristic of a modernizing society.

The process of racial segregation in modern Cape Town at the turn of the century was first marked by the respectable classes' moral panic about the threat posed to racial hygiene by the growing Black population in the old colony. Initially migrant dock workers from the Eastern Cape were primarily targeted to be excluded from central Cape Town by urban planners who sought to 'cleanse' and modernize Cape Town. The legislated residential segregation in the city began in 1890 when these dock labourers were housed in the segregated Dock Native Location Barracks (Western 1981). The systematic establishment of racially homogenous townships for Black people on the Flats began in 1902 when the migrant dock workers were resettled once again in Ndabeni, on the edge of the city, following the outbreak of bubonic plague. These residents were considered to be outcasts of the town, 'tainted with the stigma of the plague' (Bickford-Smith et al. 1999: 45).

The progressive isolation of African residents from mainstream Cape Town and the formal reordering of the Black population into coloured and African continued with the national enactment of the Urban Areas Act of 1923. This legislation was passed to enforce this population's segregation into separate townships or locations such as Langa on the Cape Flats. The wording contained in this legislation, in which Africans were equated with 'idle, dissolute and disorderly' behaviour, reflects the increasing stigmatization of this sector and its exclusion from urban Cape Town (ibid, 87).

Nevertheless, throughout the 1920s and beyond, some African families still continued to live in other, poorer, 'more notorious' parts of the city, such as District Six and Windermere shantytown, alongside coloured and Asian families, as well as in older suburbs such as Observatory, where they were surrounded by better-off whites. This situation was barely tolerated by the municipal authorities and it was only a matter of time before these areas would also be segregated.

By the late 1920s concern about the removal of the other, poorer sectors of the Black population from the European sections of the city was increasingly being expressed as a fundamental aspect of rational town planning and the establishment of spatial order. The official perception was that the uncontrolled racial mixing allowed in the slums of District Six, Windermere and Parkwood Estate would only result in the poverty that characterized these areas. Urban planners increasingly regarded racial segregation as the crux of social and spatial order. The rational style of town planning adopted by the planners at the time emphasized the separation of urban space into different zones for racially separate residential, commercial or industrial areas (Bickford-Smith et al. 1999). As a result, the administrator of the Cape Province, objecting to the establishment of a coloured township close to a white garden village, said that 'Scattering the Non-Europeans from one end of the city to the other was not in the best interests of Cape Town. The city should be completely zoned ... so that certain sections should be set apart as European areas, others as Non-European and areas where noxious trades might be established' (Mayor's Minute, Cape Town 1928: 51–67, quoted in N. Barnett ms. 1993).

During the 1930s and 1940s, the racial stratification process continued apace when low-income housing was provided for the Black population who were forcibly moved from the city by the national Housing and Slum Clearance Act of 1934 (Koen 1997, Western 1981). Living conditions were certainly appalling in some sections of Cape Town's inner-city areas such as District Six. The Slums Act was used as a measure to pressure landlords to improve their properties. However, the act also provided the city administration with an opportunity to use housing as the means to segregate the cosmopolitan working-class population along racial lines and to move the poor further away from the city. This period saw the development of racially segregated housing estates such as Epping Garden Village for whites; Athlone, Gleemoor, Kew Town, Heideveld, Crawford, Lansdowne, Silvertown and Cooks Bush for coloureds; and Langa, Nyanga and Gugulethu for the African population (Western 1981). These areas were located in concentric circles radiating out from the city, with the white residential areas located closest to the centre, the coloured townships located beyond these, whilst African residential areas were located farthest away.

Socially and geographically, coloureds were now defined as occupying an intercalary position between white and African. The coloureds' social and geographic proximity to the white population in the urban centres was tolerated until the 1950s. This situation was possible for three reasons. Firstly, the white population was numerically larger than the coloured minority until the 1950s – consequently, the latter was not perceived as a demographic threat to white dominance. Secondly, in keeping with the dominant ideology of European modernization, most urban-based coloureds were generally perceived to be members of the nation, who were inherently inferior to the white population, but who provided a necessary buffer between the 'civilized' white minority and the 'undeveloped' African majority. Finally, the coloureds were not perceived as a major social and economic threat to white dominance, thanks to the national Civilized Labor Policy of 1924 which ensured that the better-paid jobs were reserved for whites. This legislation provided whites with economic and social mobility while it set a cap on the Black workers' social and economic aspirations. Whites were also protected from coloured 'invasion' into their areas through economic means. Coloureds' lack of socio-economic resources and their dominant status as workers meant that they could not afford to rent or purchase houses in middle and upper-class white neighborhoods and, when they resided in working-class white areas, they formed homogeneous islands of color, informally separated from their white neighbors by mutual consent (Western 1981). Clearly, even when residential areas were racially mixed, a measure of social and geographic distance was maintained.

By the late 1940s, informal social and geographic segregation was no longer regarded as sufficient means to prevent racial integration and was not acceptable to the new Afrikaner Nationalist government. Economic and demographic factors threatened to blur the spatial boundaries of race in the cities, and the state perceived that stricter segregationist laws were required. By the late 1930s, the economic depression blurred the social and economic boundaries between coloureds and Afrikaans-speaking whites in the city and elsewhere (First Carnegie Inquiry into Poverty). In addition, the numbers of the lower-status coloured population had increased more rapidly than those of the English-speaking and Afrikaans-speaking white population from 1930 onwards because of their higher birth rates. By 1940, Black workers were entering the cities in large numbers, eager to acquire the jobs created by the war economy and the growth of a secondary industry. By the 1940s the Black population in Cape Town had exceeded the white population. Segregationist policies and enabling legislation were thus well established by the late 1940s.

G. Manenberg and the racial ideology of apartheid after 1950

The history of contemporary Manenberg is imbricated with the Afrikaner Nationalists' project of social and spatial engineering during the apartheid era. The enactment of the Group Areas Act of 1950 resulted in the construction of townships such as Manenberg, Bonteheuwel, Lavender Hill, Parkwood Estate and Hanover Park on the Cape Flats. This law ushered in the second phase of racial ordering of the city space and the extension of housing development on the Cape Flats. This time the coloured and Indian populations were targeted for forced removal to the outskirts of the white city, whilst Africans without passes allowing them to be in the urban area were monitored ever more intensely and forcibly removed to the Bantustan areas. The implementation of the Population Registration Act of 1954 and the Group Areas Act together created supposedly homogeneous, bounded coloured and Indian racial communities within the urban areas, which were spatially separated from white and African areas in apartheid South Africa.

However, the creation of homogenous racial communities through administrative fiat belied the actual diversity within these categories and the cultural commonalities that existed across administrative and spatial boundaries. The issue that faced the people within these reified categories was how they would negotiate their lives between the rigid state policies that confined them to bounded socio-economic and spatial locations.

Manenberg's geographic location personifies the intercalary racial and class position officially assigned to the working-class people who were classified as coloured during apartheid. The township is situated next to the Athlone industrial area, on the north-west. The Xhosa-speaking townships Langa and Gugulethu are located on the township's south-easterly border and are separated from it by a railway track and a pedestrian bridge. Other areas such as Vanguard Estate, Penlyn Estate and Surrey Estate, which were also the creations of the Group Areas Act, were islands of middle-class respectability, separated from Manenberg by the Athlone industrial area. These suburbs were inhabited mainly by the skilled artisan class, entrepreneurs and professionals such as medical personnel, lawyers, ministers of religion, educators and others. The socio-economic differences that existed amongst these residents were crisscrossed by and layered over by alliances of class, language, religion, gender and generation. These alliances at times articulated with and contradicted the social connotations that official policies imposed upon a racial or ethnic identity, to generate a unique, though permeable cultural system of meaning within these residential suburbs. This cultural system of meaning distinguished these residents as particular persons who were different from the coloureds who lived in Manenberg.

As I stated before, Manenberg was established as a place for people who were classified as coloured and who were forcibly removed from newly defined white areas. It was also inhabited by people who could not afford to purchase their own homes in the middle-class coloured suburbs. Consequently, most Manenberg residents were working-class people who were considered to be 'rough' by their better-off neighbours in the surrounding areas. These dominant stereotypes of the township as an impoverished, rough coloured place informed the popular image of the place and its people. Yet, when one examined the place and the people from their point of view and from within the township, then finer differences emerged. These differences became relevant and meaningful for these people in terms of their construction of community and their understanding of personhood. The different meanings that these residents gave to the received apartheid policies and places could be seen in terms of the different housing that was provided in the township.

Housing in Manenberg was constructed in two phases in the early 1960s and divided the area into three distinctive housing zones. As I will show later on, these three zones informed the finer, local social distinctions that the residents made when they defined the boundaries of their communities. The first area of housing construction, which I will call Zone One, rose up between 1963 and 1965 and consisted of a mix of free-standing four-roomed houses, which were defined as 'economic units,' and two-storey apartment blocks, known as 'sub-economic housing.' While the quality of the housing in this area distinguished it as a poorer economic area than Surrey Estate, its visual proximity to Surrey Estate and Primrose Park, the limited number of housing units and less dense housing differentiated it from the central housing zone in Manenberg, known as The Courts. The second phase of housing construction occurred over a longer period, between 1966 and 1980, and provided housing in two distinct zones, the central zone, locally known as 'Die Korre' or 'The Courts' and a third zone, Zone Three, which The Courts residents refer to as 'Die Koephyse' or the 'Ownership Homes.' The Courts comprised the largest housing area in the township. Most of the sub-economic units, which provided approximately 70% of the housing in Manenberg, were situated in this area.

Zone One was situated relatively closer to the business districts and central health centres in Rylands and Athlone as well as the public transport to Cape Town. It was situated along the central road along the northwestern perimeter, Klipfontein Road, and extended in an easterly direction along Duinefontein and Ruimte Roads. Klipfontein Road was a central route that connected the Cape Flats residents with central rail and road transport hubs and served as the key public transport route for buses and mini-bus taxis passing through Manenberg. The central business district in Rylands and Athlone provided a rich diversity of stores and services, as well as the major sports and health centres such as the Athlone sports stadium, a number of medical and legal offices and the privately owned Gatesville Hospital. The old African townships, Langa and Nyanga, were located at its northeastern end across a road bridge and the railway tracks respectively. Duinefontein Road was a key transport link to Mitchell's Plain in the south-east. The state-run G.F. Jooste Hospital as well as the Nyanga railway junction, containing a shopping mall and a central railway station, were located on this main road. Duinefontein Road also linked the older 'phase one' houses with the more densely constructed dwellings that were built during phase two. Philippi Ring Road formed the southern border of the first phase housing.

Like Zone One, Zone Three houses were less densely constructed than The Courts. In this zone, housing consisted of freestanding units with only eight blocks of apartments. Residents who lived here registered their social distinction from The Courts when they stated that they lived *'in die koephyse'* 'in the purchase houses'. The housing contrasted with that provided in the numerous, densely constructed double-storey apartment blocks in The Courts. Zone Three was situated within visual proximity of middle-class Sherwood Park and adjacent to two major transportation routes, namely Duinefontein and Landsdowne roads. These residents were situated closer to the large number of corner shops, wholesalers, gas, hardware stores and the private medical surgeries located in Sherwood Park. Like the residents in Zone One, these residents' proximity to the major transportation routes also provided them with a sense of connectivity to areas beyond the dense township.

The Courts, or *Die Korre* as the area was colloquially known, was the poorest section in the township. In contrast to Zones One and Three, it was perceived to be the most marginal in Manenberg. The apartment blocks that provided the only form of housing in this zone were constructed in two formations in this area. In the first formation, a number of these blocks were constructed side by side along the entire length of the street, resembling giant dormitories. In the second formation, two blocks were constructed on either side of a concrete courtyard, so that the staircases to the second-floor apartments in each building were situated exactly opposite each other. Similarly, all the apartment entrances to each building were located directly across from each other and faced the concrete courtyard, creating a spurious sense of intimacy between the inhabitants. Laundry lines ran across the width of the courtyard and extended between the second floor of each building, connecting the buildings like giant strands of thread. On most days laundry fluttered gaily from these wash lines, like many multi-coloured flags, and lent a festive quality to the otherwise drab buildings. Housing was the densest in this zone and the first-time visitor would be forgiven for assuming that a sense of community naturally existed amongst the residents in these apartments, as they were thrown together by racial categories, hemmed in by bricks or sewn together by laundry lines. As I show in the next chapter, however, the dense housing construction belied the atomization and the social alienation that most of the original residents experienced when they were first resettled in Manenberg.

Manenberg Housing Zone 2 (Elaine Salo 1998)

Chapter 3

Clearing the Wilderness:
Defining Identity from Within.

'Skollies were winning the 'Battle of Manenberg"
(*Cape Herald*, 2 August 1969).

'Julle kan ma' New York toe gaan, ek bly innie Manenberg.'
You can go to New York, I choose to remain in Manenberg.
(Abdullah Ibrahim, from his song 'Manenberg').

'Council ready for war. Strategy plan for staff safety on Manenberg.
The Cape Town municipality is to provide escorts, safe routes and
evacuation plans to protect staff at council facilities in
the 'war zone' of Manenberg.'
(*Cape Argus*, 11 February 1998).

Da's niks eintlik fout hie'nie. My familie is naby,
die mense in die pad is vriendelik.
There's nothing really wrong here. My family is close by,
the neighbours are friendly.
(Manenberg resident 1999).

The newspaper headlines from the Cape Argus and the Cape Herald reflect the common perception of Manenberg and other Cape Flats townships that existed in Cape Town over the past 30 years. These headlines, read by many coloured readers, convey the message that, historically, Manenberg was and remains a marginal space, a notorious, dangerous place in the city landscape, and an aberrant area beyond the rule of law. This view is commonplace among most middle-class Cape Town citizens, regardless of race, and few dispute this image. This opinion is also inscribed within the local research discourse. Social science researchers based at the University of the Western Cape readily use adjectives such as 'crime-infested gangland' (Koen 1997),

'Murderburg,' and 'poverty-stricken, coloured ghetto' (Sauls ms.1999) to describe Manenberg. The City Engineering Department publication describes the area as 'a problem area, with a high incidence of crime and social disturbances' (n.d.: 18). The contemporary discourse contained in the media, as well as city council and newspaper reports, construct the image of a township on the social and geographic margins of the city. Taken together, they reflect the dominant perception of Manenberg as a dangerous, deviant space in the city landscape. Paradoxically, the thirty years that separate the two newspaper headlines hint that the Manenberg residents, who have always been a part of the urban poor, pose as great a threat for the stability of the city during the buoyant time of the 'rainbow' South African nation in the 21st century as they did during the regimented, racial order of the apartheid state.

Manenberg residents acknowledge the negative image of their township in the wider urban and national context. However, they add a resistant rejoinder – *'ma ons bly lekker hier'* (but we live contentedly here); *'da's niks eintlik fout hie' nie'* (nothing's fundamentally wrong here). Similarly, the line from Abdullah Ibrahim's song, quoted above, strikes a discordant note which dances defiantly across the media images of a township in economic and social chaos. In contrast to the pejorative media labels, residents prefer to call Manenberg *Die Tjatjies* (the Jazztown) or 'JunkyFunky Town' – names that capture the tone and atmosphere of daily life in the township more aptly, despite the harrowing experiences of gang violence. These names accurately epitomize the predictable rhythm of everyday life here; one marked by rich social and economic improvisation that is sometimes sharply fragmented by the volatility of violence. They also allude to the rich variation of lifestyles, multiple identities and social differentiation that local residents recognize within the area. The verve and zest with which residents celebrate events such as weddings, matriculation or high school graduation and twenty-first birthdays resonate with the same vitality and fervour that mark their grief at the funk of violence and death.

A view of Manenberg (Elaine Salo 1998)

The names *JunkyFunky Town* and *Die Tjatjies* are laced with a sense of affectionate familiarity, of rebelliousness and a refusal to acquiesce in the derogatory meanings that the more powerful city inhabitants ascribe to the place. They are suggestive of the residents' tacit recognition that their current sense of residential security is built upon a history of earlier dislocation and loss. They also reflect their sense that social and economic security is elusive and that change is the only consistent feature of life here. These names are shaded with a recognition of the violence which erupts like a jagged rent in the social landscape, and resignation about its inevitability. Many residents speak despairingly of the gang fights and the loss of life that ensues. They indicate that they hope that the gang violence will end, at the same time that they express their satisfaction with life here. The juxtaposition of contentment with life here, with a hope for peace, suggests that these residents recognize that violence and change are the inevitable underside of the vivacious quality of their lives.

This rich texture of life in Manenberg, made up of multiple threads of diverse histories and memories of disparate places, opulently interwoven, and overlaid with stories of collective journeys, is lost in the dominant public discourse. The public discourse of the media and the discourse of the Manenberg residents themselves reflect two perceptions of the township. The media representation is heavily embedded with the connotations of a disorderly space that is filled with violence and upheaval. The representation by the residents themselves is suggestive of a strong pride in a place that has enabled the routing of memories, and the space in which their identities are anchored. At the same time, they recognize that their beloved township is founded upon their very dislocation and distress. These two mutually opposed images of Manenberg hint at the duality that is inherent in the residents' continuous construction of identity and community.

The Manenberg residents' opinions of themselves and their township indicate that they do not necessarily accept outside attempts to impose an *a priori* definition of their identities and the meanings of their township upon them. In spite of, and counter to the attempts to impose an official construction of coloured identity onto them, these residents create their own notions of personhood in the local context through a variety of means. The different types of persons that are found here are multifaceted and multiply determined in the complexity of everyday social interaction within the spaces of the township as well as in relation to state processes. Thus personhood is characterized by a dialectic between the official state-imposed racial hierarchy and the round of quotidian social interaction in the township. It is partly based upon and includes aspects of the officially imposed coloured identity, against which the social norms and cultural values of white and other racial identities are set. But it also includes other facets such as that of being a Manenberg resident, located in a particular type of housing in the area, being a member of a specific type of household, possessing a particular gender, having a distinctive sexual preference, and being a member of a particular age cohort. Some or all of these multivalent aspects of personhood are expressed in the warp and weft of everyday social relations within specific social contexts in the township and in relation to a particular set of social or moral values. The processual construction of personhood through the dynamic interplay of history with factors such as gender, age and space during social interaction is not new. It has been illustrated ethnographically by Donham (1999), Kratz (1991, 1994), and Comaroff and Comaroff (1993).

The notions of personhood that people hold at the local level within townships such as Manenberg have remained hidden for the most part, partly because the academic narratives of forced removal reflect the dominant theme of loss and destruction only. This dominant theme is narrated in the contemporary histories of urban South Africa (Bickford-Smith et al. 1999, Fields 2001) as well as in museum exhibitions such as the Apartheid and District Six museums. These narratives were a necessary and important corrective to the dominant apartheid discourse which represented the original Black residents in urban South Africa as non-persons residing in impoverished townships filled with social chaos, shame and disrepute.

However, in recuperating the social vibrancy of these old areas, the authors portray the areas of resettlement as places without history, that exist only as timeless, alienating spaces by those who were resettled there. As I show later on, in the early years following their removal, these removees did in fact experience a profound sense of alienation from their new homes. Nonetheless, over three decades have passed since they were first resettled here, and two successive generations have been born here. Through these residents' social and physical labour in this space, the township has acquired multiple social and physical meanings. Yet, in the dominant representations of removal, the authors fail to reflect the social and physical changes that have occurred in the resettlement landscapes such as Manenberg. Consequently, they have also failed to indicate how the residents continue to define and contest the meanings of personhood, thereby imbuing the place with a particular social significance that reflects both the common experience of loss suffered through removals as well as the common experience of gains made through reconstructed social networks.

The historic creation of Manenberg, the first residents' experiences of resettlement in the township and the subsequent development of their households incorporate a number of mutually interconnected and interpenetrating developmental processes through time and space. In this chapter I explicate three of these processes, namely the common histories of dislocation and of loss of the old communities, the common experience of alienation from the new place, and finally the subsequent reconstruction and location of communities, households and persons within this space as well as within the bureaucratic location of coloureds within the hierarchy of deprivation.

I have already referred to the finer spatial and socio-economic diversity that can be discerned in Manenberg in chapter 2. As I explain later in this chapter, residents make an even finer social distinction within the township and divide it into a number of local communities that vary in size from those consisting of a number of courts across a few streets to those located within a single street or court. I use the local definition of community to focus specifically on the life histories of the residents of Rio Street. First I indicate how these local residents' diverse stories of origin locate the township's beginnings in these common histories of dislocation that reflect multiple, kaleidoscopic, hybrid urban origins. These residents' shared notions of personhood are also rooted within the common historic loss that they experienced when the old web of social networks anchored in the multiple locations of origin was disrupted by removal. Secondly, their common experience of resettlement is also rooted in all the original residents' narratives of their initial rejection of and alienation from the new, empty place. However, over the passage of time, armed with the memory of community and household in the old places, a common sense of loss, and the reconstruction of households, these residents have been actively engaged in the recreation of a shared moral economy and its associated ideology of respectability. The first residents' common histories of dislocation, loss and resettlement become a key facet of this collective moral economy and its associated ideology of respectability or *ordentlikheid*. Later, in chapters 4, 5 and 6, I show how this ideology becomes the means whereby the Rio Street residents pass on history to the successive generations, through which they create and contest personhood and structure their lives.

In his study of Ilongot headhunting, Rosaldo (1980) has indicated that the presence of history 'as an active force in the lived-in present' (ibid, 23) is both structured and generated. Rosaldo uses the system of cohort analysis to illustrate how the composite biography of a particular group can be transformed into 'a collection of individual biographies in their historical, cultural and social-cultural contexts. [By this method] ... subjects of the study were defined by that formative historical moment when their collective identity was formed and... by their enduring character as a self-conscious group in society' (ibid, 110). In this chapter, I apply the method of cohort analysis to indicate how the Rio Street residents' common experiences of dislocation, loss and resettlement assist to forge community.

A. Coming to Manenberg: Erased histories and displaced persons.

Most of the literature written on the forced removals of people classified as coloured from newly declared white areas focus on the anger, the brutality and the pain of the experience. These studies illustrate the human cost of the racial cleansing that occurred throughout urban South Africa. They also illustrate how persons were rooted not so much in a race as much as in the space of their local communities, their lived histories within these social spaces, layered by the round of their daily lives within them. These removals reflect the state's attempts to reshape individuals' identities from one where 'being coloured' was just a single aspect of a multifaceted notion of personhood, to one where a reified racial category, coloured, became the only identity rooted in a specific place.

John Western's *Outcast Cape Town* (1981) is a classic study of people's experiences of the Group Areas removals. Western conducted his research in Cape Town in 1978, just after the forced removals of coloured residents from Mowbray, a middle-class area located in the newly declared white southern suburbs. He returned to Cape Town in 1995, after the first democratic elections, to continue the story of apartheid removals and their impact on the city's landscape. His study of Group Area Act removees from Mowbray is a powerful examination of the way in which power relations in apartheid South Africa were and continue to be reflected in spatial distribution. He identifies the processes in which spaces like Mowbray and the Cape Flats were politically and socially produced, thereby acquiring a specific racial identity within a given set of power relations. Western's study is rooted in Mowbray, one of the original spaces of the Group Areas removals. Using ethnographic methods he eloquently mirrors people's experiences of these processes, especially their profound distress as they found themselves dislodged from familiar social worlds. A Mr Abraamse, one of Western's informants, expressed his distress in the following way:

> I was very unhappy coming out here to the wilderness (the Cape Flats). Coming out on the bus I was thinking where is he riding me to, out all this way? I felt so degraded to leave our house in Mowbray. One night soon after the group areas put us out here, I'd had a couple of tots and I got off

the last bus, couldn't find my way to this house; some children had to bring me to the house. (Western 1981: 218)

Western contrasts this sense of alienation with the Mowbray residents' experience of community in their old area. He portrays the image of a vibrant, lively community in which individuals such as Mr Abraamse were identified as persons, whose identities were determined in relation to a diversity of other persons and shaped within a set of social and cultural values. His experience of personhood was inextricably intertwined with social spaces that included the corner store, neighbours, a customary route to work or school on weekdays and the soothing interior of the mosque or church during worship. Western's description above evokes a powerful sense of loss of closely knit communities and personhood. However, in his effort to register the loss of the original community, Western's descriptions do not reflect how the difference between communities and persons was constructed within the city's social geography prior to forced removals; a process that both continued and was elaborated upon in the new urban spaces like Manenberg.

The description above is not only rooted within a sense of loss of social relations and shared values within a closely knit community. It is also predicated upon and rooted in loss of the sense of difference between Mr. Abraamse and his white neighbors, between his Christian identity and the Muslims in the local Mowbray context, as well as the socio-economic difference between the Mowbray residents and those residing in other, more destitute areas such as District Six or the numerous squatter camps located in backyards on the Cape Flats that were also earmarked for removal during the same period. Mr Abraamse's sense of self is reflected in, and buttressed by, the web of local social relations in which he is embedded, as well as in a sense of the difference between Mowbray and other areas in Cape Town.

Western argues that his informants' everyday consciousness of their 'inferior' racial identities in Mowbray was brought to the fore only through their awareness of their residence within a 'pocket of (less-well-off nonwhite) space' surrounded by the majority of better-off whites. He indicates that this awareness produced a sense of racial group cohesion. Coloured racial identity was spatially defined within the local context, relative to local whites. What Western does not indicate is that, at the same time, these coloured residents in Mowbray did not display a common sense of racial identity with coloured residents who lived in Claremont or District Six or for that matter, those who lived on the Cape Flats. Western's informants also exhibited a lively consciousness of the heterogeneity within this community, cut across by religious, economic and occupational statuses:

> an old (Christian) Coloured lady... said to me: 'there were no other Frederickses in Mowbray.' 'Yes, there were,' I said... 'Oh you mean *Malays*!...yes, there were.' (ibid, 206).

Residents' conscious racial solidarity in Mowbray was not necessarily transferred to the racially homogeneous Cape Flats townships to which people were moved, nor did similar racial classification or a consciousness of common victimhood foster an immediate sense of community. Western found that many coloured ex-Mowbrayites spoke disapprovingly of their neighbours, describing them as '*Skollies* [ruffians or scavengers], alcoholics or rough types.' The important factor that was central to a community in the old neighbourhood, namely the web of personal histories that crisscrossed and connected families in a specific local place, was missing. It was these Mowbray residents' shared personal histories lived in common spaces that assisted individuals in identifying specific persons within their community and that provided them with the social values with which to judge personhood. The definition of persons that emerged and that was contested in relation to the moral meanings assigned to social interactions within certain spaces as well as the means that was used to mark off difference to other communities was suspended when the removals destroyed these areas.

In short, the meaning of colouredness for Western's adult ex-Mowbrayite informants is overwhelmingly tinged with the distress of being forcibly removed from their old neighbourhood and familiar social networks, as well as a familiar sense of difference to other places, to be dumped on the wind-swept Cape Flats alongside strangers whom they initially distrusted. For the ex-Mowbrayite, the meaning of 'being coloured' is very different from that of the ex-Claremont resident. For the experience of 'being coloured' is tied to a specific local place, namely

Claremont, Mowbray, District Six or a squatter settlement in a Cape Flats backyard.

It is not possible to compare the depth of different individuals' distress during the forced removals. However, the individual's social location within the life cycle, the developmental cycle of his or her household, as well as his or her socio-economic status at the time, shaped his or her experience to a great extent. Most of Western's informants, like the older generation of Manenberg residents, were the adult residents and heads of households who were removed from lower-middle-class Mowbray in the mid-1960s. At least half of Western's informants were house owners. Consequently their stories of removal were dominated by the emotional distress they experienced when they were forced from their homes, the economic loss they suffered when they lost their home ownership, as well as their descent into a lower social class as they were moved next door to *skollies* (ruffians) and the unfamiliar 'rough types.'

For Western, located as he was at the single point of dispersal, the Mowbray story of removal became the only story of removal. Consequently, the diverse stories of other experiences of removal, from the numerous locations within the city, from men and women of different generations and from households located at disparate points in the developmental cycle, remain untold. Likewise, the stories of people constantly arriving in the Cape Flats townships over the years, after the great influx of Group Areas removees in the 1960s and '70s, which reflect the social dynamic of this place as a living space, were not narrated. Many of the Mowbray residents Western interviewed, as well as removees from other areas in the city, began anew in areas like Manenberg. They all brought with them both the common memory of their removals as well as the fragments of the value systems that they used to define and judge persons. They used this social capital to assist them in building community anew and to fill in the social vacuum in the new place.

The story of the removals that peopled Manenberg and other areas on the Cape Flats is not a single story. It is the collective pool of diverse, individual streams of memories that were shaped by people's locations in the life cycle, by their households' developmental cycle, by their sense of difference to other communities in the city, and by the diverse places, they came from to the new areas on the Cape Flats. A different historical and spatial location is necessary in order to capture the wealth of these other stories. My own historical location at the cusp of the 21st century looking back to the 1960s, and from within the place of resettlement looking out, enables me to recover the diverse histories of arrival in Manenberg that were lost in the dominant representation of forced removal. This historical location also privileges a perspective that shows how the initial stories of removal to the sandy wastes of these townships have been transformed through the years to stories of arrival in a place augmented by the social and physical accretions of life over time.

At the time my research was conducted, between 1997 and 2000, many adult inhabitants had lived in Manenberg for over thirty years. In Rio Street, situated in The Courts housing zone, where I worked most of the time, I found that the majority of the residents had arrived there more than thirty years ago, between 1967 and 1970. They had been some of the first inhabitants whom the state had declared illegal occupants in the newly declared white areas like Mowbray, Claremont and Newlands, and who had been forcibly uprooted from their earlier communities to be resettled in the little houses on the sandy Cape Flats. Many Manenberg residents who had been forcibly resettled expressed a great deal of ambivalence about their forced move to the area. They had arrived from disparate areas in the city, travelling with their belongings in trucks and cars on the N2 from the poor inner-city areas such as District Six, middle-class Mowbray, or from the numerous squatter camps located in backyards or on the sand dunes elsewhere on the Cape Flats.

They narrate their journey to Manenberg through time and space as one marked by the memories of earlier homes, and of grief evoked through their subsequent loss. Through their stories of dislocation, they indicate that it is the loss of the social meanings attached to these places that was most distressing. In doing so, they underline the point made by human geographers such as Lemon (1991) and Harvey (1973) that places are socially produced and are not only passive, physical spaces on the landscape. These Group Area removees summon up recollections of kin and communities in newly declared white areas such as Claremont and District Six or the dense backyard settlements in the brash, aspirant coloured areas of Surrey Estate and Belgravia. For the removees from more respectable areas such as Claremont and Mowbray, their forced move is poignantly remembered as a loss of social status which was located in the place. Removees from the dense, backyard and squatter settlements register the appalling living conditions in their old locations. But like their companions from Mowbray and Claremont, most often they remember their relationships with the people who lived there and the distress they still experience when they recall how they lost their community. They note that it is within these social relationships, forged within the woof and weft of habitual activities in familiar spaces, through the seasonal cycles of work and festivities that they were identified as persons.

While the ex-Mowbray residents in Western's study registered regret at the loss of their solidly constructed middle-class homes, most adults who lived in squatter settlements prior to their move said that they were pleased to be occupying more formal residences where the physical conditions of life had improved. However, they bitterly regretted that whilst their living conditions had improved, it was at the enormous cost of the loss of their earlier social networks. The following case illustrates a Rio Street resident's ambivalence about being moved from her previous community in a backyard squatter camp.

Aunty Frances is a 53-year-old woman who lives in a four-roomed apartment in Rio Street together with her adult son and daughter and their respective families. She has been living in Manenberg for the past 29 years. She and her husband lived in a squatter community located in a backyard, commonly called 'Die Jaart,' in Surrey Estate before they moved to Manenberg. Earlier, they had moved to the squatter camp when her father was forced to sell his two plots in Rylands when the area was declared an Indian group area under the Group Areas Act. She and her spouse were newly-weds at the time and so the move presented them with an opportunity to move into their own place in the Surrey Estate squatter community while still remaining in close proximity to their kin. Aunty Frances and her husband chose to move to the yard because her sister already resided there. They lived there for approximately ten years. She says that a government official visited their camp in 1974 and marked each house with consecutive numbers. The official informed them that they would be obtaining their own formally constructed homes the following year (1975). They waited another four years before they were finally moved to Manenberg in 1979. Aunty Frances was 33 years old at the time.

The sanitary conditions in the yard in Surrey Estate were very poor. All the residents shared an outhouse. During the rainy season, Aunty Frances's house leaked constantly and puddles of water remained in the yard for weeks. Their shacks were damp in the winter and as a result, her children were always coughing. Aunty Frances said that for these reasons she was very happy to move into a more sanitary abode in Manenberg. She said that *'Dit is baie lekker om op my eie te bly in 'n council huis'* (It is good to live by myself in my very own council house). However, she missed her old social network very much. *'Ons het nou all'ie jare bymekaar gewoon en geheg geraak aanmekaar'* (We've lived together all these years and we've grown attached to each other*)*. She reminisced about the different characters that populated the yard.

> *'Da' is goeie mense wat gewoon'it op die jaart. Nou my suster – ek en sy het soe mekaar uitgehelp met die kinners of huiswerk. Dan is da' Ouma Tries. Hoe! Sy is 'n kwaai Aantie. Djy't nie da' weggekom met onbeskofdheid nie. Sy konnie soe lekker loep nie, so sy't altyd ve die ouere kinners gevra om winkels toe te gaan. Elke einde van die maand, as ons nou geld gehad het, dan het 'n heel paar van ons die bus in Parade toe geniem. Dit is lekker. Ons het in ons beste klere gegaan, amal soe spoggerig in hulle outfits. Da't ons nou groceries en soe gekoep, en lekkergoed ve die kinners. Op Saterdaemiddae, dan het ons grootmense gesit, drinks gedrink en lekker gesels.'* (There were good people who lived in the yard. My sister lived there – she and I assisted one another with childcare or with housework. Then there was Grandma Tries – my, but she was a stern one. She never allowed anyone to get away with a surly attitude. She couldn't get around that well so she'd send the older children to the shops to run errands for her. At the end of every month, when we had a bit of money, then a group of us would take the bus to the Parade. It was great. We'd dress up and we looked so smart in our outfits. We'd do our groceries and buy treats for the children. Every Saturday afternoon we'd hang around, have a drink and talk.)

The children attended the local primary school and her family belonged to the local church. After they were moved to Manenberg, her family still attempted to maintain their links with the old neighbourhood. The children returned to the same school and her family still worshipped at the old church. However, they found the cost of local transport to Surrey Estate prohibitive and so they sought institutional ties closer to home. Her sister was allocated a house further away in Valhalla Park. Aunty Frances takes the bus to visit her sister every weekend.

As Aunty Frances reminisced about the community in the Surrey Estate yard, she was invigorated by the memories of the place and its people. Her face was animated with laughter interspersed with alarm and then a wistful sadness as she recalled 'the good old days.' Her reminiscences are suggestive of the powerful role that memory plays in bridging the gulf of the temporal and spatial disjuncture in the story of her identity, brought on by her own and others' forced removal and resettlement. Her memories of the backyard embed her own and her children's identities within the web of social relationships shaped and located there. Through her recollections of the backyard, she speaks of herself as an agent who chose her previous place of abode. She had lost her childhood home when her father was forced to sell his plots when the Group Areas Act was implemented. Still, she indicates that she was able to exercise some choice about where she wanted to construct her new home. She says that she chose to live in the yard, in close proximity to kin and friends. In this location, physical living space overlapped with the social networks in which she was embedded from the time of her earlier home. While the squatter camps provided less than suitable living conditions, residents lived in close physical proximity to others with whom they had intimate social relations.

The individual household member's personhood was affirmed within these intimate social relations. After they were told to move, they were unable to exercise control over their place of residence. And so they were unable to relocate to new homes close to the people who knew them intimately, namely their old friends and family.

The process of becoming coloured through forced removals did not only imply being separated from the heart of the city. It also meant being removed from backyard squatter communities so that mixed coloured and Indian suburbs like Belgravia and Surrey Estate which were established before the era of removals would be transformed into respectable suburbs for the aspirant middle classes. For most of those inhabitants forced to move, the destruction of the social networks within a specific locality – the very social networks that affirmed the individual as a social person – was at the core of their pain. Without these networks, they became misplaced bodies, dislodged from their multi-faceted identities that were embedded in and shaped by a familiar web of social relations, shared histories and a common understanding of difference, as well as the objects that marked their selves with meaning. It is through the acts of remembering and narrating that they are able to suture together their individual histories of personhood, of the disparate places of origin in Cape Town and social relationships in which their identities were forged. Through memory and the recollection of forced removals, Manenberg residents have created an imagined history of common coloured identity.

B. The loss of personhood and identity

The older generation, who were the first to be resettled in Manenberg, narrate their loss of their earlier homes as a story of lost personhood. Their stories are enmeshed with the deep sense of loss of collective social power in defining persons within the social relations in their immediate communities as well as in relation to the extant perceptions of difference. They also express a sense of alienation and bewilderment at the lack of social relations in which personhood is rooted in the anonymous new place.

For adults like Aunty Frances, their own sense of personhood is affirmed by the children's obedience to their elders' directives. The enforced break-up of their squatter yard community and the spatial dispersal of its members meant that the shared histories of overlapping life cycles of the older and younger generations, required to affirm personhood, were lost. Adults like Aunty Frances express this loss as the lack of respect among the younger generation in the resettlement area, Manenberg:

'Daai tyd toe is da' meer dissipliene en die kinners h't meer respek ve die ouere mense gehad. Hie ondervind 'n mens alles hie. Jy hoor hoe kinners vloek mekaar 'jou ma se die.' Hie is da mense van all over the world.' (At that time children were more disciplined. They had more respect for the older generation. Here one experiences everything. The children curse each other: 'your mother's this [cunt].' Here there were people from all over the world.)

The curse Aunty Frances refers to is considered an outrage and a threat to the cultural building blocks of community. It registers the younger person's refusal to recognize the authority of the older mother over him or her. In so doing s/he challenges the age hierarchy between persons of the older and younger generations that informs, defines and oils the relations of respect between them. Finally, it registers the user's refusal to give due respect to, and therefore recognize, the older woman as a person in the community. This curse is generally used against those who are not mutually recognized as persons and suggests that such people are dangerous strangers who have falsely paraded as persons, but who are out of place and who do not belong. The insult also implicitly suggests that many men have intimate knowledge of the mother's most intimate physical aspect, namely her vagina, through which she births potential persons. This curse is considered to be one of the most powerful insults delivered against someone, striking fear into the hearts of people and evoking enormous anger. It labels the individual as a non-person and condemns him or her to a social death. To insult one's mother in this fashion is to imply that she is morally equal to the prostitute whom everybody knows sexually but who is socially unknown. The prostitute cannot be recognized as a person, for her sexuality exists outside the purview of social relationships. It is not embedded within this set of relationships, and so cannot be controlled by its identifiable configurations. Worse still, her sexuality does not reproduce any potential persons biologically, and, by extension, she cannot be recognized as someone who is capable of reproducing others socially.

When I told Christine, a community activist, about Aunty Frances's remark, she noted that respect is only accorded to those adults who have contributed to one's social reproduction as a person: '*wie my ken van kleins af, voor wie ek opgegroei h'?* (who have known me since I was little, who witnessed my growth [into adulthood]).

Her comment confirms Kratz's (1991) point that the use of curses implies that respect is relational. In the case above, respect is due to an older woman if she has assisted to produce the younger individual as a person. The curse reflects that the cursed has not done her social duty and so its utterance turns her into a non-person. The prostitute and the mother who is cursed as being a prostitute have not invested in the production of persons, remain unknown and so are undeserving of respect.

For many adults, their experience of the forced removals is expressed as a rupture in their personal history. Aunty Frances's reference to the diverse origins of her neighbours is also indicative of her initial sense of personal anonymity in Manenberg. More profoundly, it illustrates her perception of rupture in her own personal history and of her knowledge of herself, for the people and the social relationships through whom she knew herself at a particular point in her life have been dispersed. Similarly, Christine laments the loss of the older generation's social investment in nurturing individuals like herself who were entering adulthood, in another context, at the time of the removals. She expresses this loss through her sorrow over the apparent lack of communal discipline over the younger generation in Manenberg:

> '*Daai tyd is djy amal se kind. Ma hie' as djy 'n kind wil reg bring dan kom die ouer en hulle wil wiet 'Waarom slat djy my kind?'* (Then you were everyone's child. But here if you want to discipline a child then the parent wants to know why you would want to beat *their* child.)

These grievances signify recognition that a rupture had occurred in the tacit, naturalized view that the oldest residents were able to exercise undisputed authority over the younger ones when people were resettled in Manenberg. Christine's memory of a time when a child was *amal se kind* (everyone's child) is located in a time and place prior to the removals when the relationship between the older and younger generation was buttressed by a firmly woven safety net of social relations. Her despair over the loss of communal discipline of children is premised upon her recognition that this form of discipline can only occur when it is embedded within the accretion of social relations built over time. Her comment is also a tacit acknowledgement of the erasure of time within the life cycle, marked by the gap in social relationships brought on by the removals. At the same time, Aunty Frances's and Christine's grief were also suggestive of their recognition that a sense of place is created through the social work that is carried out through relationships over time, as well as the intensive social and material energy that had to be invested anew in the creation of persons within this new place. Their common sense of loss of the old communities, the moral values assigned to space and the quotidian interactions from which personhood emerged were carried over to the new place and overlaid with the difficulties of alienation and disorientation and of starting anew in a space that was a social vacuum. Yet these painful experiences also mark the poignant beginnings of community as people began to provide the social and cultural values that fill in and thread through the township's stark physical architecture.

C. Peopling Manenberg: Stories of arrival

Most adults recall the sand and the bush as the most common image that dominates their first memory of arriving in The Courts. The bush takes on varying degrees of alienation and fear for members of different genders and generations. When I asked some older women about their earliest memories of their life here, Aunty Nellie, a fifty-six-year-old woman, who arrived in The Courts in 1968 and had lived in the area for the past 31 years, made a sweeping gesture with her arm, as she pointed out towards the schools and the netball field that formed the border between The Courts and Zone Three housing:

'Toe ons net hie gekom het, da', da', da' is net sand en bos. Ons is bang om da' te loop, in case die jongens met mens lol. Ons moes deur die bos loep om die bus te kry werk toe of kerk toe. En as die wind so waai is die hys vol sand. Ons't niemand geken nie.' (When we'd just arrived here, over there, over there, that was just sand and bush. We were afraid to walk over there, in case the gangsters interfered with us. We had to walk through the bush to take the bus to work or to church. And when the wind was up, then our homes were covered in sand. We didn't know anyone then.)

She paused, then said:

'So oorie jare het ons mense leer ken. Ons kinnners het met anners vrinne gemaak en hulle het so saam-saam voor ons opegroei.' (Over the years we learned to know our neighbours. Our children befriended other children and we have witnessed them grow up here together.)

82

This story of arrival mirrors the older woman's perception of the place when she came here via the route of forced resettlement, as a young woman in her early twenties. She roots her memory of arrival in her perception of the proximity of the bush to her new house. The adjacent bush symbolized the increased social and physical distance from work and her church community, as well as the danger that the lack of social networks posed to her sexuality. Moreover, her fear of the bush indicates her ability to discern the extent to which the township was wild, undeveloped and filled with unfamiliar people, who could not vouch for her safety. The bush represented the alienation from this landscape, and from the amenities such as the schools and stores that were inaccessible to the newly arrived population. It also signified the huge social and physical obstacles that they had to traverse to access them. Given the uneven but steady infrastructural and social development in Manenberg, and in the Courts where Aunty Nellie lives, the terrifying aspect of the bush recedes from her story of arrival. Temporality shaded the area with accretions of familiarity as she became acquainted with the local people and acquired intimate knowledge about the successive generations. The bush's recession was marked by the younger generation's development, as they bridged the physical and social gaps between the place of origin and the new township as well as the temporal gap between the younger and the older age groups. These young people's lives were vertically nested within those of their parents, the other elders and their own children, and laterally enmeshed with those of their peers.

Aunty Nellie's daughter, thirty-five-year-old Maureen was four years old when their family arrived here. She then took up the story of arrival from her mother:

'*Ons het lekker hier opgegroei. As ons clubs toe gaan innie Athlone, dan het ons soe saam in 'n groep sommer so deur die bos gestap – ek, Illie, Noreen en Judy. Dan kom ons hie twaalf uur by die hys en niemand het ve ons aangeval nie. Nie soes nou nie–- nou skiet hulle gun, en jou eie mense val jou aan.*' (We enjoyed growing up here. When we went clubbing in Athlone, then we'd walk in a group, just like that, through the bush – myself, Illie, Noreen and Judy. We'd return home at midnight, and no-one hurt us. Not like now. Now they shoot with guns, and our own people attack us.)

For Maureen, the bush takes on much less fearful proportions as she returns to memories of a time when leisure amenities like clubs were more established in the area. By then, in the late 1970s, her own and others' fears of the bush had receded. Its size had reduced as more buildings were constructed. Furthermore, it had become a familiar, neutral space that she and her friends were able to traverse without fear. Aunty Nellie's and Maureen's perceptions of development of communities in Rio Street, in The Courts and in greater Manenberg, were marked by the decreasing significance they accord the bush in their stories of arrival. Similarly, other residents who arrived in Manenberg in the late 1970s, after they had been assigned a house there, also do not accord the bush the same significance as Aunty Nellie does.

Vonna is Aunty Nellie's 38-year neighbour. Her story of arrival in Manenberg is more indicative of how central events in her life cycle colour her impression of her cycle of arrival in Maneberg and her departure from here.

'Net voor my ma-hulle uit Lansdowne gesit is, toe's ek mos al groot, toe't ek besluit om op my eie te gaan bly op 'n kamer in 'n vriend se huis in Lansdowne. Later, toe besluit ek maar om met my ma hie te kom bly. Maar toe trou ek en Broer Greg, toe't ons aansoek gedoen vir 'n huis in Manenberg. Hulle't gese hulle gaan vir ons op die waglys plaas. Toe trek ek en hy uit van my ma-hulle en ons het op 'n kamer gaan bly weer in Lansdowne. Toe trek ons agerna na 'n kamer in een van die koephuise hier in Manenberg. Die vrou da' het baie gedrink. Toe kry ons 'n kamer in Black Riverstraat. Na vyf jaar op die waglys, toe kry ons die huis, in dieselfde pad soes my ma.' (Before my mother and our family were forcibly removed from Lansdowne, I decided that I wanted to live on my own. I was an adult by then, and I was able to move into a room in a friend's house in Lansdowne. A little later, I joined my mother here in Manenberg. Then I married Brother Greg and we applied to the municipal housing authorities for a house. They said that we would be placed on the housing waiting list. We moved back to Lansdowne and occupied a room in a house there. Then we found a room for rent in one of the ownership houses here in Manenberg. But the landlady was drunk all the time and so we moved out to another room in Black River Street. After five years of waiting we were assigned this house in the same road as my mother.)

Residents like Vonna were not Group Area removees but extended family members who shared an overcrowded house elsewhere on the Flats while they waited patiently to be assigned their own homes. The newest township occupants also became more visible as they occupied the numerous Wendy Houses or *hokke* that were constructed in the backyards from the late 1980s. These residents' origins were as diverse as those of the original township. They arrived in Manenberg as recent migrants entering, or as ex-residents returning, from surrounding townships, rural towns, or from elsewhere within the township, who had come to join their extended family, or to establish their own dwellings. These waves of arrivals have all contributed to clearing the social and natural wilderness from the township. The diverse stories of arrivals that I have narrated above indicate that the first residents, the early Group Area removees, began spinning the social webs that created community here by drawing on their shared memories of loss and of marking themselves as persons. Vonna's narrative of arrival illustrates that the next generation was also drawn into the area as they sought to move closer to their parents. Thus loss was overlaid with generational continuity in the new place as these residents sought to reproduce and renovate the notions of personhood. In this fashion, the different persons who were identified from within, and in relation to, the new township space diversified a sense of colouredness.

D. Clearing the social and natural wilderness: Defining colouredness in the new place.

Establishing a way of life in Manenberg, especially in The Courts, required not only a physical struggle to clear the bush. It also required and continues to require a social struggle against the wilderness of economic and racial prejudice from the outside, and a struggle to develop a common sense of identity and community within the fragmented, atomized population in the local context. From the time the township was established, three distinctive processes were set in motion by various key actors in the local context, to forge a common sense of personhood and identity within Manenberg. These key actors consisted of local representatives of political groups that supported as well as resisted the state policies, community activists and the other local residents themselves. The processes that these actors set in place have been shaped and anchored in the township's development as a physical and social space over the past 34 years. At the same time their activities informed, created and struggled with the diverse notions of colouredness in the local context. These were linked to, and differentially utilized, the coloureds' structural location in the national political and economic context.

The infrastructural development in the area, which was mainly provided by the state, through the Coloured Management Committee, slowly mitigated against the encroaching physical wilderness. The state also used the infrastructural development to foster a notion of colouredness as a modernizing identity that was spatially and socially located between white and African. So, while the state spent fewer resources on the development of infrastructure and the provision of public services in townships like Manenberg than they did in white areas in the city, these resources were certainly more than those spent in Xhosa-speaking townships like Langa and Gugulethu. Local newspaper reports would carry stories about local members of the Coloured Management Committee proudly claiming how a new building or school in the township was due to their efforts in developing their communities (*Cape Herald*, 17 May 1969).

The community activists' organizational efforts served as another means to clear the social and physical wilderness, in ways that were oppositional to the state. Through their efforts, these activists attempted to create a common consciousness of colouredness as a Black political identity, in which Black people as a whole were defined both as the subjugated victims of the apartheid state as well as its adversaries who were able to forge their own visions of community. As I show below, they mobilized residents around the lack of amenities such as adequate transport or housing and the fight against crime in the township. At times their actions self-consciously tied these struggles to the broader struggle for a non-racial, democratic South Africa. On other occasions, the needs in the local context were emphasized and the links to the national struggle were implied only cursorily. Their efforts were often an uphill struggle to create a common sense of political identity in a context which was initially so spatially and socially fragmented. Simultaneously within the immediate, densely constructed residential spaces, residents themselves were clearing the social wilderness by fostering a sense of colouredness based upon a moral economy in which persons were identified and recognized. Often these three efforts to clear the physical and social wilderness in Manenberg in diverse ways, and to foster a common sense of identity, coincided and were mutually reinforcing. At other times, however, these efforts collided, and strident disagreement and contestation about coloured identity would ensue.

At the time of Aunty Nellie's arrival in 1968, few amenities such as schools, sports fields and stores existed in the area. Other residents registered their alienation from the stark township landscape through their complaints about the high crime rate in the area and the lack of recreational, transport, educational and other amenities such as telephones. One 1969 newspaper report told of the new telephone service linking Cape Town with South Korea, but of no available telephones linking Cape Town with Manenberg, due to the lack of telecommunications services in the township (*Cape Herald*, 2 August 1969). Like most resettlement townships elsewhere in South Africa, public services and amenities such as garbage removal, building and road maintenance, the provision of street lighting, libraries, schools and health clinics in Manenberg were inadequate at best, absent at worst. This is in stark contrast to the excellent public amenities to be found in the well-maintained white residential areas in the city's southern and far northern suburbs.

Historically, the apartheid state's provision of public amenities in Black areas is woefully inadequate when compared to those provided in white areas. When these amenities were provided, they were used as a political carrot to win over public support for the state's separatist policies and to reinforce the ideology of racial hierarchy and modernization. Consequently, while public amenities for coloureds in Manenberg were inadequate to serve the population's needs, they were marginally better than those in the Xhosa-speaking townships located across the railway tracks. The pro-state Coloured Management Committee used the provision of public amenities as a means to win over coloured support for the state's separatist policies, especially when local elections were held to elect coloured officials who served on the separate local councils. Electoral candidates would draw attention to the amenities they had developed in the area. On the other hand, anti-apartheid groups mobilized against these efforts and from the early 1980s they discouraged local residents from using the state political structures to lobby for improved amenities.

Public services and amenities, beyond those that the state provided in its initial plans, were often acquired only through local organization, public protest, political organization and the threat of rent or bus boycotts. By the late 1970s, the township had acquired two high schools and, after the national education crises in 1976 and 1980, educational facilities were improved. During that time another high school was built and the number of primary schools was increased to eleven. Three of these primary schools were located in The Courts area. During the apartheid era, they were only allowed to enrol children who were classified coloured. Now, in the post-apartheid era, students attend these schools from Manenberg as well as from the surrounding Xhosa-speaking areas, such as Nyanga and Gugulethu.

At the time it was established, the township's marginal position in the city was emphasized by the poor public transport system that linked it to the central business and industrial districts. Over the years, transport services have also improved both as a result of the improved public infrastructure and social struggles for affordable, efficient modes of transport. The main bus route was established down Manenberg Avenue, linking all three Manenberg housing zones with each other, with the diverse business districts nearby and with the transport nodes to the city. Historically, few residents have had the means to own private cars, and, since their resettlement in the area, residents have come to rely heavily upon public transport to travel to shopping districts and other amenities in the city. In this manner, Manenberg residents mitigated their physical and social isolation in the Cape Flats bush. During the late 1970s and early 1980s, they experienced frequent increases in public transport costs and constantly complained about these increases, but to no avail. In 1980, they joined other Black city residents in a bus boycott against proposed fare increases. The boycott ushered in diversified forms of public transport. Entrepreneurial local residents who owned private vehicles began illegal, low-cost commuter services for the township residents, and provided new links with areas that were not serviced by the bus or metro rail networks. This practice was also common in other Black townships and spread like wildfire across the

Cape Flats. Through this means, the mini-bus taxis became synonymous with the townships. Being coloured in townships like Manenberg implied being an active public commuter, crisscrossing the divided city landscape between the multiracial workplace and the apparently homogenous racial townships. Being coloured meant that one would spend a substantial part of one's day walking to public transport stops and waiting for, or travelling in, buses and taxis that traversed the city.

In addition, a small number of local businesses were initiated in Manenberg Avenue, including a general store, a hairdressers' salon, dry cleaners, a public health clinic and one or two private medical and dental practices. The jazz club, Montreal, was established in Zone One in the late 1970s and nurtured the city's most famous musicians such as Abdullah Ibrahim, Winston Mankunku, Jonathan Butler and Sathima Benjamin. People from all walks of life and every part of the city patronized the famous club, characterizing it as an illicit, hybrid space of social and inter-racial fusion. Religious institutions and sports clubs were also well-established in the area by the 1980s. Today, two mosques, serving Sunni Muslims, and twelve churches representing the wide spectrum of Christian denominations exist in the area. By the early 1990s a new centre, Nyanga Junction, was constructed across the railway tracks that divided coloured Manenberg from Xhosa-speaking Nyanga. The Junction, as it is commonly known, incorporates the railway station within the shopping mall. It serves as a new hybrid cultural space, where Xhosa-speaking and coloured shoppers and commuters mix freely.

From the beginning of the 1970s, local residents formed different civic organizations to fight crime in the township and to address other civic concerns such as building maintenance, high rentals and poor services. Through their activities, these organizations were constructing colouredness both as a subjugated political and economic identity in relation to the apartheid state, as well as its adversary. The first civic organizations were the anti-crime organizations that the residents formed during the townships' early history. They were formed in response to the lack of civilian policing in the area, and to control the high frequency of crime here. They were also formed to resist the popular perception and media representations that depicted the area as a crime-infested hole inhabited by the lower, impoverished, violent coloured classes. Small anti-crime organizations, such as the reservists, emerged from more localized responses, within the individual housing zones. These small organizations failed after a short time because their members were closely associated with the very gangs whom they were supposed to disband.

The Peace Makers were the best-known and most successful anti-crime organization formed in Manenberg during the 1970s. Their longevity and success were due to their ability to organize their members across the diverse housing zones and micro-communities that constitute Manenberg. They also combined their anti-crime activities with other civic actions such as establishing communal savings clubs and providing assistance to destitute households. The organizations' members consisted of local men and women. The men volunteered as vigilantes to clear the area of criminal gangs, while women policed the individual apartment blocks where they resided. At times they collaborated with the old South African police. However, the ever-present distrust for the state police and the criminal justice system as well as the ambivalent sentiments the members expressed about the local gangs in the area tainted the group with shades of political insurrection and illegality.

Local anti-apartheid activists founded the Manenberg Residents' Association and the Advice Office in the 1980s to mobilize and protest against the poor living conditions in the area, and to link these local issues to a wider political struggle for racial and economic justice. The Advice Office, which was staffed by senior members of the Residents' Association, was established to provide residents with paralegal assistance. It mediated with the various state departments such as welfare and labour on behalf of the residents. By then these activists had defined the state-run services such as the housing offices and the police as adversaries of the Black population. The Residents' Association organized its members according to a decentralized model. In The Courts, a residents' committee was elected in each set of apartments, to record residents' grievances and to resolve any conflicts that arose between them. Residents were similarly organized in Zones One and Two on a street-by-street basis. Through these small committees, the Residents' Association was able to harness the boundaries of the micro-communities for its own ends. These various residents' committees then reported to a central body, who took up key issues with the City Council. At the same time, this association also served as a means of political education, linking the poor socio-economic conditions in Manenberg to the apartheid state's political program. The organization, together with the Advice Office, articulated the residents' dissatisfaction with their lot and mobilized their anger into small-scale political protests in the local context.

By 1985 local branches of the anti-apartheid organizations such as the United Democratic Front were formed and drew most of their support from politicized high school students who had participated in school protests in 1980, and the adults living in The Courts, who worked as activists in the Residents' Association and the Advice Office. One example of this localized protest occurred in 1987 when a small group of residents were angered by the infrequent garbage removal in the area and the common sight of trash casually dumped in close proximity to their homes. Activists from the Residents' Association and the Advice Office organized the residents into a small but vocal band of protesters, and accompanied them on a march to the local rent office, carrying full garbage containers. There they dumped the garbage in the offices and handed over a petition to the local rent officer, in which they demanded better garbage removal.

During the 1980s, at the height of widespread national civil unrest, the activists brokered a peace deal between some local gangs and harnessed their support to protect local activists from police harassment, and to provide an informal crime watch as well as a local justice system. Through their political networks, they were able to raise funds to construct a community centre in the heart of The Courts, named Manenberg People's Centre (MPC). The centre was and continues to be used as a cultural and social space. Throughout the 1980s musical and dramatic performances supporting the anti-apartheid vision of a non-racial, non-sexist South Africa were held there. In this manner, the space was self-consciously defined as a new South African place, through which colouredness was being imaginatively located, and transformed into, an anti-apartheid agentive identity. Local residents were encouraged to claim the centre as their own and to participate in activities where cultural forms from the Cape Flats would be celebrated. For a while, residents could enrol for lessons in music, dance, drama, sports and language there.

At the height of the state of emergency, the centre became a focal point for political protest meetings, music and other cultural performances that critiqued the status quo. Events at the centre, such as poetry readings or jazz performances by local musicians, were publicized as anti-apartheid activities, attracted a variety of people from all over the city and representing diverse racial and economic backgrounds. A number of non-governmental civic organizations and sports organizations such as the Community Counseling and Training Centre, the South African National Civics Organization and the Manenberg Soccer Board were also located at the centre. Like the civic organizations, the sports organizations were also affiliated to the anti-apartheid sports board, the South African Council on Sport (SACOS). Through their activities, these civic, advisory and sports organizations were redefining colouredness as a self-conscious political identity wholly centred around anti-apartheid activities. In this way, they cleared the social wilderness that plagued individuals' existence in Manenberg from the time of resettlement.

However, through their focus on anti-apartheid activities the activists from the MPC, the Residents' Association and the Advice Office defined identity and community solely within the political and economic spheres. In this arena, residents' existence within the habitus of everyday spaces and activities was pushed to the periphery. As a result, political activists, as well as the official representatives of the old state institutions, often overlooked the emergence of identity and personhood within the enmeshed accretions of quotidian actions and local spaces and the gendered or generational meanings they took on for local residents. While the activists were attempting to identify colouredness and personhood primarily in relation to the national socio-economic and political arena, residents wanted their personhood to be affirmed within and in relation to the spaces they occupied and to the people who inhabited them. Residents create and differentiate between diverse persons through the distinctions that they make between spaces in the local context, as well as the meanings they give to the daily or weekly temporal passage through their social relationships and their activities.

E. Defining identity from within the local spaces: A view from the periphery within

During my first few visits to Manenberg, I was struck by its physical and social density. I first entered Manenberg via Vygekraal Road, which separates it from middle-income, predominantly Muslim, Surrey Estate. Vygekraal Road rapidly passes a strip of *koephuise* or ownership houses on the outermost perimeter of The Courts and then twists into little more than a concrete strip that runs between an industrial dump site and the largest soccer field, The Greens, on the southwestern boundary of the township. As I entered the central Courts district, I travelled along a tarred strip, Downs Road, that intersects with Manenberg Avenue at the heart of the township, and divides Zone Three from The Courts. The intersection is surrounded by the densest housing in Manenberg. Blocks of two-storey apartment buildings stretch out from this central point as far as the eye can see. The Courts' spatial design creates a visual impression of a giant, compact Lego-town, laced together into a single unit by a maze of streets and narrow passageways below and laundry lines above. There were few empty spaces in this densely constructed area. The two-story apartment blocks, locally referred to as 'Die Korre,' characterize The Courts and set them apart from the single-storey *koephuise* that are located in Zones One and Three.

The Courts' physical density is enhanced by the network of streets that are filled with pedestrian traffic. The streets in The Courts, like others in the township, were laid out in a grid-like pattern, and run off four major perpendicular roads. These major roads, such as Manenberg Avenue, are the busiest traffic routes through the area. The street names are not without irony. All the street names in the township refer to natural phenomena in the South African landscape such as mountains, rivers or farmland. The connotations of grandeur or rustic quaintness suggested in names such as Manenberg Avenue, The Downs Road, Rhinoceros Street and Vygiekraal (Fig Orchard) Road were not linked to the visible presence of mountains, elegant oaks, green fields, wild animals peacefully feeding or flowering succulents. Instead, they evoked suggestions that the old state, albeit unintentionally, attempted to define this population's racial character as more natural and primordial in relation to itself. They also serve as cynical reminders of Manenberg's previous rural history as a farming community, and, possibly, of coloured history as slaves and farm labourers. The main roads such as Manenberg Avenue and The Downs Road serve as the centre for commerce and traffic. Fruit and vegetable vendors' stalls, as well as some small businesses such as the local supermarket and hairdressers' salon, are located along Manenberg Avenue, while the Saturday morning flea market is held in The Downs Road.

The apartment blocks that provide most of the housing here were constructed in two distinctive patterns in the area, as self-contained U-shaped centres, or in a linear fashion running the length of the street. In the first pattern, two apartment blocks, consisting of eight compact four-roomed dwellings were constructed parallel to each other around a narrow tarred strip. A small children's playground equipped with see-saws or swings is located at one end of the strip, completing the U-shape of the Court. Laundry lines tied to steel posts run the length of the tarred strip. Above it, more laundry lines crisscross the space between the two apartment blocks like a giant spiders' web. These laundry lines are never empty – a variety of clothes flutter from them like numerous, multicoloured flags overhead. They are public symbols of the women's frantic efforts to keep dirt and dissolution, the classic signifiers of impoverishment and disrepute, at bay.

In the second pattern, apartment blocks consisting of four units each sit cheek-by-jowl along the length of the street. In these blocks, two units are situated on the ground floor and two on the first floor. Adjoining apartment blocks are separated by narrow passageways approximately one meter wide, referred to as *gangetjies* or passages. These *gangetjies* lead into the backyards of apartment blocks in the adjacent road. First-floor apartments that are situated at opposite ends of adjoining blocks are separated by a meter-wide landing, accessible by a narrow concrete staircase. The ensuing web of common *gangetjies*, staircases, and landings creates a visual illusion of a single giant dormitory constructed along the entire length of the street. This physical density blurs the physical boundaries between public street and private domestic spaces.

The physical density is matched by population density. In the period of research, eight thousand people lived in Manenberg, and overcrowding is common here. The average household size for a four-roomed dwelling varied between four and eight people (City of Cape

Town 1998). Informal housing suggests that the figure was higher. A vast network of informal housing settlements called *hokke* or cages crowds into small back or front yards to provide extra accommodation for extended family members. These are one-roomed wooden or corrugated-iron structures that occupy the available space in front and backyards. The prefabricated wooden structures are the uniform dark brown of treated wood and are generally preferred to the cruder corrugated-iron structures. Some of these iron structures are painted in bright colours, while those that remain unpainted occur in the familiar hues of tarnished silver and rust, reflecting different stages of weathering. They are home to the residents who cannot be accommodated in the available housing. These residents have created their own shelters in the available open spaces just far enough off the street to be considered private. The social and physical density in the township increased through the 1980s, as the population grew through natural increase and immigration. These *hokke* began to appear in the township during this period as a necessary means to stave off the acute housing shortage, and at a time when the state relaxed its strict control over housing in favour of security control. The use of the *hokke* has diversified and some are used as churches, Islamic madressas, stores, video game shops or nightclubs. Given this physical and social density, residents in the *Korre* are in constant contact with each other. In this manner, the *Korre* flow almost seamlessly into a single geographic unit.

The Court's social and physical density is bounded by the broad, spacious four-lane roads on the north-west, north-east and south-east perimeters and the industrial wasteland, *die Bos* (the Bush) in the west. For the urban planners, these physical boundaries serve as economic and racial borders that separate Manenberg from other townships. For the Manenberg residents, in contrast, these boundaries form a *cordon sanitaire* around the area, and as I will indicate, later on, mark or separate the stranger from the resident and home from the dangerous, unfamiliar places. In this local context, ordinary people create the meanings of racial or ethnic identities, often in resistance to, but also at times in complicity with, those imposed upon them both by officialdom and the political activists.

Ordinary people adapt and reshape these meanings to suit their own ends, through the process of localization, through the use of the local categories of space and temporality in the daily course of interaction, as well as within the rounds of daily social exchange. In this way, they may give prominence to coloured identities in the local context that deliberately eschew racialization. Through the web of their social relations within the local context, these people push the racial identity 'coloured' to the margins of inquiry. Their interactions allow for new identities or persons to emerge that are based upon a moral economy that is both rooted within the local context and articulates with the social and economic locations of coloureds and coloured women in particular in the regional and national structure. In the next section, I examine the economic status of The Courts' residents and its implications for identity and personhood in the local context. I then examine how residents differentiate between the diverse communities that exist within The Courts area itself and identify the numerous social spaces that exist within these communities. At the same time, I show how they infuse these spaces with social and moral meanings that shift with the daily and weekly passage of time in the local context. These finer distinctions that The Courts residents make within the local space and the moral meanings that they associate with them are suggestive of how they actively create or contest identities in the local context.

F. Thirty years after the move: The economic and cultural aspects of identity in the local context.

Residents like Aunty Nellie and Maureen recognize their earlier sense of isolation, signified by *die Bos* – the Bush – and the social and physical labour required to clear it. However, like other residents in The Courts, they speak fondly of the history of their lives in The Courts. In reply to my query, whether she would move from The Courts or from Manenberg, Aunty Nellie replied:

'*Ons woon al die jare hier. Ons bly oraait hier. Die mense hie' hou mens se mond oop. Ek kan vir help vra, enige tyd wat ek dit nodig het.*' (We've lived here all these years. Our lives have been okay here. The people here sustain our open mouths. I can ask for assistance [from the neighbours] any time that I need it.)

Similarly, when I posed the same question to Tessa, a young 17-year-old, she replied:

> '*Nee, ek sal nog nooit trek uit die Korre uit nie. Ek 'it al my vrinne hier. Ons het saam-saam opgegroei en ons kom aldie jare aan.*' (No, I'll never move from The Courts. I have all my friends here. We have grown up together and we've come along together all these years.)

In both these responses, the earlier recognition of the township's physical and social alienation disappears completely. Now both respondents emphasize the social relations between people and their importance to individuals' identities as different persons in the local context.

In her response, Aunty Nellie implicitly identifies the key moral and social qualities that signify personhood or identity within The Courts, namely the ability to sustain people through material assistance and the recognition of their social worth. Local residents in The Courts utilize the gendered bureaucratic provisions of the state welfare system as well as the fine differentiation they themselves make between places in the local context to construct a moral economy in which they redefine, create or contest identity and personhood. Through the moral economy and the local meanings of personhood that emanate from it, individuals and households are socially and physically nurtured and reproduced.

G. The economic capital of local identity

Household incomes in this area are inadequate and people are unable to maintain their households without monetary assistance offered through formal welfare and informal networks of friends and neighbours. At the time I began ethnographic research in 1997, official statistics estimated that 24% of households in the township did not have any cash income, while approximately 64% had incomes ranging from less than US $20 to less than US $40 per month. Approximately 30% of men and 48% of women in the township identified themselves as unemployed and looking for work (SA Statistics 1996). While the official statistics do not draw distinctions between the different areas in Manenberg, poverty is clearly greater in the densely populated Courts.

97

Women who are employed or who are primary security grant recipients are most relied upon to provide the economic means to support the impoverished communities here. Until the recent effects of trade liberalisation on industries in the Western Cape, coloured women living in the townships like Manenberg were more likely to be permanently employed in the local economy.

While the Coloured Labour Preference Policy racialised labour preference in the Western Cape, the nature of the local Cape Town economy gendered it. The clothing, textiles and leather industries, as well as community and social services, form a major part of the Cape urban economy. The clothing, textiles and leather sectors employed 25% of workers within the Western Cape manufacturing sector in 1995 (Western Cape Development Council 1998). Until the late 1990s, these sectors were protected against international competition and have had the greatest degree of labour feminization (Lundt 1996). Townships such as Manenberg have been a key source of female labour. The feminization of their workforce placed employed, coloured, working-class women in a powerful economic position as breadwinners of households. While manufacturing relied on female labour, the position of working women was more secure than that of men, who were largely confined to casual labour at the docks or in the construction industry. These women provided material support for their own and other households within the local community. However, given the high unemployment rates in the township, even these women breadwinners were also likely to be unemployed in many households and they relied heavily upon the state welfare system for relief.

For most of these households in the township, state security grants constitute their lifeline to survival. Like most other aspects of state expenditure between 1960 and 1990, welfare policies and the ensuing benefits followed the hierarchical racial order. State maintenance grants benefited whites, coloureds and Indians primarily, with the size of payments also following that order. Welfare benefits for Africans excluded those people living in the Bantustans and were limited to those who were 'legal residents' in the old white South Africa. In its efforts to create an equitable social assistance programme, the democratic state passed the Social Assistance Act of 1994, which makes assistance available to all South Africans in need. At the time of this research, the old state maintenance grant was being phased out, ending the racially structured welfare system on 1 April 2001. The effects of the former social assistance program were still operative at the local level during the time I conducted my research.

Between the 1970s and 1990s coloureds and Indians benefited most from welfare benefits as the number of grants allocated to them rose steeply, and as whites were excluded as their standard of living rose (Lundt 1996). Data for 1990 indicate that by that time, coloureds received the lion's share of the total number of State Maintenance Grants allocated for children – 48 benefits per 1000 children as compared with 40 benefits per 1000 Indian children, 15 per 1000 white children and 2 per 1000 African children (ibid). Similarly, data for the 1996/97 year, in the post-apartheid era, indicate that the old social security system was still in place. The social security budget for the Western Cape was still the largest in the country and the average monthly allocation per head in this province was the highest (US $56). The data tell of the importance of child welfare grants as one of the primary sources of income in coloured households. These grants were often the primary source of income in Manenberg households where unemployment among adults older than 15 years was estimated to be 30% (City of Cape Town Urban Policy Unit 1996).[1]

Grants for child support were and still are allocated to women as mothers and not to households. Consequently, mothers were and are empowered to decide how the monies should be spent. They have to navigate the state's bureaucratic system, complete the numerous application forms and be subjected to social workers' interviews in order to access these grants. As a result, these women build up a substantial store of knowledge about the state bureaucracy serving the poor. As we will see in the next chapter, this knowledge translates into substantial symbolic capital in the local context. What the social welfare data do not indicate are the social and cultural significances given to state maintenance grants in the local context and how these meanings are played out at the level of the household or within communities such as

---

[1] Unemployment is defined here as being older than 15 years, being unemployed and currently looking for work. It excludes those who were not working and not looking for work, home-makers, disabled people, and those not working and wishing to work.

The Courts. These meanings will unfold, as we examine later on how personhood and identity are constructed and interpreted within the moral economy in this local context.

H. The spatial and temporal capital of identity: defining local communities

In a township with a population estimated to be between 46,000 and 80,000 people, who are the local community and how is the community defined? To the outsider, Manenberg appears to be a homogeneous racial township, a single geographic and social unit. Certainly, it is discursively described as such in newspaper reports and city planners' maps. However, for the residents of Manenberg, socio-spatial boundaries crisscross the apparently continuous geographic unit, dividing it into multiple small communities. The social and physical density in The Courts enables the social and physical reproduction of people here. Residents use The Courts' physical design as well as the patterns in social density to define the boundaries of the diverse local communities that exist within it. These communities are also further differentiated into diverse social spaces that residents imbue with different social meanings that in turn are activated to define the diverse persons who reside here.

During the first planning stages of research in Manenberg, I relied heavily on my older brother, Bertram Salo, for his insight into the social issues in the area. He is the rector of the area's aptly named Anglican church, the Church of Reconciliation. During a visit to his house in November 1997, I told him of my plans to conduct ethnographic research in Manenberg. He reached for a map rolled up on a bookshelf in his cramped study. 'You have to be aware of the gang turf in the area,' he said. 'Work in a single gang turf. Don't work across gang turfs; you could endanger your life unnecessarily.'

He unfurled the map and spread it out on the tabletop. The now familiar map of Manenberg township that the city council planning unit had produced had been transformed into eleven discrete units. 'This is the map we [i.e. he and the church council] use to locate parishioners and to predict which communities would be caught in gang violence when gang war erupts,' he said.

He had used different coloured felt markers to demarcate the boundaries of each geographic unit in which a particular gang dominated. He pointed out the turf of the different gangs: the Hard Livings and the Americans controlled the largest areas. The remaining area is divided between the smaller gangs, namely the Young Dixie Boys, Clever Kids, Naughty Boys, the Junky Funky Kids, Respectable Peacefuls, Wonder Kids, School Boys, Scorpions and Yuru Cats. He explained that young men who resided within the boundaries of each gang turf would be identified as members of the local gang by rival gangs on the outside, even if they did not actively associate with gang activities. Young men living within each community marked its boundaries with the peculiar graffiti associated with their gang. The letters HL$ demarcated the Hard Livings' territory, whilst YDB$ stood for Young Dixie Boys; WK$ referred to the Wonder Kids; SB$ for the SchoolBoys; JFK$ for Junky Funky Kids; RPF$ for Respectable Peacefuls; SB$ for SchoolBoys; CT$ for the Cape Town Scorpions and YC$ for Yuru Cats. By coincidence, I had befriended the young residents in Rio Grande Street, the single street controlled by the Young Dixie Boys (YDB$).

In Manenberg, graffiti is scrawled on almost every perimeter wall, building and even road sign. The graffiti I had seen scribbled on the walls in the Courts now took on new meaning. For the uninitiated outsider the arbitrary letters along with the cryptic, yet ubiquitous dollar sign, $, seem at best benign, to be nothing more than mindless, meaningless vandalism in a township ghetto (UCT Monday Paper, March 2001). The scribble's apparent meaninglessness also seemed to be confirmed when I asked Sharlien about it and she dismissed it with a wave of her hand, replying that '*Ag, dis ma net die jongens wat soe hulle gangse name skryf.*' (Oh, it's just the lads who write their gangs' names.)

The meaning of graffiti takes on new significance when it is clear that, unlike other urban media such as company advertisements splashed on huge billboards, the creators and the symbolism are intended to be secret. The graffiti's message, though recognized by all in Manenberg, is commonly understood to hold significance for a select few only, namely the all-male members of the individual gang and its rivals. Later on, in chapter 5, I show how this peculiar discourse actively confers meaning on place and person. I indicate that not only does it mark off the boundaries of local community, it confers both gender and identity upon a particular sector of the community, namely the young men residing outside its borders. This process of conferring identity and gender upon individuals, as well as maintaining the boundaries of local communities, are especially pronounced during gang warfare.

By coincidence, I had befriended the young residents in Rio Street, the single street controlled by the Young Dixie Boys (YDB$). The male members of these gangs take on the responsibility of safeguarding the local residents and defending the community's reputation. These communities are often no bigger than a single street in The Courts, or a block of apartments. In chapter 5, I show when and how the boundaries of the local community are identified and activated.

Within the communities, residents also distinguish between the street and the home as two semi-autonomous, though conjoined, spaces. The boundaries between the private, domestic space of the individual apartments on the one hand, and the public space of the street and the *gangetjies* on the other, are blurred by the extension of activities such as domestic tasks from the home to the street. The small landings that are shared between second-floor apartments allow one to overhear conversations or keep an eye on activities occurring well within the private household sphere. At the same time, one is able to obtain a bird's-eye view of the street. The almost unobtrusive flow between the outdoor, public world and the indoor activities of the household reconfigure the distinctions between private and public space. The dominant, affective meanings associated with the private and public realms flow seamlessly across these permeable boundaries. The street and the *gangetjies* are reconfigured as an intimate, moral space while retaining notions of the public arena. The street is a space where emotions such as anger, frustration, pride and humour are displayed. At the same time, it is the space where men and women display their moral and personal integrity and subject themselves to public scrutiny. Likewise, their absence from the street, at the times when they are expected to be seen, is indicative of some moral dilemma and is discussed intensely. The street is the space where the rhythm of life is played out, where public opinions about morality and identity are challenged or reinforced, and where the daily or weekly cycle of time is marked. The street is the space where certain types of comportment are expected and judged, and where the various aspects of personhood are displayed. It is also the physical space where community is actively defined. These displays of personhood may vary with gender and age, as well as with the temporal cycle of the day or week. At the same time, they are all anchored within and generated from women's ability to reproduce the community through birth, through material support as well as their ability to reproduce the community through social recognition and affirmation of individuals as persons.

The weekday in Rio Street begins when workers and students are disgorged from the sleepy comfort of their homes onto the street. Even residents who remain indoors can be seen looking out expectantly over the street, constantly watching from apartment windows located on the second floor. The streets bustle with the school children and workers walking hurriedly off to school or to catch buses or taxis to work. They are often joined by those who leave early to seek medical assistance from the public health institutions or the various state and privately run welfare institutions. On the days that the clinic schedules for maternal and child healthcare, young mothers can be seen walking, carefully cradling swaddled babies in their arms. These women are dressed neatly and usually wear headscarves to signify their modesty. All these departing residents are watched from the sidewalks and windows by the housewives and the unemployed. Most people do not own private vehicles here, and so invariably have to walk for some time before they reach their destinations. They remain within the purview of their neighbours' and family members' gaze for a short time until they disappear around corners or onto public transport.

Women then return to the interior of their homes, to busy themselves with domestic work while unemployed men and the elderly still cling to the warmth of their beds. During the mid-morning hours, some women can be seen emerging from their apartments carrying plastic containers filled with laundry ready to be hung out on the lines. Small groups of women occupy the makeshift seats lined just outside entrances as they enjoy a respite from domestic chores or walk to the stores. As the women sit or stand in their little conversation clutches, they quietly share their stories of hope or talk with modest pride of a child's achievement. They also share their stories of concern, such as the lack of income in the household. These stories serve as indirect appeals for material assistance from the other women. The woman making the appeal is careful to insert this request almost seamlessly into the conversation so that she is not embarrassed by possible refusals, and others are not burdened by a request that they cannot reasonably meet. As they talk they watch the flow of activity in the street. If a school student is seen coming home from school earlier than usual, the women inquire about their absence from school.

By this time, others return from their visits to the local health clinic or the state welfare institution, and they stop to exchange greetings with one or another group of women, sometimes informing them of the outcome of their visits. The young mothers returning from the clinic are expected to give a detailed account of their infants' health. This is followed by individual women offering stories of advice and admonition about childcare. Soon the women return indoors to complete their domestic tasks and to await the children's imminent return from school. In a few hours, they are replaced by schoolchildren returning home to play intense games of street cricket or soccer. Sometimes a woman is overheard scolding an errant child who is caught playing whilst still dressed in school uniform. Children are expected to change their dress immediately after school, in order to keep their uniforms clean for the next day. The older children and adolescents are rapidly dispensed on errands to charge up electricity dispensing cards, or to purchase household items at the local house-shops or small supermarket in the area. Others are seen walking in groups to visit friends or to attend netball or soccer practice sessions. Most sportsfields are occupied in the weekday afternoons as the various local clubs practice for the league games they play on Saturday afternoons.

Dusk sees the increase in automobile traffic as buses and taxis noisily disgorge returning workers. As they enter the street where they live, they are accompanied home by the ever-watchful gaze of the housewives. In a short while, the activity on the street thins out, but it never quite ceases. The children and most of the women go indoors. But the streets are never quite empty even during the dark night hours, unlike those in the city's more affluent suburbs. The street becomes a masculine domain after nightfall and street-wise men can be seen strutting through the dark, into the deep night. Rival gang members often confront each other in the street, in the small playgrounds and on the sports fields after dark. In doing so, they display their acts of courage and bravery to each other, under the cover of darkness. No respectable woman would be caught on the street after dark.

Despite the physical density of The Courts, activities within certain spaces remain hidden from the public purview of the people on the streets. This is partly due to the tacit assumption that these spaces are inherently neutral moral spaces and so should not be as severely policed as others, such as the street. One such space is the home. For most residents, the home represents the private space of moral sanctity and a place where all activities are geared towards the social and physical nurturance of those who live there. Young women who spend most of the time indoors after school are assumed to be completing household chores as expected and are described as *goeie dogters* or good daughters.

Another such space is the small postage-stamp size backyard behind some apartment blocks. Most backyards are undeveloped spaces, where old household bric-a-brac, scrap metal pieces and the rusting skeletons of old bicycles and refrigerators are stored until some use can be found for them. Some may contain chicken coops or dog kennels. Adjoining backyards are separated by tall corrugated iron fences, creating a sense of semi-privacy. Second-floor windows overlook these backyards as well, and so activities here can be monitored as well. However, no-one would spend time looking into backyards, because they are not the primary place where people are expected to display or perform their various identities. In the afternoons, groups of unemployed and adolescent men can be seen entering these backyards in groups. Here they sit in furtive groups, smoking 'white pipes' – the name given to the potent mix of marijuana and powdered mandrax tablets. Soon they lapse into a drug-hazed silence, interrupted only by someone spitting occasionally to get rid of the excessive saliva brought on by the drug. Women do not frequent the backyard during these times and do not join in the communal smoking. Some men have confined their smoking to backyard *hokke*. In this way, some backyard *hokke* have become known as the exclusive hang-outs for the local gangs.

Hokke serve many functions in The Courts. Most are used as small, informal house shops where local residents can obtain basic supplies such as bread, milk or eggs. Some *hokke* also carry candy, soft drinks and cigarettes, which are sold singly. The latter goods attract the custom of the adolescent youth in the area and soon become their local hangout.

These *hokke* then become the popular space amongst teenagers of both genders and are often furnished with pool tables and video machines. Teenagers can be found here most afternoons, sizing each other up, playing the available games or sharing a cigarette clandestinely. Most of these *hokke* are also equipped with stereo sets, tuned in to the popular local radio station, Radio Good Hope. This radio station often plays the latest rap, R'n'B or *kwaito*[2] hits and keeps its listeners informed about the latest movies on the circuit, or about planned activities at the popular disco clubs such as the Galaxy in nearby Rylands. Sometimes the young people teach each other the latest dance steps here or even experiment with alcohol that they drink furtively from cheap wine containers. Adults are almost never seen in these *hokke* and parents will usually send other children to extricate their older teenagers from this space. The daylight hours during weekday afternoons, when the adolescents are to be found there, mark their activities as harmless. Teenagers can engage in these leisure activities and still emerge from the *hok* with their reputation as good children intact. They risk tainting their reputations if they are found there after dark, however. This threat poses even greater danger for young women than for young men.

Friday afternoons mark the onset of the long-awaited weekend and the end of the week's daily routine. School students are dismissed from school at midday so that Muslim students can attend the Friday Jumu'ah services. Most students saunter home from school casually in counterpoint to the more hurried pace of their Muslim counterparts. Muslim men wearing the customary long, white, shirt-like garment and kufiyas, displaying their religious devotion, hurry off to mosque to worship. These are the first signs that mark the onset of another, more leisurely pace of time. It is as if the social pressure to display one's identity as an industrious, productive worker, housewife or student has eased off and with that the need to police the efforts taken to perform these identities. Local people refer to this process as a time *'wanneer ons uitrafel'* (a time when we unravel). The children are allowed to play in their school uniforms after school and no threats are issued about dirtying their clothes. They, like the adolescent women, are allowed to

---

[2] Kwaito is the popular music form that has emerged from the Black townships in the 1990s. It draws on rap music's use of spoken repetitive words or phrases against the background of dominant bass guitar and drum rhythms.

remain outside on the street until well after dark. Their presence increases the general sense of social effervescence that pervades most Friday nights. The children's shouts as they play in the dark lend to the festive atmosphere that has taken hold in the street. Workers arrive home later than usual, some having stopped over at the supermarket in Athlone for groceries while others stop for a chat and a beer at the local *hok*. Some young adults buy a case of beers and sit in a front yard drinking them while listening to a popular song played on a stereo system.

On Saturday mornings, most adolescent women can be seen hanging out school uniforms that have been washed by hand, in readiness for the next school week. Shortly afterwards they and their male peers are seen dressed smartly in the latest fashions, ready to hang out at the local *hok* or at Nyanga Junction. Some of their fortunate peers can be seen walking to the local bus or taxi rank, where they will take a bus or a mini-bus taxi to the Cape Town city centre. Often some families will travel to relatives living elsewhere on the Cape Flats, where they will visit and spend the weekend. Most soccer and netball matches are scheduled for Saturday afternoons and the few sports fields are filled with supporters of the local teams as they urge them on to win. Netball teams draw their members from women of all ages from within the local communities in the township. As a result, adolescent and older adult women who live in the same street or set of apartments can often be seen playing in the same team. During these times, the women consider each other as equal teammates or competitors and the customary respect for age is set aside during these matches. Young adolescent women can be heard cursing as loudly as the adults, hurling insults at themselves or at their teammates as they commit fouls or give away ball possession to their opponents.

Soccer is the most popular game in the township and from the age of five years, boys are encouraged to play club soccer on Saturday mornings. Like the women's netball teams the respective soccer teams are also associated with individual local communities. The outing to The Greens on Saturday afternoons to watch the local soccer matches is a gay affair. Local fans transform the space into a festival as they drink beers and eat the fast food and sweets sold by local vendors while they urge their favourite players on. During times of gang warfare, however, the atmosphere at the soccer field becomes tense, as rival gangs back opposing teams. On these days, soon after the match fixtures have ended in the late afternoons, fans hurry home shortly before the space is transformed into a battlefield, filled with the sound of gunshots, people running and angry cries. However, most Saturdays, the games end peacefully, and the fans go off, sometimes to celebrate the team's win in a local *hok*.

Some *hokke* serve as versatile leisure spaces that serve their teenage audiences during the weekday afternoons while transforming into informal nightclubs for adults over weekends. These *hokke* tend to be more sophisticated than those that serve adolescents exclusively. The better-furnished *hokke* contain basic pub tables and chairs situated on the perimeter of a tiny dance floor, as well as a small disco sound system. A mirrored ball suspended from the ceiling marks the *hok* as a place of glamour and worldly sophistication. The *hok* owner often relies on the profits he rakes in from beer sales over weekends as a main source of income. On Saturday and Sunday nights these *hokke* are crowded with local adult revellers, who have come to party. Alcohol is consumed here in large amounts and often drunken fights break out as the night wears on. The silhouettes of lovers making out can sometimes be seen in a narrow *gangetjie*, or in a backyard, where they seek some modicum of privacy in the dark. Their lovemaking may be noticed by passers-by or overheard from a second-floor window or landing, but goes unremarked. In The Courts, where the social density and the lack of private cars prevent couples from finding a suitably safe, private space for intimacy, night offers them some relief from the residents' constant surveillance. The constrained spaces in the tiny backyards and narrow passageways are obscured from the street and provide some semblance of physical intimacy.

The effervescent, jazzy, Saturday night street crowd is replaced by formally dressed churchgoers walking purposefully to church on Sunday mornings. Their resoluteness seems to suggest that they are once again knitting together the more rigid patterns of the workday schedule as they prepare for the week ahead. In some *hokke* however, the pace and activities on Sunday afternoons unravel once again into noisy drinking sessions, as some revellers try to regain the previous night's gay atmosphere. However, the activities on the street are more subdued, as many adults take the obligatory Sunday afternoon nap while the children play.

The numerous spaces that exist within the confines of a single community within The Courts, as well as the daily or weekly rhythm of life here, provide the terrain as well as the cultural resources through which identities and personhood are produced, reproduced or contested in this local context.

Chapter 4

Making Mothers, Producing Persons:
The Gendered Ideology of Orality and Space in the
Local Community

'Sy't deur swaar tye deurgemaak en sy't nooit haar eie vergeet'ie.'
She had made it through hard times and she never forgot her own
people.
(Obituary for an 80-year-old grandmother,
Manenberg, January 1999).

'Terwyl my ma nog lewe, is ek maar nog steeds 'n kind.'
While my mother lives, I still remain a child.
(27-year-old Christopher, a Rio Street resident).

'Ukwanda kwaliwa ngumthakathi.'
My daughter, it is the witch who denies human increase.
(Sindiwe Magona 1937, Forced to Grow).

The Rio Street community, like others in The Courts, has been knit
together over the past 34 years by individuals' social interaction through
time and within the diverse spaces in Rio Street such as the home, the
street or the *hok*. In the previous chapter, I argued that these places are
not just innocuous, benign spaces, but that they are imbued with social
significance and play a particularly meaningful role in creating
community in Rio Street. The accretions of the everyday engagements
in these local spaces have created and reproduced the community here
over time. The process through which these locales acquire social
significance is imbricated with and moulded by various individuals'
interpretation of their personhood that they bring with them to the
everyday social exchange and the local moral economy from which these
identities emerge.

In chapter 3, I have argued that the apartheid economy, racial
legislation and urban planning provided the economic and cultural

capital in the local sphere for the emergence of local identities and placed adult women in powerful positions in local communities such as Rio Street. Apartheid's spatial, cultural, legal and economic location of coloureds defined this group as a hybrid, buffer race, situated between whites and Africans. In this chapter, I argue that the unintended effect of these laws created the material and social interstices in which particular gendered identities such as the *moeder* emerge that are pivotal in, and give meaning to, a local moral economy that itself is generated and reproduced through social interaction in key sites.

The moeder identity was buttressed by three structural processes. First, national welfare and housing legislation governing coloureds' access to economic resources such as social security and housing placed women in a favourable position to obtain these resources on behalf of their communities. Secondly, the regional economy of the Western Cape is dominated by secondary industries such as textiles, leather and canning industries. Until the liberalization of the South African economy in the late 1990s, these industries relied on a feminized labour force that they employed on a permanent basis. Thirdly, Manenberg's impoverished economic circumstances mean that the majority of people living there rely heavily on the women's economic statuses for their sustenance. These structural processes provide the economic and cultural capital for the construction of personhood and identity in the local context. They affect the moral values assigned to physical space, through which personhood is shaped or defined. In the following sections, I indicate firstly how these structural factors shaped, ordered and gendered space and temporality in Rio Street so that a pattern of gendered practices associated with household nurturance and reproduction was brought into sharp relief. These practices instantiate and reproduce a set of moral values that valorize nurturance and social reproduction as well as the *moeder* identity associated with them.

A. Gendering housing and welfare access, gendering household formation

While national policy such as the Group Areas Act sought to order urban space along racial lines, Cape Town city council's housing policies reordered coloured households spatially to suit the nuclear household model. However, many other households in communities like Rio Street attempted to work through and around these regulations as they sought to acquire housing in the township in close proximity to their original kin. Fields (2001) and Paulse (2001) define the household loosely as the people occupying a discrete physical housing unit. However, they also indicate that this definition did not apply to all cases in practice. Taken together, their works illustrate how households were multiply constituted in relation to the members' socio-economic resources. They also indicate that household membership was fluid prior to Group Area removals. In squatter areas like Windermere or backyard settlements in Athlone, extended kin occupied a number of shacks in physical proximity to each other, while in more formal housing areas like District Six or Tramway Road in Sea Point, poorer families rented single rooms from landlords. Multiple family households sometimes formed household management committees to determine common house rules (Swanson and Harries 2001: 70).

Most often a married couple and their children rented a single room in a house, which was similarly occupied by unrelated tenants or by other kin. Most often the wealthiest homes were multigenerational and incorporated some unrelated individuals, who were then scripted into the household as social kin. The terms 'Aunty' and 'Uncle' were and still are commonly used by the younger generation as a sign of respect to older women or men who are not blood relatives but who are acknowledged as social kin. These wealthy households consisted of the homeowner (usually male), his spouse, children, his parents, and/or his wife's parents. Often single adults who were social kin, tenants and servants also resided in the house or in backyard rooms.

Fields and others have indicated that households took different forms in relation to their socio-economic resources and that membership was shifting and fluid prior to removal. Unfortunately, their research does not elaborate how the social processes within households, such as the growth of the younger generation, ageing, divorce or death – in short, what Goody (1966) called the developmental cycle of domestic groups – also influenced household formation. Nevertheless, the city council ignored these multiple determinants of household formation as they formulated housing policy.

City council housing regulations attempted to fix once diverse, fluid and shifting household formations and reify them to suit the nuclear or matriarchal household model. According to these policies, housing was provided to households with a male breadwinner who was married or to a woman with dependent children (interview with Manenberg housing manager, Mr Cleophas, June 1998). In this manner, the city council housing policy denied house owners, landlords and tenants their right to determine who would become members of their various households. These housing regulations biased housing allocation to households with mothers of dependent children, thereby skewering the population distribution in these townships so that women and dependent children predominate. The regulations also made men into members of these households solely on the basis of their roles as heterosexuals, as husbands or as sons of senior women heads of households. However, they could never be formally recognized as household heads in their roles as single fathers, or as single household heads, regardless of sexual preference. These regulations moved men to the social and economic periphery of the household and of the community. Women in their roles as wives and mothers were recognized as and ultimately became, the de facto household heads through city council regulations.

Many single men faced a housing crisis as a result of the cumulative effects of the Group Areas Act and the city housing regulations as these interacted with the developmental cycle of their households. At the height of removals in the late 1960s and the 1970s, the plight of single men in households who did not fit this model was highlighted in the Cape Herald newspaper, which was aimed at Black readers. Headlines such as the one from the Cape Herald dated 24 May 1969 read 'Let's have some sense from the council marriage brokers.' The article reported on the plight of two single men, one a Mr James Matthews, who was divorced, and the second, Mr Harry Simon, who had been widowed. Mr Matthews had originally been allocated a house in Manenberg on the grounds that he was married. Soon after, he had been granted a divorce and on those grounds, the city council did not consider him to be a suitable tenant any longer. In desperation, he had advertised for a wife in the Cape Herald. The report read that his story 'had a happy sequel …. Mr Matthews is now remarried and settled in the house he wanted so much' (ibid). In the second case, Mr Simons and his aged mother had been evicted from their home in Waterkant Street in the city centre by the Group Areas Act. He had applied for a house in Manenberg, but could not qualify for one because he was a widower. He too was advertising for a bride so that he and his mother were not left homeless. These two cases indicate that the developmental cycle of households that was shaped by social processes such as divorce, death or ageing affected household formation, increasing its fluidity through time. City council housing regulations did not accommodate such changes through time, thereby alienating persons such as single, divorced or widowed men in the provision of housing.

Unsurprisingly, the household membership in Rio Street did not fit the city council's nuclear household model. The majority of households consist primarily of women and their adult or dependent children. Single women overwhelming head the majority of households (88%) or consist of three generations of kin headed by a heterosexual couple. If one used the city council's definition of household, namely a two-generational household consisting of a heterosexual couple with dependent children living in a single housing unit, to assess the households in Rio Street, then only two out of 17 households, or 12%, would be defined as such. Eleven out of 17 households (65%) were headed by single women, three (18%) consisted of three generations of kin, headed by a senior heterosexual couple and included their effloresce adult children and their children, while two (2%) fit the nuclear model. In addition, young children move between households for a variety of reasons, challenging the idea of households as discrete physical and social units. Clearly, the definition of 'household' employed in city housing policy does not accurately describe the fluid and complex social processes that households and persons employ to ensure their socio-economic survival and to generate and reproduce the cultural values and practices that sustain persons in their community.

Like housing policies, social welfare policies also apply to the nuclear household model as they identify single women with dependent children or women with unemployed husbands as eligible grant recipients. Men as fathers are unable to apply for child welfare grants. Similarly, these social welfare policies move men, especially unemployed men, to the socio-economic periphery of the household and of the community. In a township where total unemployment is estimated to be 60%, the majority of men would draw upon rather than contribute to these households' meagre socio-economic resources. At the same time, as I indicated above, coloured adult women were considered to be the favoured employees in the feminized textile, canning and leather industries in the Western Cape. The bias towards mothers in their role as welfare recipients, their central role in housing acquisition, as well as their favoured employment statuses, provide the structural form within which the moral economy and the central role of women as mothers are elaborated.

Stack's (1997) research on African-American households in a north-west American city indicates that statistics on households do not capture the complex social processes that their members utilize through time and across space to acquire the necessary socio-economic resources to survive. A key activity that she identifies is the practice of child sharing. However, she reads this and other diverse social processes within and between households only in relation to and as determined by these households' economic strategies for survival. She does not consider the possibility that while the economic strategies shape and inform a community's cultural value systems and practices, these systems and practices are prioritized and may, in turn, determine and elaborate upon the economic strategies that originally gave rise to them. In other words, communities initially generate and recreate a set of cultural practices and values to meet socio-economic exigencies. However, with the passage of time, these cultural practices and values become self-reproducing, sometimes shaping and partly determining economic values and practices.

Initially, as households move into Rio Street, the women as mothers are responsible firstly for ensuring that housing is secured. I have already indicated above how women, as wives and mothers, were central to a household's claim to housing and to a household formation in the township. Women as mothers thus beat a regular path to the local housing offices in Manenberg during the day, defining this bureaucratic space as a feminine space. With natural population growth and the progression of the households' developmental cycle, applications for housing in the area increased. This situation was exacerbated as kin sought housing as close to their natal households as possible. Consequently, housing became increasingly difficult to acquire in the township. At the time of research in 1998, the housing manager for Manenberg indicated that they faced a 20-year backlog in housing provision and that at the time they were providing housing for households who had applied for accommodation in 1986 (Interview with Mr Cleophas 1998). Once again women as mothers were the primary applicants. Informants who had moved into Rio Street in the 1980s, and who were part of the second wave of arrivals there, speak of being on the housing waiting list for 15 to 20 years.

Women like Vonna speak of arriving at the housing office early in the morning to obtain a favourable place in the queue. These women wait patiently in line, week after week, month after month, year after year, to make their inquiries about housing. Finally, a white envelope is mailed or given to them across a wooden counter, informing them of the address of the house that has been provided for them, the date that they would be able to move into the new abode, and the monthly rent. During my research I witnessed women, dressed in formal apparel and clean headscarves, accompanying each other in twos and threes to the housing office. Upon their return home, they share their experiences with the other adult women kin and neighbours amidst exclamations of sympathy and commiseration if their visit was unsuccessful or shouts of jubilation if they had finally been assigned a dwelling.

Households' applications for child welfare grants follow a similar cycle. Once again women in their role as mothers make inquiries about acquiring grants for dependent children. As I show later on in this chapter, their efforts are successful only after numerous, often humiliating interviews with state social workers. Here too, women are required to exercise discipline over their need to express their frustration at another failed application and endless patience.

Their display of stoicism, discipline, quiet resilience and patience as they face the endless waiting for housing or state welfare has been recognized as the hallmark of women's identities as mothers in Rio Street. These characteristics bear testimony to and underline the sacrifice they are willing to make on behalf of their households. In this manner, stoicism, resilience and patience have become two of the key values of the moral economy through which personhood is recognized. Another value that emerges as a central feature of the moral economy is that of child sharing and rearing amongst adult women in different households.

An examination of childbirth, childrearing, child sharing and nurturing practices amongst women, between and within households, in relation to the critical housing shortage in the township, rather than a focus on household membership per se, reveals finer details about the social and moral value system that underpins personhood and sustains the importance of women as mothers. The critical housing shortage in the township has meant that young heterosexual couples with dependent children cannot move out of their natal homes for a long time, even though they may desire to do so. Consequently, new fathers and mothers remain members of their original households for years, while their offspring are shared between the households. Initially, when their child is born, she or he remains a member of his or her maternal household through infancy. However, this situation changes once she or he is weaned. Often parents reside in separate households while their children shuttle constantly between them, knitting maternal and paternal kin as well as households together over time. While men accept parenting responsibilities to some extent, senior women in both households are acknowledged as the children's primary nurturers and caretakers. Consequently, children's household membership switches constantly right into adulthood, until they inherit a housing unit after the death of the senior generation.

Child sharing between women of different households is clearly used as a survival strategy and a means by which the costs of child-rearing are shared. However, it is not the only reason why children are shared between households. Child sharing also becomes a cultural practice that implicitly identifies and recognizes parenting as senior adult women's communal responsibility as well as a means of indicating the primary biological mother's trust in and willingness to learn parenting skills from other, senior women in her own and her partner's household. Similarly, as the child is shared between women over the years, she or he is identified as *almal se kind* or everyone's child. The practice of child sharing also extends beyond biological kin, to incorporate the children of individuals who have been made into social kin as women and households share the quotidian difficulties and pleasures of everyday life through close interaction. In this manner, women's communal child rearing or child sharing expands beyond the confines of the domestic space and extends across domains to incorporate the monitoring of children's behaviour in different households as well as the public space, the street, especially during the daylight hours. Women's practices of child sharing and communal monitoring of children effloresce outward from an economic survival strategy in the domestic household space and elaborate into a key value and practice of the moral economy, namely communal mothering. In this way, women as mothers share the responsibility of identifying and making persons such as the tough men or the good daughters in this community.

In the previous discussion, I have argued that women's practices as mothers define the dominant values of the moral economy, namely stoicism, resilience, discipline, patience and child sharing, and the matrix in which persons are identified. However, women themselves have to be made into mothers, or *moeders*, the central persons through which other persons are identified. Below, I examine how even young, childless women are incorporated into, and assume, the identities of moeders through biological and social child rearing.

B. Making *moeders*: A daughter's rite of passage into adult womanhood

The process of household formation in Rio Street over time illustrates the core role that different generations of mothers within the same household play to ensure its continuity. A young woman's first steps to becoming a *moeder* are marked by her initiation into adulthood through pregnancy. Most women express the desire that their daughters should first marry or have a *skoon troue* (a clean marriage) before they bear children, in keeping with Christian and Islamic sexual mores. Mothers take great pride in their daughters who remain chaste because they embody their own successful careers as respectable parents. Yet most women here have at least one child before they officially marry. When a young, single woman's pregnancy is revealed, it precipitates a temporary crisis for her mother's moral career as a respectable *moeder* in the community and marks a shift of power in the developmental cycle of the household. Through her pregnancy, the young woman embodies and signals the break from her dependent status as a daughter. This crucial moment in the young woman's life generates both rupture and continuity within the household. Through the act of pregnancy, the

119

young woman and her partner have initiated her own passage into a new phase of life. In addition, the young woman's pregnancy has also signalled the shift in relations of power between mother and daughter and of a change in the household structure. The women's narrative of pregnancy, illustrated in Liesl's story below, indicates how the crisis, that is precipitated when the younger women's active sexuality is revealed, is managed so that the older woman's reputation as a respectable mother is restored while enabling her daughter's rite of passage into motherhood.

During my first few visits to Grande street, Charlene introduced me to her 55- year-old mother, Mrs Andries. She was a mother of three daughters. The eldest, 22-year-old Pokkel, was married and lived in the Wendy House[3] with her husband and infant son. The other daughters, 16-year-old Leisl and 8-year-old Kaylin lived with their mother in the main house. On that wet Monday afternoon, we sat chatting in her well-furnished living room. She listened as I told her about my project – then it was still firmly focused on the lives of adolescent women and sexuality.

> '*Ek wil wiet hoe groei die meisies hie' op, wat maak hulle ve entertainment, op watter ouderdome hulle nou met outjies sal uitgaan, of hulle seksueel aktief is, of hulle family planning gebruik en dies meer*' (I want to find out how the young girls grow up here, what they do for leisure, at what age they start dating, whether they're sexually active and whether they use family planning), I said.

Nannies then began telling me about her daughter's lifestyle.

> '*Ja, Leisl is sestien jaar oud, maar sy's nog op skool. Sy gaan nou wel met 'n outjie uit – Aan' Gwen se seun, Peter, ma' sy's 'n goeie kind. Sy en haar suster bly nounet heel dag hier in die huis na skool, doen nou huiswerk, en sal nou kook. Hulle gaan so te sê, nou nie baie uit nie, net nou hie' oorkant na vrinne toe, of sy sal nou saam met Peter na sy ma se huis toe gaan. As hulle Owen se hok toe gaan op 'n Saterdagmiddag, dan gaan sy en Pokkel en Peter saam. Hulle sal nou net da' sit en 'n drink drink, miskien dans, of kyk hoe dans die ander. Hie' agtuur is hulle al in die huis. Verlede Saterdagaand toe gaan ek en my berk na die hok toe, toe kyk ek my verbaas aan ve die jong meisies, hulle was ma' nog kinders, ma hulle sit oek da' innie hok, mit lang, lang sigarette, die rokkies is soe kort en hulle is vol make-up gesmeer. Ek is ma net*

---

[3] A Wendy House is a portable two-roomed log cottage that Manenberg residents use to accommodate extended family members. It is usually located in small backyards.

dankbaar dat my klomp nie soe is nie. Ek vra toe myself wa's hulle maens dan om te kyk hoe gaan hulle hie laataand aan.' (Yes, Leisl is sixteen years old but she still attends school. She has a boyfriend – Aunty Gwen's son, Peter, but she's a good child. You will find her and her little sister at home [indoors] after school, busying themselves with housework, like cooking. She hardly ever goes outside – often only to visit her friends across the street, or accompanying Peter to his mother's house. When they go to Owen's hok on Saturday afternoons, her eldest sister Pokkel and Peter accompany her. They'll hang out there, drinking soft drinks, maybe dancing or watching others dance. At eight o'clock they're home. Last Saturday evening, when my boyfriend and I visited the hok, I stared in amazement at some young girls who were there. They're mere children but they were there too (at night, in adult company) smoking long cigarettes, wearing really short dresses and heavily made up. I am grateful that my lot are not like that. I wished that their mothers were there to observe how their daughters were (mis)behaving. You'll never find my lot in that crowd.)

Nannies said this with satisfaction.

I then arranged to interview Liesl herself, in the next week. However, before that happened, Charlene informed me that Liesl had had a baby. Amazed, I inquired how that was possible. Grinning at my reaction, Charlene replied:

'Sy't dit van a'mal wegestiek. Heel Vrydag kla sy by ha' ma dat ha' maag pyn. Nannie't toe ve ha' Harmans druppels, en koliek druppels gegie, ma' niks het gehelp nie. Laat daai aand, ga't sy toilet toe, en toe begin sy ve ha' ma te skreeu. Nannies se toe't sy net betyd aangekom want toe' die kind se kop al halfpad uit.' (She hid it from everyone. On Friday she complained constantly about a stomachache. Nannies gave her Harman's and Colic drops,[4] but nothing seemed to ease her pain. Later that night she went to the toilet and then called her mother frantically. Nannies said that she arrived just in time to see the baby's head emerge.)

We returned to Nannie's house to visit the new mother. I congratulated Liesl on the birth, while Charlene said in jest *'Jy't gou*

---

[4] Popularly known as 'Dutch medicines' and commonly used to treat sundry ailments.

gewerk!' (You worked quickly!). Leisl smiled modestly and proceeded to show us her little son snuggled against her breast. Nannies had watched our entry warily but relaxed visibly when we offered our good wishes. She began to tell us about her experience of the events that led up to the infant's birth.

'*Een oggend, toe kom Peter saam met Aan' Gwen om te kom sê. Ek was bitter kwaad met hom. Maar hy't darem gesê hy's jammer dat hy ve Liesl bederf het, en hy't belowe dat hy die kind sou onderhou. Wat kon ek nou daarna vir hom en sy ma sê .. .ek't net gesê ek aanvaar sy verskoning en ons moet maar net dankbaar wies ve die kind. Liesl het net in die kamer gesit met die kind. Hulle't nou hulle bed gemaak, hulle moet net daarop lê. Sy ma't belowe dat sy ve hulle sal uithelp met kindersorg as Liesl wil terug skooltoe volgende jaar. Ek't oek ve hulle gesê ek sou ve hulle uithelp waar ek kan.*' (One morning Peter arrived with his mother, Aunty Gwen, to 'come and tell.' I was angry but he apologised about Liesl's pregnancy. He promised that he would support the child. I accepted his apology and said that we should be thankful for the child. They've made their bed, now they must sleep in it. His mother said that she would assist with child care if Liesl returned to school. I said that I would do the same. I don't know how she managed to hide it from me that well. Every month she used to ask for money for sanitary towels. I assumed that she was having her periods regularly so she was healthy. I don't know how it [the conception] could have happened.)

Liesl continued to breastfeed the infant on the sofa, with her eyes lowered whilst her mother spoke with us. Then Nannies said with pride '*He's a greedy one, wants to stay latched onto the breast.*' The time for shame and regret was ending. It was time to celebrate the life of the infant and, clearly, he was being warmly welcomed by the ready network of caring kin. Months later, Liesl informed me about how she and Peter were able to engage in sexual intercourse, despite being surrounded by the apparently vigilant mothers and other family members. In her diary, she wrote:

'*Ek en Peter het uitgegaan ve twie jaar vandat ek 14 jaar oud was. Hy't nie ander meisies gehad nie. Na twie jaar toe begin hy met my te praat van seks. Ek't ve hom gesê dat ek noggie gereed was nie. Maar toe een aand, toe my ma hulle by die hok was, toe't ons allien hie gesit en TV kyk, toe druk hy my vas. Hy't gesê ons gaan al lank uit en hy't lank genoeg gewag. Toe gebruik hy ve my.'* (Peter and I were dating steadily for two years, from the time I was 14 years old. He wasn't seeing any other girls then. After two years he began talking to me about having sex. I told him that I wasn't ready yet. One evening, when my mother was out at the *hok*, we were home watching TV by ourselves when he got hold of me. He said that we had been going together for a long time and he had waited long enough. Then he used me.)

Nannies's narrative about Liesel's reputation as a good girl, followed by the revelation about her pregnancy, characterizes the moral cycle that marks the woman's rite of passage from *a goeie dogter* or good daughter, to her new identity as a respectable *moeder* or mother. The rite of passage into respectable motherhood is marked by recursive emotional shifts that are reflected within Nannies's narrative. During the first stage, the narrative is dominated by Nannies's story of successful motherhood and her obvious pride in her daughters' ability to understand the relationship between local spaces, gender and personhood in Rio Street. Good girls who stay home, occupying themselves industriously with housework, attest not only to their own modesty but also to their mothers' respectability. Whilst they may be seen on the street, they appear only during daylight, usually in the company of other girlfriends. Nannies's story shows that her daughters have internalized the values of modesty and respectability, and take on the responsibility to police themselves and their friends. This apparently internalized self-policing aspect won them some degree of leisure time in spaces such as the *hok*, at least during daylight hours. Nannies proudly indicates that her daughters were not only able to perceive the moral meanings of local spaces such as the *hok*. They were also able to discern the nuanced shifts in these meanings as the *hok* was occupied by different bodies at different times during the day, as well as the inherent threat the *hok* posed to their moral reputations as young, *goeie dogters* (good daughters) if they transgressed the rules of occupation. Nannies' story reflects that she had taught her daughters the lessons of morality, gender and space very well indeed – they had learned the local, cultural grammar of personhood well, thus distinguishing their mother as a respectable *moeder*.

In the second stage of the moral cycle, the older woman's shame and anger dominate, as the young woman's pregnancy is revealed. Nannie's reputation as a respectable *moeder* is threatened by Liesl's transgressive action, as well as her reinterpretation of, and challenge to, the dominant meaning of the home as a moral space. In this case, Liesl's partner Peter was acknowledged to be 'an honourable man' – he visited her at home openly, thereby showing respect to mother, daughter and the household. In addition, the couple were welcomed into Peter's mother's home. The mothers' acceptance of their children's partners in their homes indicated that the relationship was honourable. Yet the facade of respectable spaces such as the home also allowed the young couple some agency. This private space is defined as the quintessential space of respectable, sexually inactive adolescent women. Yet Liesl's diary records that they were in the home, the space of feminine respectability, when they had first had intercourse. Liesl's and Peter's actions indicate that spaces such as the home, and temporality, in this case, daylight, may only appear to possess a fixed, predetermined moral significance within the local moral economy. The moral significance of time and place ultimately emerges from the social actions of particular persons at particular times. In this way, the categories of significance that make up the local moral economy are rendered open, emergent and contingent. When Nannies acknowledges that she was temporarily deceived, her anger and shame embodied and disclosed these tensions and contradictions that emerge, as the moral significance of the home, which was implicitly assumed to be fixed and mutually shared, is contested through, and instantiated in her daughter's rite of passage to adult motherhood. Liesl's pregnancy allowed for the potential reinterpretation of Nannies' claim to having been a respectable *moeder* who had vigilantly policed her daughter's sexuality.

Nannies' angry claim that

> I don't know how she managed to hide it from me that well. Every month she used to ask for money for sanitary towels. I assumed that she was having her periods regularly so she was healthy. I don't know how it [the conception] could have happened.

reflects the fact that she had been policing her daughter's sexuality as she was expected to do. Through her claim, she implied that Liesl had 'stolen' her adulthood from her mother through deception. Liesl's adult status is registered in Nannies' dissociation from her deliberate, independent decision to deceive her mother and subvert the moral definition of the home as the space of the *goeie dogter* (good daughter). The reputations of the mother and the home momentarily exist in a liminal moral space and local residents speculate whether they were deceived by women who deceived them, and who parodied the respectability of good mothers and daughters.

Nannies' anger and shame, along with the public threat to her reputation as a respectable *moeder* are dissipated, and her own, as well as her household's reputation, are restored, when the young man, accompanied by his mother, claims paternity through *ga't sê*.

Peter's claim to paternity, through the ritual *ga't sê*, allowed Liesl to prevail as a new adult woman and *moeder* while their households' and their mothers' moral reputations are restored. *Hy't ga't sê* is the phrase commonly used to refer to the prospective father's ritualized visit to the girl's parents, and more importantly, to her mother, to inform them about the pregnancy. This visit marks the first time that the girl's parents claim they learn about her situation. They express initial shock at the news even though they are likely to have learned about her pregnancy from other sources prior to the man's visit. It is also the time when the man apologizes for bringing shame upon the girl and her household and indicates his intention of honouring her by supporting her through the ordeal.

This act signifies that the man has considered the girl respectable enough to apologize to her parents. It is also the means whereby he claims formal responsibility for the pregnancy and paternity of the child. Throughout the conversation, the young man expresses a spirit of contrition and humility. The girl's mother berates him for bringing shame upon her home. He is expected to remain silent throughout this time. The girl, who usually happens to be present in an adjoining room, is called into the conversation at this point, and she is also scolded. After the scolding, the parents could either continue the conversation by asking the couple about their future plans, or the young man could be told to leave the house. The parents indicate their willingness to support

125

the couple when they choose to continue the conversation. If the young man is asked to leave then it serves as a sign that his apology and contrition have been inadequate. He would be expected to pay another visit to the girl's parents later.

Often the young man is accompanied by his mother during this visit. Her presence not only attests to her own and her son's honourable intentions but also reflects that her household, as well as the one she is visiting, are respectable. If a young man does not claim paternity at all, then aspersions are cast upon the young woman's as well as her mother's moral reputation. In such cases, rumours fly through the community, claiming that the young woman had been sexually active for a long period of time, was promiscuous, and worse, had used birth control to prevent pregnancy. The mother is cast in a dim light as a bad or *slegte moeder*, who has not policed her daughter's sexuality. Happily, Peter and Liesl had adhered scrupulously to the local notions of respectable persons-in-the making. Yet they were still able to manipulate the apparent rigid set of cultural rules about personhood and sexuality in order to assert their own transformation into adults, with no harm done to their mothers' respectable reputations.

In the final stage of the moral cycle, the newborn is celebrated as a sign of the households' continuation, and pride dominates the young woman's transition into adulthood. During this period, usually, both households display a keen interest in and claim on the newborn child and the new parents. The grandmothers are solicitous in their concern for the new mother and her child. Usually, the new parents visit the households in their community to show off their new infant, and the *moeders* enthusiastically offer them advice on childcare. During these visits, the infant is introduced to the local community, and, by extension to the people who will nurture it in the local cultural and moral practices. During this public display of pride in the newborn, the new parents also publicly register that their loyalty towards each other and their respect for each other's households have always been honourable. Peter had amply demonstrated that he was 'man enough' to assume the responsibility of fatherhood by acknowledging parenthood and by apologizing to Nannies for the conception. His mother's presence attested to his honourable intentions and his links to a respectable home, as well as to her own reputation as a respectable mother. His claim to paternity through the ritual *ga't sê* also indicated that he had the moral fibre of a responsible man.

Once the respectable reputations of the expectant woman and her mother have been restored, the community reads the pregnancy as public proof of the young couple's loyalty to each other and of their willingness to accept adult responsibility associated with parenthood. Liesl's pregnancy served as a public indication that they had not used any birth control, and were willing to bear the consequences. In contrast, the use of birth control devices such as condoms, injections or oral contraceptives, is associated with immaturity, irresponsibility, selfish sexual motivation and sexual promiscuity. More importantly, the local community regards women's control over their reproduction in an ambivalent light. While many women acknowledge the control they can exercise over their individual reproduction through contraceptive use, they also fear their loss of control over younger women's sexuality and with it, their power to mould personhood. Ultimately women's reproduction is perceived as a threat to two core local values that are central features of the *moeder* identity. The adult women's ability to reproduce the community socially and biologically is threatened, thereby undermining the mothers' powerful positions, and ultimately, their collective ability to maintain the cultural logic that sustains this reproduction.

Liesl's pregnancy had precipitated an apparent crisis within Nannies' household. However, her successful rite of passage into the *moeder* identity had resolved the crisis by accommodating the subtle reconfiguration of generational power within the household when a daughter became a mother too. In most cases, young women like Liesl are able to make the transition from *goeie dogters* (good daughters) to *ordentlike moeders* (respectable mothers) successfully. The young woman's transition to adult motherhood marks the beginning of her career as an *ordentlike moeder*, but it does not guarantee that she will retain this identity throughout her life. She now has to work hard to illustrate that she has the moral and emotional resources to remain an *ordentlike moeder*. In the following life history, Sharlien's experiences as a *moeder* illustrate the vicissitudes and challenges that an *ordentlike moeder* encounters in her moral career. It also indicates how the cohort of *moeders* acts to sustain each other in their moral journey.

C. Policing the moral career: Maintaining respectable mothers

I climbed the grey concrete stairs to Vonna's first-floor apartment one Tuesday afternoon. I had had a busy morning running errands and relished the thought of sitting quietly in Vonna's small, tranquil living room chatting with her. Sharlien had introduced me to Sister Vonna during my initial visits to Rio Street. When I first met her, she was seated on an upturned milk crate outside her gate chatting with a few older women during their early afternoon respite from housework. Vonna was modestly dressed in a checked housecoat that covered a knee-length skirt and blouse. She kept her head covered like the other senior women, constantly tucking in her hair under a woollen, crocheted hat. She greeted us with '*Die Here is goed, Sharlien, kannie kla nie*' (The Lord is good, Sharlien, I can't complain), as we approached the group. I later learned that this phrase was Vonna's customary manner of greeting. I also learned later that she disapproved of my wearing a pair of jeans or an unlined skirt. '*Elaine is 'n ma en 'n getroude vrou. Die manne kan alles sien*' (Elaine is a mother and a married woman. The men can see everything), she would chide me gently, referring to me in the third person as a mark of respect to offset the rebuke.

As I climbed the stairs to her tiny apartment, I thought about how time took on another, slower quality in Rio Street. I cherished these visits when I could sit down, spend time drinking tea and listen to Vonna's reassuring voice. I realized that she had become more than the 'expert informant' – she had become a close friend and a cultural mentor. She guided me through the behavioural codes expected of me in Rio Street and mediated my relationship with the more senior women. In return, I assisted her by running errands in my car or obtaining catering jobs for her through my network of professional friends.

I looked back over the street when I reached the small landing. The day took on a mellow, more tranquil tone. The sounds from the street consisted mainly of people's shouts and laughter interspersed with an angry reprimand or the occasional noise of a passing car. Some women stood around in a conversation clutch, chatting and idly monitoring the activities in the street. The few private cars in Manenberg meant that while people were confined to transacting their affairs in the area, they could also take possession of the streets. Residents were able to stroll at leisure in the streets, while children played street cricket or pushed each other in pushcarts they had constructed from milk crates, some planks and tin cans. The peaceful street scene belied the constant worry about unpaid bills or empty food cupboards that gnawed away relentlessly at every *moeder's* peace of mind, or the copper-tasting fear that filled one's mouth every so often when a gun battle erupted suddenly.

I entered Vonna's simply furnished, immaculate living room. She had created a tranquil home environment above the grit and dust of Rio Street. Vonna's living room, like most others in the area, was filled with framed prayers and family portraits. These objects celebrated family life and distinguished the domestic space as a place of warmth, social order and respectability. On one wall, framed family portraits or pictures of individual family members were displayed. On another, a framed prayer entitled '*Wat is 'n moeder?*' (What is a mother?) was prominently displayed. In Muslim households, these prayers would be replaced with the framed images of the *Ka'bah*[5] or the gold and black *rakams*, which consist of Koranic quotes or prayers written in gold Arabic calligraphy on a black, velvet background. Every surface and object in the room, like the rest of the house, was polished to a high sheen. The sparkling cleanliness silently communicated the energy that women like Vonna expended doing housework. I found her sitting in an easy chair enjoying a cup of tea. She greeted me with the usual phrase '*Die Here is goed*' (The Lord is good), and then rose to fetch me some tea too. Soon I was gratefully sipping the warm, sweet liquid. Vonna's religious invocation, which most adult women, whether Christian or Muslim, customarily used to greet each other, also served to indicate that she was unruffled by everyday crises because she lived in accordance with divine guidance.

Vonna asked me,

'*Het Elaine van Sharlien gehoor? Sy gaan mos nou met 'n gangster uit. Sy hou net uit da' by Alim en Kleintjie se hok. Drink net biere. Ek wietie wat gat aan met ha' nie. Elaine moet met ha' ga' praat.*' (Has Elaine heard about Sharlien's doings? She's seeing a gangster. She spends most of her time at Alim and Kleintjie's hok, drinking beers. I don't know what's happening to her. Elaine has to speak to her [about this situation].)

---

[5] The holy rock of Islam that pilgrims visit during the hadj or pilgrimage.

Vonna's concern about Sharlien's reputation was well-founded. At the time, Sharlien was the only source of income in her household. She lived with her parents, her younger brother, Lindley, and her two daughters. Her mother was chronically ill and was unable to seek work. She kept house for the six-member household. During the summer her father and brother were employed as casual manual labourers in the dockyards. However, during the stormy winter months, shipping traffic thinned out and there was very little work available then. Her father and brother would remain unemployed until the summer when the rains ended and the dockyard or construction companies would be looking for labourers.

Until recently Sharlien worked at Bonny Textiles factory as a casual worker. She had hoped that they would change her employment status to that of a permanent worker after she had worked there for three months, as required by labour legislation. However, the employers had terminated her contract shortly before the three-month cycle ended, in keeping with the new labour casualization practices. They did this in order to avoid employing a worker permanently, thereby incurring the extra costs of medical and other insurance benefits. The factory supervisor promised Sharlien that she could renew her labour contract after two months. Until then, she had to rely on the small welfare benefits of R200 (US $20) per month for her two minor daughters and R60 (US $6) that she received from their father for child maintenance. She used this small sum to purchase food for the entire household. She frequently asked Sister Vonna or me for assistance in the form of small cash loans or groceries when their household supplies ran out, usually after only two weeks.

By risking her *ordentlike* or respectable reputation Sharlien was risking her own as well as her children's social and material strategies for survival in Rio Street. The street community sets great store by a woman's reputation, especially if she is a mother. As I indicate in the discussion below, her moral reputation as *ordentlik* (respectable) or *sleg* (bad) holds serious consequences for her children as well as for herself. If a mother gained the reputation of being *sleg* then her own social, and by association, her economic, network would shrink. To be *sleg* also means that the friendship network of a woman's offspring, especially that of her daughters, would be curtailed. Other '*ordentlike* women' would not allow their children to spend time with them for fear that they too would gain the reputation of being *sleg*. Adolescent girls live in fear of acquiring a reputation as *sleg* through the gossip network.

I was concerned about Vonna's account of my friend's behaviour. Vonna's appeal to me to talk to her, however, indicated that Sharlein's reputation could still be rescued. The community, and more particularly the *moeders*, had yet to pass final judgement about her recent behaviour. She had not yet been written off as *sleg* even though she was known to be spending an inordinate amount of time in Alim's *hok*, where the Dixie Boy gang hung out. When Vonna requested me directly to talk to Sharlien, she was not only asking me to advise my friend to stop her potentially dangerous liaison. She was entreating me to use my own reputation as a respectable woman and, as Sharlien's friend, to help swing the current ambivalent opinion about her still untarnished reputation. I knew then that the mothers in the street were carefully monitoring the people with whom I was seen to be associating, in order to make a judgement about my own reputation and about those whom I chose to befriend. My decision to associate with Sharlien after the rumours were spread would cast doubt upon the opinions that she had become *sleg*.

Sharlien was the first woman I had befriended in Rio Street and she introduced me to the *moeders* in the community. Sharlien had also reassured me that I would not find the local gangsters threatening. She had subsequently mediated my relationship with the young men in the area and over time our friendship had grown. During our numerous conversations, she had shared many intimate details about her life. She was a 25-year-old mother of two girls, Tammy, aged 10 and Jadine, aged 5. She had known the children's father, James, since childhood. Like most people here, he was more commonly known by his nickname, Spookie. He and Sharlien had started their relationship when she was 13 years old. Spookie's family lived in the *Koephuise* (ownership houses) section, and he was considered to be a good match because he was from a more respectable, better-off household than Sharlien was. He was her older brother's friend and a member of the local soccer team, Rio Rangers. He spent most of his free time in Rio Street with the local boys and so was considered to be a part of that community, even though he lived elsewhere. Sharlien had become pregnant when she was 15 years old and was forced to drop out of her first year in high school. She wasn't overly concerned about her economic well-being at the time because Spookie was permanently employed at a small distribution company.

When Sharlien became pregnant Spookie had *ga't sê* so that he could claim paternity of the child, and assume responsibility for her. At the same time, he was also asserting Sharlien's reputation as *ordentlik* or respectable, by claiming paternity. He had paid the formal visit to her parents one evening after work and informed them that Sharlien was pregnant with his child. Like other women in her situation, Sharlien had waited in the adjoining room, where she was able to listen in on her parents' response to Spookie's announcement. Following the ritualized conversational format, Spookie had formally apologized to her mother for 'spoiling' her daughter and indicated that he would provide material support for Sharlien and the child. In addition, he also promised to marry her after their child was born.

As expected, Sharlien's parents expressed their initial shock at the news. Sharlien was then called into the bedroom where she was informed about her parents' disappointment in her behaviour. Her mother told her how she had

'*ordentlik opgebring in 'n opregte huis*' *(well raised in a respectable home)*, how she had '*my bes probeer om jou reg groot te maak*' (tried my best to raise you properly) and how '*ek'kie wiet wa' jy geleer'it om su'kke dinge aan te vang'ie*' (I don't know where you learned to do these things, i.e. have sex).

Sharlien, who was reduced to shameful tears by then, apologised to her mother and expressed her gratitude to her for sustaining her and caring for her throughout her childhood. She said that she had emphasized that she alone was responsible for her situation and that her mother had done all she could to ensure Sharlien's sexual reputation as a respectable daughter. Spookie had recuperated Sharlien's *ordentlike* reputation by going to *ga't sê*, and this left her parents little option other than to support the couple's future plans. Sharlien and Spookie continued to live in their respective natal households but still maintained their relationship. Through the birth of their child, they had obtained tacit permission to continue their sexual relationship, without being subjected to the condemning gossip of the Rio Street community. Often Sharlien would sleep over with Spookie at his house when his mother was away visiting family or friends in another part of the city. The Rio Street community regarded them as a couple.

After Tammy's birth, they had selected a wedding ring set which Spookie had bought on a credit plan from a local department store. They had become engaged on Christmas Day when Tammy was two years old. Sharlien had obtained employment at a local clothing factory by this time. She obtained her job through the local system of introduction, *ingebring* (bringing in), which most local women relied on to obtain employment. Sharlien *was ingebring* by Morieda, an older woman who lived close by. At that point, however, rumours abounded about Spookie having fathered another child with a woman from the neighbouring street. Then another woman had accused Spookie of raping her. Sharlien had stood by him through the whole affair, paying his bail and staying off work for days to attend the court hearing. She had lost her job as a result. He was acquitted of the charge but by then Sharlien had discovered that he was having a relationship with a woman in his lift club. The woman, who was married, separated from her husband while Spookie left Sharlien and moved in with his new partner. Sharlien's parents said that they had warned her that they did not think that Spookie would follow through on his promise to marry her.

During the first few weeks that I befriended Sharlien, she spoke wistfully about her relationship with Spookie. She took pride in showing me the diamond engagement ring that she wore on her right hand and the wedding band that lay, unused, in its velvet box in her drawer. She said that she still hoped that he would return to her. She would refer to Spookie as *die kinners se pa* (the children's father). Even after Spookie moved in with his current partner he would drop by to take Sharlien on a drive in his van, ostensibly to talk to her about the children's welfare. Sharlien continued to maintain contact with his family through the two girls and I would often take Tammy to Spookie's mother's house where she would spend the weekend. Lately, however, Sharlien had heard rumours that Spookie had married his new partner, Elizabeth and that they were proudly showing off their new baby to the Rio Street community. She had told me that, one evening, shortly after she had heard of Spookie's marriage, her anger at his desertion had overcome her. She had walked to Elizabeth's house and had entered the house without invitation. There she had angrily accused Elizabeth of robbing her children of their 'bread and their father' and challenged her to a fight. Sharlien's mother, who had heard of the fracas through the local rumour mill, hurried to the house and accompanied Sharlien home. She too had shouted at Elizabeth that she was welcome to a man who refused to support his children. When they recounted this incident to me, Mrs Ally and Sharlien both spoke ruefully of the shame that they had brought upon their household.

However, Mrs Ally stated that Elizabeth was *sleg* because she had married Spookie, even though she knew about his commitment to Sharlien.

Vonna expressed concern about Sharlien's reputation as she told me of her impending downfall.

'*Ek 't ve ha gesê sy moet ve die mense wys dat she bietere is, al het Spoekie ve ha en die kinners netsoe gelos. Sy't mooi gewys dat sy die swaarheid kan deurkom. Ma' nou vergooi sy ve ha met 'n gangster. Die mense praat net van ha innie straat.*' (I told her that she has to show the people that she's respectable [better], even though Spookie deserted her and the children. She had shown that she was able to overcome her suffering. But now she's deliberately slumming it with a gangster. People in the street are buzzing about it).

I knew that Sharlien was fighting depression. I had seen her the day before when she had borrowed some money from me to buy groceries. She was unable to obtain permanent employment since she had been retrenched from the clothing factory about three weeks before. During this time she had inquired from the working women in Rio street about opportunities to 'bring her in' to employment. She received maintenance payments from Spookie, but these contributions were sporadic and could not be relied upon as a dependable source of income. Sharlien did not wish to reveal too much about Spookie's contributions to the upkeep of their daughters. It was illegal to obtain state maintenance grants for the children if their father was providing some financial support. Until recently, she had been employed as a casual employee at a local factory but was laid off when '*die werk klaar was*' (when a job contract was fulfilled). She was deeply concerned about the economic impact her retrenchment would have on the household income.

'*Net ses wieke voor Krismis*' ([laid off] just six weeks before Christmas), she said bitterly. '*Ek 't ve Tammy se pa gese sy 't skoene nodig ve Krismis. Ma' amal praat van hom en die meid. Hulle pronk net mit die nuwe baby oppie Junction. Wa' gat ek die gel' kry ve die kinners se Krismis klere? Glen werk 'ie en Brinley het ga' soek ve 'n casual. My pa gie ve ma 'n skrale R200 'n maand en dan moet sy alles uit daai gel' betaal. Die wat ek net uit die hys bly deesdae.*' (I told Tammy's father [Spookie] that she needs new shoes for Christmas. But everyone's talking about him and that low woman. They're showing off their new baby at the Junction [the local mall]. Where am I to find the money to buy the kids some Christmas clothes? Glen is unemployed and Brinley has only just begun looking for casual employment [her brothers who live at home]. My father gives my mother a measly R200 per month to pay all the bills. That's why I keep away from the house these days.)

After Vonna had told me about Sharlien's situation, I hurried off to find her. When I arrived at her home, she answered my knock on the door and let me in. Her eyes were bloodshot, her face blotchy and swollen – a tell-tale sign of the heavy drinking sessions she was now participating in at Alim's *hok*. '*Wa's djy? Ek ko' haal ve jou*' (Where have you been? I've come to fetch you), I said. '*Ons sit da' by Vonna. Ko' saam.*' (We're sitting at Vonna's house. Come along.) She shook her head vigorously as she stared beyond me into the street, her eyes reflecting hurt and anger. '*Nie, ek bly liewerste hie by die huis. Die straat se mense praat te veel van 'n mens, skinner te veel, wil te veel wiet van 'n mens se biesigheid*' (No, I prefer staying home. The people in the street talk about one too much, gossip too much, want to know too much about one's business), she said bitterly.

'*Kom saam*' (Come with me), I begged. '*Ons mis ve jou. Djy wiet tog issie waar wat hulle van jou sê nie. As djy jou kop hoeg hou en djy kom uit, kan hulle mos sien djy 't niks om weg te stiek 'kie*'. (We miss you. You know well enough that what they say about you isn't true. If you hold your head high and you come out onto the street, they'll see that you have nothing to hide.)

'*Nou wag, te'wyl ek my broek change*' (Wait then, while I change my pants), she replied, sighing heavily, possibly at the prospect of facing the women's silent, watchful eyes on the street. She removed a skirt from the small wardrobe and proceeded to the bathroom to change into it. Then she tied her hair in the customary *doek* or headscarf that most women wore here as part of their everyday attire. This was the first time in as many days that Sharlien would be appearing in public on the street and she intended to use the opportunity to silence those who claimed that she was *sleg*. She was intent on asserting her respectability or *ordentlikheid* to all the gossipers by dressing in the customary modest fashion.

I sat down awkwardly on the bottom section of a double bunk that filled the tiny entrance room. Sharlien shared the bunk with her youngest brother, Brinley, while her two daughters shared the only other bedroom with their grandparents and Sharlien's eldest brother Glen. Like most Rio street residents, the Allys used the living room as an extra bedroom to cope with overcrowding. As I waited, I tried to make mental sense of what I thought was the unnecessary pain that Sharlein was experiencing. I was angered by the severe impact that the gossip mill had had on Sharlien's freedom. She had stopped appearing on the street in her customary manner. Her absence communicated her anger at the neighbours' talk but also served as a means to alleviate her sense of shame at having contravened important codes of female respectability. First, she had behaved like a *straatsmeid* or street girl, by challenging Elizabeth to a fight; then she had begun dating a gangster and spending long hours drinking in Kleintjie's *hok*, in Rhinoceros Walk. In an effort to mitigate the shame she had brought upon herself and the household she had remained indoors or continued to seek refuge in the '*hok*' in another community.

Sharlien accompanied me to Vonna's living room to partake in conversation and shared cups of tea. It appeared as though our little group had resumed its usual intimate chatty atmosphere. Sharlien was filled with a sense of hurt and shame at the knowledge that she had become the subject of intense scrutiny by women like Vonna. However, none of these emotions were evident as she masked her face in a smile and greeted Vonna with a warm, respectful '*Hallo suster Vonna, hoe gat dit?*' (Hello, sister Vonna, how are things going?)

'*Gat goed, die Here is goed, Sharlien, Kannie kla nie*' (Things are going well, the Lord is good Sharlien. I can't complain), Vonna responded.

Our conversation consisted of words exchanged like so many soothing touches. Vonna and Sharlien each inquired courteously about the well-being of their respective household members. Then Vonna turned the conversation to the subject that filled the room. '*Sharlien, mens sien jou nie meer deesdae nie. Djy bly nou net da by Kleintjie. Die mense sê dat djy nou mit 'n Dixie Boy uitgaan.*' (Sharlien, we don't see you anymore. You're hanging out at Kleintjie's hok. They say that you're seeing a Dixie Boy now.)

'*Die mense hie praat te veel, suster Vonna. Hulle mind'ie hulle eie biesigheid'ie. Tot die mense wat ekkie gedink 'it sal van my skinner nie, praat nou van my. Van goed wat hulle niks af wiet'ie.*' (The people here talk too much Sister Vonna. They don't mind their own business. Even those I least suspected of gossiping about me do so now. About things, they know little of.)

This last comment was a veiled condemnation of Vonna's participation in the gossip.

'*Die outjie is ma' net 'n vrind. Ek kan mossie help as hy self belangstell'ie!*' (This guy, he's just a friend. I can't be blamed if he's interested in me!), Sharlien ended indignantly.

'*Ja, Sharlien, ma' djy't soe mooi aangehou, altyd mooi agter die jouself en'nie kinners gekyk, ve Spoekie gewys*' (Yes Sharlien, but you were holding up so well, always taking good care of yourself and the children), Vonna interjected.

'*Djy kannie lat jouself soe ve'gooi nie. Djy moet ve Spoekie wys dat djy bietere is, dat djy 'n ordentlike ma is. Ma nou sal hy mos ka' sien dat djy jouself ve'gooi.*' (You can't let yourself go like this. You have to show Spookie that you're better [respectable], that you're a respectable mother. But now he can tell that you're letting yourself go.)

At this point, I grew angry at Vonna's attempts to rekindle Sharlien's hopes that Spookie would ever reestablish his relationship with her. Sharlien had told me that Spookie had fathered three other children with three different women after her eldest daughter Tammy was born. He had reneged on his numerous promises to provide material support for

137

Sharlien's two daughters. She was considering taking her case to the family court to coerce him into providing financial support. Until now, her loyalty to him, her hope that their relationship could be re-established and her willingness to struggle along on state assistance prevented her from seeking legal action.

'*Ma' hy's useless, 'n gemors!*' (But he's useless, a mess!), I said angrily.

'*Dink Suster Vonna hy gie om oor hoe Sharlien moet sukkel om die kinners groot te maak? Waarom moet sy nog omgie oor wat hy dink?! Wat van wat hy maak? Hy't vyf kinners van verskillende vrouens! Daai's nie reg nie!*' (Does Sister Vonna think that he cares about what a difficult time Sharlien is having raising the children by herself? Why should she care about what he thinks? What about the things he's done? He's fathered five children with different women! That's not right!)

'*Ja ma hy's 'n man Elaine. Mans is soe*' (Yes, but men are like that), Sister Vonna explained patiently. '*Sy's 'n ma. Sy moet ordentlik wies. Maak 'ie saak wat hy doen nie. Hy moet ka' sien dat hy die vekere een gekies 'it. Want al het hy ve ha' gelos moet hy ka' sien dat sy nog steeds 'n ordentlike vrou is, sy't 'ie ve haa'self laat vegooi nie, sy't iets van ha'self gemaak. Sy moet van ha' kinners dink. Dan ka' hy dink hy't 'n fout gemaak.*' (She's a mother. She must be respectable. Doesn't matter what he's done. She has to think about her children. He must see that he's chosen the wrong woman. Even though he's left Sharlien, he must be made to see that she has remained a respectable woman, that she hasn't let herself go, that she's made something of herself. Then he can realise the error of his ways.)

We were silent after that. I certainly had trouble understanding Vonna's unwavering faith in the certainty that Sharlien would have her revenge in the distant future, when Spookie would '*sien dat hy die vekere een gekies 'it*' (realise that he had chosen the wrong woman).

'*Ma' ek gaan nie mee soe baie na Kleintjie se hok toe nie. Ek bly ma net in 'ie huis*' (But I don't spend so much time in Kleintjie's *hok* any longer. I remain at home)', Sharlien said quietly. She claimed the one space that was indubitably associated with respectable womanhood, the home, to reestablish her reputation and to quell Sister Vonna's fears that she was becoming a *slegte moeder* or a mother of ill-repute. A few days later, on 22 May, she made the following entry in the diary that I had given her: '*Ek het opgebreek met die Dixie met wie ek uitgegaan het.'* (I've split up with the Dixie Boy whom I was seeing.)

Clearly, Vonna's earnest talk to Sharlien had had the desired effect. Sharlien's relationship with a gangster certainly reflected her individual emotional need for a loving, sexual relationship. During the brief time that she dated him, she may also have made a vain attempt to recoup a 'golden age' in her life when she was free from the familial and social responsibilities that now weighed so heavily on her. During the ensuing crisis, however, older women like Vonna reminded her that she was regarded as an *ordentlike moeder* or a respectable mother in the community, but that her current actions threatened this reputation.

D. *Ordentlikheid*: the ideological scaffolding of the moral economy

Local spaces such as the street or the *hok* structure the cultural grammar and its associated ideology of respectability that underpins the *moeders'* moral careers. In this ideology, the discourse of *ordentlikheid* or respectability is used to describe, order and assign moral value to the array of actions, social relationships, character traits and the social spaces associated with personhood. More importantly, *ordentlikheid* refers to the intense, lifelong social and physical work that women have to do to keep the natural order of the *bos* or the wilderness at bay. They need to maintain a constant vigilance over their own and their community sisters' behaviour to ensure that the wilderness of social, sexual and economic chaos does not threaten the fragile order of their community. *Ordentlike* women pride themselves on the fact that they have nothing to hide. They take great care to display their integral selves through their modest dress and behaviour when they appear in public spaces such as the street. A woman's appearance on the street during daylight hours, where she is subject to the intense scrutiny of the neighbours, especially the other *moeder*s watching from their top floor windows or their up-turned milk crates, is the most eloquent testimony to her *ordentlikheid*. In addition, *ordentlikheid* also contains a temporal dimension, described through the process of moral maturation. During this moral career, the individual women constantly strive to become *ordentlike* mothers by assiduously following the cultural grammar set out in the ideology of *ordentlikheid* or morality.

Women begin their moral careers as *ordentlike moeder*s when they bear children after a *skoon troue* or clean marriage, or more commonly when their partners claim responsibility for their pregnancy. A woman's ability to control her own as well as her daughter's sexuality is the constitutive sign of respectability. Control over sexuality is marked through a number of practices. One of these is marriage. The *ordentlike* woman's sexuality can only find expression in the confines of monogamous marriage. An *ordentlike* mother would not allow her daughter to be sexually active, use birth control methods, or become pregnant out of wedlock. In addition, *ordentlike* mothers have to maintain a code of secrecy about sexuality, and discussions about sexual matters between parents, especially mothers and their daughters, are confined to metaphorical phrases such as the command to '*hou die kondensmelk blikkie toe*' (leave the condensed milk can unopened) or to '*hou jou koek in jou broek*' (keep your fanny[6] in your panties).

Conversations about sexuality between mothers and daughters are customarily considered to be taboo. Most mothers prefer that adolescent women learn about their sexuality from other women. The responsibility for the sexual education of adolescent girls usually falls upon older daughters who are usually mothers themselves, or other young mothers in the community. Ideally, discussions about sexual matters are secretive and confined to the intimate conversations between husband and wife in the bedroom, or between close female confidantes who are considered to be social equals. Adolescent women who 'fall' pregnant precipitate a crisis because the mothers are forced to engage in frank conversations about sex with them. These conversations usually take the form of an angry scolding, in which the daughter is berated for bringing shame to her mother and to the household. The mother's anger in this situation is not only in response to her daughter's abrupt challenge to her power within the household. Her ire is also precipitated by the immediate need to speak candidly about sexual matters with her daughter in a conversation that others usually undertake to mediate the secretive knowledge about sex under ideal circumstances. The secretive, illicit nature of feminine sexual desire in

---

[6] 'Fanny' is a colloquialism for 'vagina.'

this community is the source of much humour. Younger women would make ribald sexual jokes through the use of metaphor out of earshot of the older mothers, usually to indicate that they possessed illicit knowledge about sex.

Women's sexuality and respectable reputations are also disciplined through dress and hairstyles. As soon as young women enter adolescence, they are expected to dress modestly when they appear in public, especially in the street. Unassuming dress styles such as dresses or skirts that reach below the knee, school uniforms or loose-fitting pants are *de rigeur* in Rio Street. Many women also wear a *doek* or headscarf to signify their modesty. Others who are seen to be dressed fashionably and are perceived to be displaying their sexuality openly in public through their dress are considered to be emulating the sexy, flirtatious mannerisms and dress that are associated with the glamour of television and the soap operas such as *The Bold and the Beautiful*.

Hairstyles that are a marker of respectability often require the hair to be brushed flat on the head or pulled back into a ponytail, plaits or braids, or to frame the face neatly. Straight hair is valued as the most proximate sign of beauty as well as of racial and gendered respectability. Most consider straight hair to be more manageable or easily maintained in these austere hairstyles. Women with Black hair textures either wear their hair in neat braids, straighten it with chemical relaxers, curlers or hot irons, or wear their hair short. Black hairstyles such as afros and dreadlocks, described as *bos hare* or bushy hair, are looked upon with disapproval and as a sign of inherent personal chaos and impropriety. Vonna and Sharlien often implored me to straighten my naturally curly hair, *'want dis meer ordentlik'* (because it is more respectable). On the one occasion that I acceded to their request, Sharlien procured a local hairdresser, who, she assured me, was renowned for his skills in blow-drying hair very straight.

The moral discourse of *ordentlikheid* also bestows a certain degree of power on senior mothers, enabling them to decide which households are worthy of assistance and therefore survival. While bearing a child is regarded as one of the central features of the *ordentlike moeder*, one does not automatically become *ordentlik* upon giving birth.

A mother's *ordentlikheid* is ascertained through marriage or, most often, when her partner acknowledges paternity of the child. *Ordentlike* mothers who do not vigilantly police their personal moral careers could also retrogress and become *sleg*. Women claim that their sisters who have become morally degenerate are individuals *'wie nie mooi na ha' self kyk nie'* (who have not looked after themselves). *Sleg* is the umbrella term used to describe an array of behaviours, attitudes and dress codes and, more importantly, a pattern of economic expenditure that the respectable women associate with moral degeneration. A key sign of degeneration is a woman's conspicuous consumption of a household's resources for her individual enjoyment. To call a woman *sleg* is to confirm not only her individual sexual, moral and economic dissipation but also that of her household. *Slegte* women are also perceived as women who don't care about the physical and moral well-being of their household members.

Often Vonna would speak disparagingly of a woman who was on the path to becoming *sleg* because she would spend a meagre income on fashionable clothes for herself and then send her children to beg for food.

'As mens ve ha' sien dan is sy uitgevat in die nuutste klere, ma' dan kom ha' kinners kô vra ve stukkie ou brood.' (When one sees her, she's looking sharp in the latest fashions, but then her children come to ask for old bread). 'To ask for old bread' is the local metaphor that is used when destitute households request food from their neighbours. The use of the term 'old bread' is the core vocabulary of *ordentlikheid*. It registers a household's urgent need for food, communicating its level of destitution, whilst emphasizing that its members are requesting surplus food that is not essential for the donor household's upkeep. In this way, the woman making the request on behalf of her household is not perceived to be taking sustenance away from others. However, few households here have surplus food. *Ordentlike* women graciously protect their indigent neighbours' reputation by discreetly providing some food under the guise of giving 'old bread'. In this manner, the donor household appears to be giving surplus food whilst assisting the recipient to nurture and sustain her own household.

Hokke, especially those used for leisurely activities, began appearing in Manenberg in the 1980s, and the respectable women view them with a mixture of scepticism and desire. The *hokke* situated in other communities are considered to be ambivalent, dangerous spaces because they are located outside the women's purview or control. They are regarded as the places where other, insidious, consumerist leisure practices, such as beer drinking, are encouraged. Many adult women do spend a night out in the local *hok*, as a means of recreation, especially over weekends. However, they should not be seen there too often. *Ordentlike* women discourage these practices because they diminish the resources such as women's time, income and attention that should be invested in the household. The term *sleg* or 'bad' is used to refer to mothers or daughters who spend most of their time in the *hok* where they spend precious financial resources on beers and cigarettes, listen to the latest music and hang out with men who may not be members of their own community. Women who hang out in the *hokke* constantly are perceived to be *sleg* or bad. These behaviours are considered to be selfish, individualistic and inappropriate for a maturing mother whose concerns should rest with the well-being of her dependents and of her household. This conduct is tolerated amongst the adolescent women who are not yet mothers and is seen as a sign of their immaturity. They are not expected to display the important skills of frugality and altruism just yet. Fashionable dress is only tolerated when women leave the local community, to go shopping in the Cape Town city centre, attend a local school dance or a local discotheque in nearby Athlone. On these occasions, the adolescent women are usually accompanied by a group of friends that includes some young adult *moeder*s. Adolescent girls who are seen to spend an inordinate amount of time hanging out on the street, when they should be busying themselves with housework indoors, are also described as *sleg*.

Sleg women are perceived as seeking easy access to economic resources by forming liaisons with gangsters who then share their illegally acquired wealth such as *bloedgeld* or blood money. Local residents consider gangsters to signify the evil, immoral economy outside the local community where wealth is acquired through exploitative, illegal and violent means, rather than by dint of honest, hard work. This form of income is only tolerated if it is acquired through crimes committed against *die wittes* (the whites). These actions were and still are seen to be some form of revenge or popular justice served upon the white population who were unfairly privileged by a racist system.

If a woman maintains her *ordentlike* reputation, she has to display the moral ability to endure suffering and not to capitulate to the chaos of immorality through dissolute drinking, poor housekeeping, or public begging.

E. Graciousness under fire: Stoic mothers encounter the state.

Vonna's invocation of Sharlien's reputation and her dismissal of the personal pain that Sharlien experienced in her relationship with Spookie act as a powerful cultural cue. Women are expected to give priority to the maintenance of their respectable reputations, in spite of the suffering they endure in personal relationships. The mothers consider a woman's willingness to endure suffering in order to sustain her respectability as potent cultural capital that wins her enormous social power in this community. Suffering also foregrounds the local cultural pathway to *ordentlikheid* or respectability that women necessarily experience as they ensure that their households have the available means to exist. For it is through the humiliation and shame that these women suffer at the hands of the state's welfare and educational authorities that they gain respect and material and cultural agency within the local community. These women are keenly aware of their precarious economic situation, and the necessity to find economic resources through employment or social security assistance. At the same time, the encounters with the state officials are governed by a cultural grammar of power that reinscribes these women and their communities as a powerless group in the face of the state or the potential employer. They fear the interactions with employers, state welfare or education officials that starkly reveal their subordinate place in society and the possibility that their requests for work or economic assistance may be rejected. The women suffer from enormous shame and humiliation when they admit their destitution to a social worker or a school principal so that they can obtain social security assistance or renegotiate school fee payments. Their narratives of destitution and economic need further reinscribe the stereotypes of social and moral chaos that state officials hold of Manenberg and its population.

They face these encounters with the state officials or employers with much anxiety and trepidation and often request other, older women to accompany them to these appointments. The other women's familiar presence, in the anonymous, sanitized bureaucratic spaces of the local state offices, represents the local community in which the individual is recognized as a worthy person. It seems as though the local women, who embody the local community and the power of efflorescent motherhood, neutralize the overwhelming anonymous power of the unknown state officials and professionals and render it more indeterminate and negotiable. The reinscription of the woman's personhood, juxtaposed with the anonymous encounters with the state or employment officials, unravels the hegemonic image of Manenberg as a monotonous, homogenous social landscape of the powerless poor. The presence of the other women serves to remind them of their dignity and their power as persons in one of the many multiple local communities that exist in heterogeneous Manenberg. They learn to adopt an attitude of resolute stoicism during these interviews even though they bitterly resent the humiliation that they experience as they face the prejudicial views of these representatives of state authority.

The numerous interactions that I witnessed between these women and the social workers from the state agencies or employers were shot through with and starkly defined by, the latter group's stereotypes of the coloured or Black poor. In most cases, social workers addressed the women respectfully in *suiwer* or pure Afrikaans or English that distinguished them as educated individuals. These women, in contrast, were only able to reply in the creolised *kombuis* Afrikaans that is commonly spoken among the urban, working-class coloured population of the Cape Flats. During these interviews, these women have to provide detailed, intimate information about their personal lives or about their households in order to show that they are destitute and require state assistance. They are forced to reveal that they may have had sexual relationships with a number of men who fathered their offspring. In the context of an authoritarian, Calvinistic Christian ethic that pervades the welfare system's bureaucratic culture, this revelation marks the women as promiscuous or loose, and too immature to exercise control over their reproduction or sexuality. In addition, most women in Rio Street are aware that they do not possess the necessary cultural capital such as fluency in English, a sophisticated wardrobe or the confidence to relate to the social workers on equal terms. They assume a submissive attitude during the interview, speak softly and listen attentively to advice offered by the social workers from the opposite side of an official, wooden desk.

The women do not accept this subordinate status passively, however. They display a keen critical consciousness of the inequality they experience during these encounters when they review the interview with friends. They gaily chew over the interaction with the professional social workers and make astute, witty comments about their attitude or dress. Often they parody the professional woman's manner and accent, sometimes referring to her scornfully as *die meid* (that lowly girl) amidst raucous laughter from their friends. This exchange registers their recognition that economic assistance is gained at the cost of their pride and dignity. It also serves as a means to restore their own sense of dignity as a person in their community and to dispel their initial anxiety about the interview.

Similarly, women are also the ones who mediate with school authorities on behalf of their children, when they have broken school rules or behave in a disruptive manner. In these cases, women would mediate with the state authorities in the hope that some agreement is reached that would be favourable to the interest of the child. However, often the women are faced with the dilemma of maintaining their own and the household's respectable reputations on the one hand and acting in the interests of their offspring on the other. Often children's rights are sacrificed in order to maintain mothers' and households' *ordentlike* reputations during these negotiations. When more serious cases of child abuse, such as incest, come to light at school, mothers are placed in the unenviable position of defending their own and their households' reputations when this shameful family skeleton is disclosed. Most often a woman's lover is found to be the individual who abuses her children from a previous relationship. However, in keeping with the cultural grammar of *ordentlikheid*, these mothers would consistently deny any knowledge of abuse and defend their partners' innocence, in spite of their daughters' obvious suffering.

One high school principal recounted a case where a young student had been suspended from school for smoking marijuana in the school toilets. The school principal summoned her parents to an urgent meeting to discuss the conditions of her suspension with himself and the student. The girl's mother attended the meeting, in which she insisted that she did not know about her daughter's drug use. However, when the principal asked the young woman where she obtained the marijuana, she

146

said that she stole it from her mother's drug stash. The mother angrily berated the daughter for lying and argued that the girl's lies were a further indication of her *slegte* or bad reputation. After this critical revelation, the mother berated the daughter throughout the entire interview for sullying her reputation, threatening to '*ga't ve ha' uitsit, omdat sy soe ombeskof is*' (to put her out [of the house] because she is so disrespectful [to her mother]). The woman contended that her daughter was *sleg* because she failed to defend her mother's reputation. In this case, the daughter had betrayed her mother by failing to defend the latter's and the household's reputation as *ordentlike mense* or respectable people in the face of state authority, such as the school principal. The pressure to sustain and police *ordentlikheid* reinscribes generational and gendered structures of power within the household, often at the cost of sons' or daughters' well-being. Moreover, the women suffer severe strain as they strive to suture together the tattered strands of respectability in the face of their own offspring's suffering.

F. The masks of respectability: Managing the suffering from within.

Suffering is not only produced in the women's interactions with the local representatives of the state. They also have to endure the sadness, hurt and anger when they are betrayed by family members and friends in the local community. In situations such as these, the *ordentlike* woman distinguishes herself through her efforts to manage her anguish and distress and to confront her suffering with dignity. Women earn enormous respect from their local communities when they manage their suffering with dignity. The respect they garner from within their communities ultimately empowers them to act as arbiters and peacemakers in local crises such as gang violence. Much of the suffering that these women experience within their own communities is due to marital desertion and betrayal.

Couples strive to live up to the ideals of the nuclear family, in which men are perceived as the primary breadwinners and women as primary nurturers. However, in the regional economy, where labour is feminized, where women are the primary recipients of welfare payments, and where men's employment opportunities are seasonal, it is difficult for couples to sustain this mode of living for very long. The cultural ideal of the nuclear family that most Rio Street residents hold dear as one of the markers of respectability unravels in the face of the limited economic possibilities and exigencies. While the classic cultural ideal of the nuclear family enjoins women to be homemakers and men to be breadwinners, the limited employment opportunities available to the coloured working class historically provide greater possibilities for women than for men. Most marriage or relationship bonds in this community are placed under enormous strain, as the sexual division of labour associated with the traditional nuclear family is in opposition to that inscribed in the regional economy and the political economy of race. Ordinary men and women worry about making ends meet in this community. The economic strain that ordinary couples experience in the context of overcrowded homes only adds to the pressure that women experience as they struggle to maintain their own and their households' *ordentlike* or respectable reputations. Heterosexual relationships are rendered enormously fragile and are not sustained for long periods of time.

Women often anguish in private as these relationships break up and generate enormous amounts of rumour. Their own and their households' *ordentlike* reputations are invested in the maintenance of the two-parent nuclear family model. Most often the relationship is broken when men form new relationships with other women and move out to join their new partners. During these times, women in the community scrutinize their deserted colleague closely, to see whether she is able to maintain the outward mask of serenity associated with respectability, or if she will shatter under the stress and strain of abandonment. Older women like Vonna play a crucial supportive role as they teach their younger colleagues like Sharlien how to maintain the outward mask of *ordentlikheid*, to face their crises with stoicism and dignity, whilst managing the anger, frustration and the shame that they experience. Sharlien was striving to manage her distress by removing herself from her own community and taking time out in a *hok* located elsewhere. Others keenly observed her physical absence from Rio Street, and her actions further fuelled the anxious rumours about her descent into a *slegte* or disreputable woman. Vonna lured her out onto Rio Street by skilfully manipulating my relationship with Sharlien. In this way, she was given an opportunity to be able to display her ability to manage her distress in public and recapture her *ordentlike* reputation. Through these difficult lessons, these women learn that their ability to withstand individual suffering is necessary to maintain community solidarity and ultimately to ensure the survival of their households and their community. Aunty Gwen's case, below, illustrates the stoicism which some mothers display in the face of betrayal, as well as the dignity they maintain under severe strain, in order to retain community ties.

Vonna introduced me to her mother, Aunty Gwen, a 63-year-old widow, shortly after I began working in Rio Street. She was a respected mother and grandmother in Rio Street. Two of her five adult children and three of her seven grandchildren lived with her. I quickly learned of her consummate skill at negotiating social conflict in the community. She and her neighbour, Aunty Mary, commanded enormous respect from the other residents. These two women were very good friends and were often seen visiting in their respective homes. They lived in adjoining second-floor apartments, separated only by the tiny concrete landing. Often I would find one or the other woman leaning in through her friend's doorway as she maintained a neighbourly conversation while keeping an eye on the activities in her own apartment. I often requested to interview Aunty Gwen about her life history, but she met these requests with a firm refusal, saying that she did not want to talk about the past. She would only respond that *'It was 'n swaar tyd, ek willie nou van al daie seer praat'ie.'* (It was a difficult time and I don't want to dredge up all that pain now.)

One day I expressed my frustration at these constant refusals to Sharlien. She quietly smiled, then began to tell me the story of Aunty Gwen's past. When Aunty Gwen had moved to Rio Street, in 1970, she befriended Aunty Mary, her immediate neighbour. At the time Aunty Gwen was working in a T-shirt factory in the city. Her husband was employed at the city council as a garbage collector, so Aunty Mary, a single housewife and mother of three adult daughters, took care of Aunty Gwen's youngest children until the eldest son, Peter, arrived from school. Aunty Gwen's husband, Buck, lost his job after a few years and stayed home to take care of the children whilst he was unemployed. Aunty Gwen became the main breadwinner of the family. For a while, Aunty Mary's and Aunty Gwen's families continued to co-exist peacefully as Aunty Mary still helped out with childcare. After a while, rumours began to fly that Aunty Mary was pregnant with Buck's child. In time the rumours were established to be true, and Buck moved in with Aunty Mary. Two children were born during their relationship. Aunty Gwen broke off her friendship with Aunty Mary while striving to maintain the outward mask of *ordentlikheid* to the Rio street community.

After about two years or so, when all the rumours had died down, Aunty Gwen and Aunty Mary resumed their friendship, while studiously avoiding any reference to Buck's and Mary's betrayal. Sharlien said that people often talk admiringly of Aunty Gwen's conduct during that trying time. Aunty Mary, in contrast, was struck down by a mysterious illness that lasted for a few years, until Buck's death. She lost weight rapidly, suffered 'from nerves' and had disturbing nightmares. She could not eat and barely sustained herself on a diet of copious amounts of tea and cigarettes. Sharlien and others who recounted the story to me later, steadfastly maintained that Aunty Mary was punished for the suffering she had caused in Gwen's home. Throughout it all, Sharlien claims, '*Aunty Gwen het nooit skandaal gemaak'ie....nie soes ek'ie'*. (Aunty Gwen never created a scandal, not like me.)

G. Judging and mothering persons in the community.

The *ordentlike* mothers like Aunty Gwen are invested with enormous social power in the Rio Street community. They have earned respect through their ability to manage their own and their households' *ordentlike* or respectable reputations. They have prevailed in their struggle to maintain their dignity in the face of humiliating encounters with employers and the representatives of the local state, and in the face of familial crises. These women's judgements about persons in the local community are extremely influential and their willingness to 'mother' individuals of uncertain reputation or origins spells the difference between admission and nurturance in the community and social rejection.

At the same time as these women adhere to the ideology and practices of *ordentlikheid*, they are also complicit in marginalizing adolescent girls and some adult women and households in the community. Here I will exclusively examine the process by which older women are marginalized. The process of adolescent women's marginalization will be looked at in greater detail in chapter 5.

Once a woman has been labelled *sleg* the impact reverberates negatively throughout her household, as respectable residents refuse to associate with her and her children or to assist them. Not only does this punitive action diminish her social network, it also curtails her economic survival strategies, placing her household at risk of complete disintegration. One household in Rio Street was considered so degenerate or *sleg* that most residents maintained a discrete social distance from all its members. The household, like most others, was headed by a single woman, Moira, who was a mother of three teenage boys. She never spent much time engaging with other women in their conversation clutches on the street but was often seen peering out of her window, half obscured by a room wall. Sharlien and Vonna referred to her disparagingly as a *slegte* mother and claimed that they never set eyes on her in the street. They claimed that she never asked anyone for assistance and would disappear for many days at a time, leaving her sons to their own devices. They said that the house was extremely dirty and that the boys were often in trouble for stealing from the neighbours or begging for food at the traffic lights on Duinefontein road. Two of the boys had been arrested for petty theft and spent some time in juvenile detention centres.

Respectable women in Rio Street prided themselves on their almost obsessive housekeeping and micro-management in the domestic sphere. The energy they invested in housekeeping served as an outward sign of their commitment to care for their households and of their ability to manage the threat of scarcity and privation so that its chaos did not overwhelm them. Windows were washed on a regular basis and drapes were considered essential decor items. Consequently one could easily observe a household's respectability from the street by examining the apartment windows. Moira's apartment appeared quite run down in comparison to the others in the street. The numerous broken window panes that had not been replaced were filled in with old rags and cardboard and some windows did not have any drapes. The local women referred to the apartment's abject appearance and the boys' obvious destitution as signs of Moira's inability or unwillingness to manage her poverty. Moira's reputation, as well as that of her household, were considered to be beyond the assistance of the *ordentlike* women in Rio Street. Her sons were barely tolerated in the community, and most women spoke of them with barely concealed irritation, perceiving them to be social nuisances. Even in the context of the impoverished Rio Street community, they were poorly groomed in contrast to their adolescent male peers and, unlike them, did not display the subtler aspects of respect to the older men and women. Consequently, Moira and her sons were considered as unworthy of other *ordentlike* women's assistance or friendship.

When I visited Moira, she was extremely reluctant to talk to me. She had seen me visiting Vonna and others who held her in contempt and so she feared that I was set up to ridicule her. After much coaxing, she shared her story with me. She said that her struggle to keep body and soul together began when her husband was sentenced to a long prison term for armed robbery. At the time, he was unemployed and stayed home to take care of her sons, who were from a previous relationship. She maintained the household through her job at a small spice factory. Her sons were aged between three and six years old at the time their stepfather was imprisoned. They had just moved into Rio Street in 1989 when her husband was arrested. The shame she experienced over his arrest, as well as her status as a newcomer, eclipsed her hopes of befriending the other women in the local community. She felt that she could not request assistance with childcare from anyone during the times that she was away at work. She stayed home frequently to take care of her boys. She still attempted to go to work most days, locking the boys indoors by themselves until she returned home. She said that she was fired from her job because her supervisor lost patience with her frequent absenteeism.

She had no further means of support and so applied for a child welfare grant for the two boys. She said that during the interview with the social worker she felt extremely humiliated and embarrassed by the numerous questions about her past relationships and about her husband's imprisonment. In addition, the social worker required documentation from the prison authorities to support her claim that her husband was imprisoned. Moira had no money to pay for the bus trip to the criminal justice authorities located in the city. She did not know anyone well enough in Rio Street at the time to ask them for a monetary loan.

This situation only served to deepen her sense of despair and shame. She could not muster the energy to return to the welfare offices again and be humiliated once more. She tried to obtain other means of employment but was unsuccessful. She said that she relied on odd house-cleaning jobs for a few years to earn some money. These income-earning opportunities were too erratic to provide her with an income to support her family.

Ultimately, in 1995 she suffered a nervous breakdown because of the accumulated stress that she suffered over that period. She was admitted to the psychiatric hospital in Mitchell's Plain, where she was treated for one month. She felt that she could not ask the other women in Rio Street to take care of her household during her absence. She feared that they would gossip about her 'craziness' and that they would reject her request because she had not asked for their assistance in the past. Her sons were left on their own once again. At the time the eldest boys were in their early teens and were able to hustle or shoplift goods from the local shops to support themselves. By this time they had all dropped out of school. When she was well enough to return home she found that she was unable to exert authority over her sons. She said that she was too tired to struggle with them any longer, even though she knew that they would spend most of their adult lives in prison if they continued to commit criminal acts. When she felt too overwhelmed by her problems at home, and when she was depressed by her isolation in the Rio Street community, she 'strolled', or walked to the city, where she sometimes lived with a homeless community. She would return home after a few days when she felt strong again. She did not know how long she would be able to maintain her current lifestyle.

Shortly after I interviewed her, I challenged Vonna and another woman, Joyce, about their lack of empathy for her fragile mental and emotional state. They brushed aside my protests with impatient gestures, saying that they too had to experience the self-same shame when husbands, brothers or sons were imprisoned, or when they had to apply for social welfare assistance. They said that she was unwilling to develop the emotional toughness needed to brush aside the humiliating interactions with the state social workers. The only way one acquired such toughness was to confront these exchanges with the state authorities and share one's suffering with the other women. They thought that Moira considered herself above such humiliating encounters and that she placed her own pride before the survival of her household. Ultimately they rejected Moira because they perceived her as being unwilling to do the difficult emotional work needed to ensure her own and her household's *ordentlikheid*. In addition, her sons stole small household items from their own neighbours, angering the residents for stealing 'from their own'. Respectable women would not squander their precious resources on those like Moira who were unwilling to endure the suffering that all respectable women endured, and who were unable to regulate their households, their behaviour or their dress codes.

Moira's case highlights the cruel paradox that inheres in the ideology and practices of *ordentlikheid*. Moira's isolation and her subsequent decline into social and psychological marginality stemmed from her desire to manage her respectable reputation in a new community, during a crisis in her household. The unfortunate conjuncture of events, namely her husband's arrest at a time when they had just moved into the community and when she had hardly befriended anyone, illustrates that women cannot maintain their individual *ordentlikheid* on their own. A woman's moral career as an *ordentlike* mother unfolds over the accretions of time and through the quotidian acts of everyday life in relation to other women and within the social web of the local community. An *ordentlike* woman is socially produced by other women as they collectively sustain her and guide her through individual suffering and economic hardship. Through their sustenance, her household is also reproduced. The power of the *ordentlike moeders* is based upon their ability to make persons, such as other respectable women, in the local community.

The power of the *moeders* to confirm others' personhood or identity in the local context is illustrated in the case of individuals such as orphans or others who are not firmly located within family networks or households and whose identities as persons are contested. In the following case, some of the *moeders* assert the right of an orphaned 15-year-old boy named Donny to be recognised as a child and a minor member of the Rio Street community, who can claim protection from its custodians. However, the ambivalent status of these individuals as

154

members of the local community but of no household, in particular, brings to light the moments when the power that the ideology of *ordentlikheid* and the *ordentlike moeders* have over the local residents is rendered tenuous, open and contingent.

During a late winter's afternoon in June 1998, I joined the adult *moeders* of Rio Street at their usual meeting place on the sidewalk. Some of us sat on the rocks and overturned milk crates that served as seats, while others stood around in a circle. The conversation was slow that day and interrupted by long, comfortable pauses. It seemed as if we were content to seek comfort from each other's physical presence. Aunty Frances's soft, leathery face, folded into numerous wrinkles, looked at nothing in particular down the street. The other women looked out towards the little green patch of field that served as grazing land for a few cart horses and a soccer field for the local children. Suddenly Donny, a 15-year-old homeless boy, raced across the field, pursued by two women. He burst into Aunty Dollie's house some distance from us, paused briefly at the gate as he shouted: *'jou ma se poes'* (your mother's cunt) at his pursuers. Then he slammed the tall corrugated iron gate shut. The two women stopped at the edge of the field, across from the gate, and shouted angrily, *'Kom uit jou naai! Jou gemors!'* (Come out, you cunt. You trash!) They continued to shout at the gate, which remained implacably shut against their curses. Their faces were flushed with anger. The older women in our group gasped in surprise and horror at the florid public exchange of outrageous curses. Aunty Gwen rose from her crate and angrily exclaimed that Donny was nothing but trouble.

'Is daai twie susters vannie Grande Walk. Hulle's nogals ordentlik. Ek wonner wat'it Donny teen hulle gemaak dat hulle ve hom soe jag. Hy moes iets sleg gedoen'it dat hulle soe lelik ve hom insê' (Those two sisters are from Grande Walk. They're quite respectable. I wonder what Donny did to make them pursue him like that. He must've done something really ugly, to earn such a curse), Morieda said.

The women rose and began moving towards Dollie's gate, loudly inquiring from the two young women about the circumstances that had precipitated the chase. One of the sisters shouted angrily that he had cursed their mother repeatedly when they had scolded him for not

155

running an errand for them. As she spoke she began sobbing in frustration.

'My ma is nog net 'n jaar dood. Hy's 'n gemors! Wat wiet hy van 'n ma om soe my ma in te sê! En sy was altyd soe goed ve hom!' (My mother died just over a year ago. He's trash! What would he know about a mother to curse mine like that! And she was so good to him!)

Her sobs grew louder as she spoke. A hush fell over the street, broken by Aunty Gwen, who angrily murmured that Donny needed a good beating. The gate opened and Aunty Dollie and her sister Aunty Asia appeared on the street.

'Wat'it Donny gedoen?' (What has Donny done?), Aunty Dollie shouted at the sisters. Again they repeated their charge.

'Lat hom uitkô Aan' Dollie, hy't my ma lelik gevloek. Laat hom uitkô soe dat hy sy man ka' staan!' (Let him come out, Aunty Dollie, he cursed my mother outrageously. Let him come out, so he can stand his man!)

Aunty Dollie and Aunty Asia then sat down on two upturned crates that were strategically placed on either side of the gate.

'Ek's jammer dat Donny soe onbeskof mit julle gewies'it. Ma' julle wiet Donny issie reggie. Hy't ma of familie nie, soe hy wiettie reg or vekeerd'ie. Julle moettie notice vat va' wat hy sê nie' (I'm sorry that he was so inexcusably rude to you. But you know that he's not right. He has no mother or family, so he wouldn't know right from wrong. You shouldn't take any notice of what he says), Aunty Dollie shouted at the two women

'Aan' Dollie moet lat hom uitkô'!' (Let him out, Aunty Dollie!) The young woman angrily persisted, petitioning the older women to satisfy her desire for restitution from the errant boy.

'Donny! Kô'uit! Kô vra ekskuus!' (Donny, come out! Come and apologise!) Aunty Dollie shouted at the gate. Everyone waited expectantly as the gate opened and Donny appeared, wearing an angry expression, but with eyes downcast nevertheless. *"Hulle't ve my eerste uitgevloek, Aan' Dollie'* (They cursed at me first, Aunty Dollie), he shouted for all to hear.

'Ja, ma' al vloek iemand ve jou uit, moet djy nie trug vloek'ie. Vra verskoning' (Yes, but even if someone curses you, you should not curse in return), the older woman replied.

'Djy't my ma uitgevloek!' (You cursed my mother!), one of the young women shouted persistently during this exchange.

'Ek's jammer!' (I'm sorry!), Donny finally shouted, although his angry expression did not change.

'Djy! Djy dink omdat djy agter Aan Dollie-hulle skuil is djy safe! Ons gat ve jou kry! Vloek net weer soe my ma uit dan sien djy!' (You! You think that you're safe because you run in [and hide] behind Aunty Dollie and her group! We'll get you! Just dare curse my mother again and you'll see!) At this point, the young women turned away and slowly returned home, as Aunty Dollie and Aunty Asia watched them.

'Asia en Dollie moettie soe ve hom skuil nie! Hy's onbeskof! Hy't g'n maniere nie!' (Asia and Dollie shouldn't protect him! He's rude! He has no manners!) Aunty Gwen shouted these words angrily at the two old women, who remained seated resolutely outside the gate, while Donny returned to the safety of their house. After the two young women departed, the tension in the street soon dissipated.

Most adolescents who could claim rightful membership within a household and, more importantly, kinship links to an identifiable, respectable mother, could claim unquestioned protection from the adult women within the spaces of the local community. Donny's marginal identity as a homeless orphan rendered his claim to protection from the local mothers less certain and contested. During the crisis precipitated by his actions, the authority of the younger, adult women from an adjoining local community in Grande Walk was set up against the authority of the older *moeders* in Rio Street. If the *moeders* of Rio Street handed Donny over to their more youthful counterparts from Grande Walk, then they would have surrendered the jurisdiction of their authority to younger women from another community. The overt crisis about generational and gendered respect was silhouetted by a more serious contestation over the boundaries of the local *moeders'* authority as well as a potential dispute about younger women's respectable reputations prevailing over those of their older counterparts. Aunty Gwen's rage about Donny's lack of respect was not only born out of her fury at the disrespect he showed towards the younger women and the memory of their mother. She also realized that his actions had brought their own *ordentlike* reputations and their authority into question. Donny's action had challenged the implicit belief that everyone in the local community prevailed under the authority of the *ordentlike moeders* and that the local boundaries of their authority were impermeable. People's ability to move across physical and social boundaries presents a challenge to these women's authority. Yet they cannot maintain the boundaries of the local community and of their local authority by themselves. They have to look to alliances with other persons to ensure that these boundaries are identifiable across time and space within and beyond the township.

H. Conclusion

I have argued that the *ordentlike moeder* identity that is so revered in the local communities within the township developed within the local township space, and also in relation to the economic status of coloured women within the Western Cape regional economy, both of which were fixed by the apartheid legislative processes. The effects of these processes continue to be felt in the contemporary period, despite the end of racial legislation, because they are reinterpreted within the local context to reinforce a powerful gendered ideology of *ordentlikheid*. Personhood, in this context, is produced through the cultural practices that emerge from this gendered ideology, which is embodied in the identity of the adult female household head, as the *ordentlike moeder*. It is through their identities as mothers that women are able to exercise agency and to confer personhood on other residents. Women's lives continue to reflect the cultural grammar of apartheid racial legislation in the impoverished context of Manenberg township. These practices of daily life inscribe their economic roles, namely as workers and as welfare recipients with enormous moral, cultural and economic power. The women's economic roles are reinterpreted in the local context and anchored within a moral economy so that women are primarily perceived as mothers and as central players in the social and material reproduction of the local community.

However, in order to socially reproduce their communities, they have to display and constantly police their reputations as *ordentlike moeders. Ordentlike moeders* are able to confront and mediate the local state authorities such as the employers, welfare officials and education officials on behalf of their community. They withstand the shame, humiliation and suffering that ensue from these interactions with stoicism and courage. They also manage the suffering inflicted on them when they are betrayed within their own community and ultimately prevail with their respectable reputations intact. Women who are unable to display their ability to endure suffering are considered to be *sleg*, and they and their households are marginalized. The power of the *ordentlike* mothers is contingent upon the demarcation of the community boundary, and its surveillance. Women's roles as *ordentlike* mothers have to articulate with men's roles as gangsters in order to preserve the spaces in which their authority is exercised. In the next chapter, I examine how men demarcate and maintain these boundaries through their gang activities.

Chapter 5

Mans is ma soe:[7]
Men, *Moeders* and Ideologies of Masculinity

Die system kan jou afbriek, innie tronk ka' hulle ve jou afbriek ... ma' jou ma ken ve jou.

The system can break you down, they can break you down in jail, but your mother knows who you are.

(18-year-old Enver, member of the Young Dixie Boys gang.)

Women control the community with men's permission. Women respect men and fear men for their violence.

(Irvin Kinnes, Manenberg peace activist.)

Like Grande Street women who desire to be identified as *ordentlik*, men desire to be acknowledged and respected as men, as persons. Young men's affirmation as persons is inherently tied to the ideology of *ordentlikheid* and adult women's roles as *moeders*, the social and biological nurturers of the social community in Rio Street. One means whereby men desire respect and recognition as persons is to be identified as breadwinners and heads of households. However, a number of social factors militate against men sustaining this vision. These include the high unemployment rates in this township, cited officially at 30% (Statistics South Africa 1996) and working-class coloured men's lack of appropriate educational skills to compete for better-paying jobs. At the same time the legacy of discriminatory racial policies which trapped these men in low-paying, low-skilled jobs continues to bedevil the post-apartheid South African economy.

Also, as I have indicated in chapter 2, the feminization of labour in the Western Cape industries has historically excluded coloured and African men from the few opportunities for permanent employment. Few work opportunities exist in the region for under-skilled, working-

---

[7] Men are like that.

class Black men. Those that do exist are unskilled, low-paying labourers' jobs in the fishing, construction and services industries. These jobs are usually seasonal and of a temporary nature. These men are unable to access the cultural capital, such as permanent employment or a living wage, that identifies them as wage earners, breadwinners and heads of households – characteristics that are enshrined in the dominant ideology of masculinity as crucial characteristics of manhood in the South African context. Instead, the men's historic familiarity with, and experiences of, the processes of racial and gendered exclusion through the lifecycle have exposed the accretions of individual toughness acquired through time. These lifelong processes of exposure to systemic violence and the associated emotional and physical toughening are colloquially referred to as 'making strong bones'. The men's ability to stoically withstand and survive any form of physical or social violence is upheld as the quintessential marker of masculinity in communities such as Rio Street. Men who display 'strong or tough bones' are shown great respect in this community. As a result, toughness is valorized throughout the male lifecycle in this context as alternative routes to manhood are constructed through the persons of *Ouens* (streetwise lads), fathers, ex-convicts and religious *Broers* or brothers. This alternative, subordinate meaning of masculinity and the persons identified through it, are defined in relation to the imposition of dominant white masculinity through societal laws and institutions and the associated constraints placed on coloured men. More importantly, they are shaped and conditioned by the moral economy and its associated ideology of *ordentlikheid,* in response to coloured women's roles as *moeders* as well as through men's social interaction in the township spaces. These alternative ways of being a man at once resist, partly combine with, and ultimately reproduce, the dominant image of men as breadwinners, heads of households and wage earners.

A. Strong bones: Making a coloured man.

A wet afternoon in June 1998 found me sitting in Aunt Dopie's house, talking to Uncle Booi and a few of his friends. The four men were quietly welcoming home a friend who had just completed his prison term. The men were seated closely around a coffee table in the tiny living room, drinking beer, whilst Aunty Dopie sat respectfully nearby. The living room was devoid of its usual occupants, the other members of the large household. They had vacated the room as a mark of respect to Uncle Booi and his guests. They could be heard on the other side of the curtain panel that separated the room from the rest of the apartment, talking in muted voices.

It was clear that these men were no ordinary visitors, but guests to be shown the utmost respect the household could muster. Uncle Booi and his friends were informing their newly released guest, Alim, about the whereabouts of their other acquaintances, as well as other changes in the society since his imprisonment. Alim's face was marked with blue tattoos, some of which he had obtained in prison. Tattoos signify a man's rank in the notorious prison numbers gangs and prisoners fill empty stretches of time designing and completing these bodily markings. Alim said that he had completed a *blou baadjie* term of imprisonment for armed burglary. *Blou baadjie* is the colloquial phrase to refer to terms of imprisonment that are eight years or longer.

Alim was currently living with his sister until he could find a job and another place to live. Pointing to his tattoos, he said, '*Ma' wie gaan ve my huur met hier'ies? Dit het iets bedoel da' binne ma' nie hier buite nie.*' (Who will employ me with these? They had meaning in prison, but not out here.) He noted that while the tattoos gave him some power within the prison gangs'[8] system of hierarchy, in the eyes of potential employers they

---

[8] Men held in South African prisons have organized themselves into the notorious 'numbers gangs' since the early 1900s (Van Onselen 1985). The most notorious of these gangs are the Twenty Sixes, Twenty Sevens and Twenty Eights. Each gang is reputed to specialize in a specific criminal activity in prison. The Twenty Sixes are known for 'bloodletting' or assassination and physical assault, the Twenty Sevens are renowned for their skills in obtaining financial resources, whilst the Twenty Eights are renowned for raping other men in order to exercise power over them. Some of the Twenty Eights may form affective relationships with the men they raped initially. The latter are then known as *wyfies* or female partners. Their gangster partners provide them with protection from assault and with other, scarce resources such as cigarettes, etc. All these gangs are organized according to a hierarchy that emulates military organization. The most powerful gang leaders take on titles such as corporal, sergeant and general. Each gang has its own set of tattoos that distinguishes it from the other gangs and that signifies each member's rank and progress through the hierarchy. These tattoos may range from the simplest design, depicting the number of the gang, such as '28' or '26' to the more complex, depicting a rising sun, signifying face up (i.e. depicting the dominant position in male-to-male sex, thereby illustrating the power of the 28s gang). Prison gang membership exists throughout the national prison system as well as

163

marked him indelibly as a gangster and an ex-prisoner. He could not utilize the usual channels or procedures to inquire about formal employment. He pointed to a tattoo depicting a sunrise and said that he belonged to the same prison gang, the '28s', as Uncle Booi, and that he had come to inquire from Uncle Booi about other means to earn a living, such as 'broking' (selling) vegetables or as an informal security guard.

When I first began working in Manenberg, I feared Uncle Booi. His neck, forearms and torso were covered in tattoos, the trademark of a gangster. His forearms were marked with the number '28,' the insignia of the feared prison gangs. I encountered him often in the street and thought that he appeared to be either morose or drugged. Initially, I would greet him quite apprehensively. When we passed him in the street the first time, Sharlien greeted him with lowered eyes, as a mark of respect, and then whispered that *'daai man is ve niks en niemand bang nie'.* (that man fears nothing and no one).

However, as I show later in the chapter, he had assisted in averting a major gang fight and neutralizing the tensions between the Young Dixie Boys and the Naughty Boys. After this incident, my curiosity about him grew. He had fearlessly confronted the armed men who threatened Paul, Aunty Gwen's son. A few days after the gang fight was averted, I asked him about the incident, inquiring whether he did not feel threatened by the Naughty Boys, who were armed. *'Eks nie bang ve die goed nie'* (I am not afraid of that lot), he said contemptuously, waving his arm in the air dismissively, as he brushed away any suggestion of fear.

'Hulle's 'n klomp laaities. Ek 'it al twee bloubaadjies agter my rug. Hulle wiet nog niks van wat da binne aangaan nie' (They're a bunch of kids. I've served two blue jackets. They know nothing about prison life), he growled, emphasizing his experience of being toughened up and surviving in the institutions that mark many working-class coloured youths' life path to manhood. *'Hulle wiet van niks. Ek loep waar ek wil, al gangfight hulle, ek's nie bang ve hulle nie.'* (They're still green. I go where I want, even when there is a gang war. I am not afraid of that lot.)

---

outside the prison walls. Prison gang loyalties extend across and override gang loyalties and boundaries in civil society. Men are bound by oaths to support their numbers gang brothers at all times and not to assault or kill them (interview with Irvin Kinnes, November 1998; see Steinberg 2005).

These were no idle words. Earlier, I had learned from Aunty Dopie that Uncle Booi earned his living as an itinerant one-man security force for any organization in the area that wished to hire him. At the time, he was safeguarding a marquee that had been erected by a travelling evangelist who was visiting the area for a week. His responsibilities included patrolling the outer perimeter of the marquee grounds through the night. Before that, he was employed as a security guard at the local primary school after school hours. Here he was expected to deter local gangsters from despoiling the walls with gang graffiti to mark their turf. He was respected and feared by most local residents in Manenberg.

Uncle Booi was about fifty years old and married to Aunty Dopie. He recalled that in the 1940s he grew up *'tussen die wit mense'* (amongst white people) in Aberdeen Street in Woodstock. He said that

'Daai tyd het ons tussen ordentlike mense gebly. Ons 'it by my ma-hulle gebly, in 'n groot huis. Ek en Dopie het ons eie kamer gehad. Net kort nadat ons getrou h't, toe 't hulle ye ons da' uitgesit. Toe moes ons hie'natoe getrek. My eerste werk was by die Docks. Maar dit was altyd 'n stone van werk ye 'ii paar wieke en dan was' da nie meer werk 'ie.'

(At that time we lived alongside decent people. We lived in a big house. When we were married [in the early 1960s] Dopie and I were given our own room in the house. Shortly after that we were forcibly evicted and made to move here. My first job was at the Docks [as an unskilled labourer.] But it was always a situation where there would be work for a few weeks and then there would not be work.)

Uncle Booi became a member of the Mongrels, a gang from the nearby township, Hanover Park, that had associations with his extended family. He had burgled a number of houses *'net innie wit areas, by die rykes'* (just in white areas, [we stole from] the rich). He was arrested for housebreaking and theft and was jailed for eight years. He rejoined the gang immediately after his release, but he was re-arrested for burglary shortly thereafter. He was found guilty and given a sentence of thirteen years. During both prison terms, he was an active member of the notorious prison numbers gangs. During his first term he was initiated into the '28s', the gang notorious for using rape as an exercise of power over fellow prisoners. When I asked him why he had become a member

165

of the prison gangs, he replied that *'Djy moet leer om te survive in die tronk. Is of ek of djy da.'*(You have to learn to survive in prison. There the rule of 'either you or me' holds.) He said that when he entered prison for a second time, his eldest daughter, Bridget, was only eight years old. When he was released, she was a twenty-one-year-old woman and had a son of her own. He spoke wistfully about being absent from his children's lives during their youth, and his subsequent sense of loss. At this point in the interview, he stared intently at a small brass vase on the battered display cabinet in their living room. He rose, picked it up, and said to me, *'Die ding, die ding het value, ek't betaal met my lewe ve die ding.'* (This thing, this thing has value. I paid for this thing with my life.) In this poignant gesture, he implied that the vase, an item he had stolen during a burglary, symbolized the long years that he had spent in prison.

For the older men like Uncle Booi, the experience of being toughened up, of becoming a man, consisted of a progressive cycle of gendered, economic and racial denigration. Their display of manhood finds expression in their proud though poignant narration of their emotional and physical ability to withstand these processes of subordination and denigration, indeed even find the courage to laugh in the face of such derision. For Uncle Booi, the process began in the early 1960s, just as he entered adulthood when he and his family were evicted from their homes in the newly declared white areas, such as District Six, Woodstock and Claremont. Thereafter, his adult life was marked by the continuous search for secure employment as well as the means to support his family. Men like him were able to find jobs as unskilled labourers in the dockyards, on fishing vessels or building sites, where they were subjected to being called 'boys', the infantilizing term commonly used to refer to Black, unskilled labourers. These adult men attempt to meet the demands of dominant manhood by supporting their families through illegal informal activities such as burglary. They are convicted and subjected to a seemingly endless cycle of imprisonment. As they attempt to fulfil the practices of dominant masculinity prescribed to them, they are constrained by structural factors such as lack of suitable employment that would provide them with the economic resources to become breadwinners or to be independent.

In his attempt to unpack the concept 'patriarchy', Connell (1987) has argued that while men, in general, enjoyed 'the patriarchal dividend ...

the advantage gain(ed) from the overall subordination of women' (ibid, 79), not all men shared in this power equally. He argues that a hegemonic notion of masculinity exists, subordinating all other masculinities. Such a dominant notion of masculinity defines what it means to be a real man and prescribes the culturally acceptable values and practices associated with this image. Building on Connell's thesis, Morrell (2001) has argued that the meanings of masculinity, whether dominant or subordinate, are not fixed across time and place, but that 'they are socially and historically constructed in a process which involves contestation between rival understandings of what being a man should involve' (ibid, 7). Morrell indicates that the dominant and subordinate masculinities in the South African context emerge in relation to structural factors such as the racial and economic ordering of society during the apartheid era. These values and practices continue to inform South African masculinity albeit to a waning degree in the contemporary post-apartheid period.

Consequently, dominant white masculinity dictated that white men were expected to be the protectors of the white community and their households, be heterosexuals, demonstrate their racial superiority over Black men, be wage earners and be God-fearing and moral. Societal laws, practices and institutions enforced this dominant masculine image. Laws such as the job reservation act forcibly placed white men in senior positions over Black men in the employment sector, while sodomy and marriage laws imposed a racially exclusive heterosexuality on them (Gevisser and Cameron 1994). Finally, the compulsory conscription of white men into the South African Defense Force (Cock 1991) officially defined white men as the legal protectors of white households and communities in the face of the *swart gevaar* or Black threat. As white men performed the values and practices associated with this masculinity, they exercised social and physical violence over Black men and women. Breckenridge (1998), Guy and Thabane (1984), Field (2001) and Morrell (2001) indicate that Black men developed a resistant masculinity through social interaction in various gendered sites such as the mines and the rural reserves, as a means of adapting to and surviving the exercise of dominant white masculinity. Black men's display of violence and toughness became a key aspect of their resistant masculinity and, Morrell argues, in the process of such display they validated the very masculinity they sought to resist.

Men require emotional and physical toughness to prevail and to be recognized as persons throughout their lifecycle in communities like Rio Street while finding alternative routes to becoming a man. Uncle Booi and his friend who had been released from prison have become men through a successive, lifelong process of toughening up, burying emotional sensitivity in self-deprecating humour in order to withstand the everyday erosion of dignity and respect. These men are finally identified as persons, as men, in their own right in mid-adulthood, after they have adequately demonstrated their 'tough bones'.

B. Teaching toughness: Preparing boys for manhood

Women begin to socialize boys into toughness during infancy. I often witnessed young mothers slapping their male infants' hands until they cried, to the hearty amusement of others. The mother in question would then hug the child, comforting him until he stopped crying. Sometimes mothers of young male toddlers would urge them on to beat each other until one or both of them cried. They would also then comfort the children later. When I observed this practice for the first time, I was horrified and scolded the adolescent mother for inciting the children to fight. She responded swiftly, saying, *'Nee, hulle moet leer om taai te wies. Die is Manenberg die. Hulle ka' nie moffies hie wies nie.'* (No, they must learn to be tough. This is Manenberg. They can't be effete men here.)

Throughout childhood, young boys are expected to be less physically and socially constrained than girls. As is the case elsewhere on the Cape Flats (Field 2001), sport, specifically soccer, becomes the initial means whereby young boys learn to become tough and to submerge their experiences of physical pain. Many young boys sign on with local soccer clubs as junior members. There, older players take them under their wing, often incorporating them into the adult men's leisure activities after games have occurred. Young boys can often be seen on the edge of the adult players' social circle, watching the latter enjoy beers or eagerly waiting to be asked to run errands. Young boys are generally allowed a greater degree of freedom to roam in the township without requiring parental permission than are their girl counterparts. They learn rapidly that they have to display a tough streetwise attitude towards other boys of their age cohort, acquiring a reputation for fearlessness and thereby enabling their social mobility. They also learn that they have to display their toughness to a male audience while demonstrating respect and obedience as *goeie seuns* or good sons to the senior *moeders* in their own household as well as those in the wider community. The boys learn that through their performance of personhood for two gendered audiences, they are able to retain their membership of and identity within the moral community while still retaining a reputation for disrepute and toughness among the men.

This Janus-faced aspect of masculinity in Rio Street is elaborated upon during late adolescence and early adulthood in the context of the male gangs. Through the aesthetics and practices of the gang, these young men reproduce the central role of women as *moeders* as well as their own personhood in the local moral economy. During late adolescence and early adulthood inexperienced young men are eager to demonstrate that they have acquired the requisite toughness to be identified as rightful persons. However, their ambivalent status in the lifecycle, somewhere between dependent childhood and independent adulthood, without the requisite reputation for physical and emotional toughness, prevents them from being acknowledged as men. They establish their potential ability to endure a lifelong process of toughening up through their ganging practices and aesthetics. They are identified as *Ouens* or streetwise men through these ganging practices and gain the sought-after reputations of toughness. However, as I show below, these young men's ganging practices and aesthetics also articulate with the women's practices as *moeders* as the latter affirm these youths' identities as *goeie seuns* or good sons. In this manner, the young men's identities are asserted through the moral economy and their membership of the local community is established. Most analyses of gangs in Cape Town have read gang members' identities and practices as working-class coloured men's resistant practices that are targeted solely at the apartheid-imposed laws and the capitalist economy which subjugated these men in terms of class and race (Scharf 1986, Pinnock 1984, Stone 1991, Field 2001). Unfortunately, none of these analyses interprets these men's personhood dialectically in relation to working-class women's gendered identities. Consequently, they are unable to explain why adult women in the township vociferously defend these men's personhood when they are arrested and put on trial for various illegal activities. As I show in my

169

analysis below, if one examines how young men are made into masculine persons, namely *Ouens*, in relation to *moeders* as gendered persons, as well as in relation to dominant state institutions, then these women's actions will be better understood.

C. Becoming men through the *moeders*

Uncle Booi and his cohort's life experiences poignantly illustrated his ability to acquire the necessary strong bones of a man and to prevail over life's hard knocks. Young adult men, however, still have to experience the lifelong process of being toughened up, and demonstrate that they are men. They are eager to illustrate that they too can be recognized as men who are able to acquire strong bones. Those who survive the high mortality rates associated with the frequent gang fights will in the fullness of time be toughened up into men. The ideology, practices and aesthetics of young men's gangs mark the beginnings of the toughening-up process. The gangs' beliefs, practices and aesthetics create an alternative ideology of masculinity that affirms the masculinity of these young, working-class men. At the same time, these beliefs and practices also affirm and reinforce the ideology of *ordentlikheid* and the power of the *moeders*.

Men's acknowledgement as social persons becomes crucial during early adulthood, when they find themselves searching for appropriate roles after they have dropped out of school but are yet to find employment, in order to be recognized as working men or find a long-term, marriageable partner in order to be identified as husbands and/or fathers. Gang practices become the passage through this liminal state and young men's passage into manhood. These practices are often of a violent or criminal nature and fall outside the precepts and the practices of the moral economy. Furthermore, they are not associated with individuals who are recognized as persons in the local communities such as Rio Street. The ideology, practices and aesthetics of gangs exist beyond the bounds of the local moral economy and are antithetical to the ideology, practices and aesthetics of *ordentlikheid* in every respect. However, the men whose biographies are intimately interwoven with the *moeders* in the community are the very individuals who carry out these otherwise reprehensible acts. The adult women, in their role as *moeders*,

170

draw on the ideology of *ordentlikheid* to assert these young men's personhood, defining them as close kin, as good sons or *goeie seuns* who act to demarcate and protect the boundaries of the moral community. In doing so, the *moeders* actions render the gang ideology, practices, and aesthetics socially invisible to the ordinary residents. Even as men create an alternative ideology of masculinity that venerates toughness, this ideology is rendered invisible by the very ideology and practices that it sustains.

Women's ability as mothers to affirm the men's personhood has to be recognized within the boundaries of the local community, which is considered to be a moral community, the sphere in which the physical and social reproduction of various persons is prioritized above all else. This is the community where moral and social obligations to others take precedence over economic instrumentalism. Here values such as loyalty, mutual respect, generational hierarchy and mutual assistance shape relationships and are valorized. It is the community within which the adult women's power dominates, and where persons are identified through them.

In the following section, I indicate how young men define the limits of this community, through particular masculine practices. I argue that through young men's practices as gang members they affirm their own right to be identified as persons by other men. At the same time, their actions are reinterpreted through the modes and practices of *ordentlikheid*. In doing so they sustain the older, adult women's central roles as *moeders* while they still uphold an alternative ideology of masculinity that asserts or displays their claim to male personhood amongst their male cohorts. I intend to show how, through their gang practices, young men define the boundaries of the local, moral context in which the *ordentlike moeders* enjoy the supreme recognition of their social power.

D. Gendering boundaries, gendering persons: A lesson in defining community

During my initial visits to Rio Street in November 1997, the local boundaries of community appeared insignificant and did not appear to affect the Rio Street residents' round of daily life. Indeed, except for the occasional reference to *die skollies* (the ruffians or the gangsters) and the *Ouens* (the streetwise men), no one made reference to the gangs or to their territory. The notorious gang members, whom I had been warned about by others, were all but invisible during my early visits to Rio Street. As I specified in chapter 3, I became aware of the influence gangs had in differentiating local communities during the first planning stages of research in Manenberg, in November 1997, when my eldest brother, the Anglican priest, indicated how the gangs used graffiti to mark out their turf.

In Manenberg, graffiti is scrawled on almost every perimeter wall, building and even road sign. The meaning of graffiti takes on new significance when it is clear that, unlike other urban media such as company advertisements splashed on huge billboards, the creators and the symbolism of the message are shared amongst an exclusive group. The graffiti's message, though recognized by all in Manenberg, is commonly understood to hold significance for a select few only, namely the all-male membership of the individual gang and its rivals. This peculiar discourse actively confers meaning on place and person. Not only does it mark off the boundaries of local community; it confers a special gendered identity upon the young men residing within its borders, as well as those residing beyond them. These processes of conferring identity and gender upon individuals, and of maintaining the boundaries of local communities, are especially pronounced during gang warfare.

Men in their roles as *Ouens* embody the limits of the local community. They establish the limits of the geographical community, policing and maintaining them through their violent acts beyond the limits of the moral community. Local boundaries are particularly meaningful for men who live beyond these limits, and they become impermeable during gang conflict. These are particular types of men, namely those who had been made into *'n Ou* (a streetwise man), a member of the brotherhood (*bras* or *broers* in the gang) and who carry the indelible mark of their masculine territorial and communal allegiance, the *tjappie* or the tattoo. In contrast, only the adult *moeders*, the aged and the very young are regularly allowed access to any community. The reasons why these various groups are allowed to cross local boundaries varies in accordance with the social power they wield in and across these communities. The very young are generally perceived to be socially invisible while the elderly, especially elderly women, are considered venerable persons who are accorded the highest level of respect in the community. While the elderly men and women embody the ability to prevail over a lifetime of denial and struggle, the *moeders* wield the power to identify persons both within and across communities. In contrast, as I show in chapter 6, young single women are not allowed passage across community boundaries because their roles and statuses are inextricably tied up with the personhood of young men as fathers and that of women as *moeders*. Young women enable men's passage to the one masculine identity, namely fatherhood, that is associated with a relationship that allows a public display of emotional warmth and trust. In addition, young women's mobility poses a challenge to the ideology of *ordentlikheid* and is also a threat to the older women's respectability and power as *moeders*. Through their ganging practices, the young men collaborate with and affirm the older *moeders* power and the legitimacy of *ordentlikheid*, by actively constraining these young women's mobility across local boundaries. Some of these dynamics can be seen in the following extended description of events that occurred in Rio Street in 1998.

I became acquainted with, and gained knowledge of, gang lore and practice gradually as I continued to work in Rio Street. In early 1998, I had befriended 18-year-old Enver and his adolescent friends. They appeared to be just another group of young men from impoverished homes, who were at a loose end, undecided about whether they should return to school or get on with the endless search for informal or casual jobs. Then, during February 1998, a gang war erupted between the Hard Livings (HL$) gang and the Clever Kids gang (CK$). The war, like so many others, had ostensibly erupted over turf expansion and the control over the fairly lucrative local drug trade (Cape Times 25 Feb 1998). One Sunday, senior members of the Hard Livings gang abducted three teenage members of the Clever Kids gang from a shebeen situated in a neutral zone. According to local rumour as well as newspaper reports, the three were taken to the Hard Livings headquarters, *Die Hok* (The Cage), where they were beaten and tortured. All three were later shot and killed. This incident sparked off a major conflict between the HL$ and the CK$.

In the days that followed the killings, two smaller gangs, the Young Dixie Boys (YDB$) and the Wonder Kids (WK$) had become embroiled in the conflict, each siding with a primary antagonist. The YDB$ had formed an alliance with the CK$ and so were also in opposition to the HL$ and their allies, the WK$. The two small gangs occupied adjoining turf. Whilst the members of the YDB$ lived in Rio Street, the WK$ could be found in the parallel street, Rio Walk. Tensions rose in Rio Street during this time and the young men spoke fearfully of crossing WK$ or HL$ turf. At this time, the young men such as Zahir, Paul, and James, whom I had first perceived to be at a loose end, hanging out, openly spoke of their allegiance to the YDB$.

During the time of the conflict, Enver, a resident of Rio street, was especially anxious about crossing WK$ territory where he would be at risk of being beaten or shot by the gang's members. He relied heavily upon the older women's goodwill for food and shelter. Most Rio Street residents identified Enver as a marginal member of the Rio Street community. When I first asked Vonna about him, she identified him as *'n weeskind,* an orphan, but proceeded to add that *'Hy 't soe voor my ma-hulle opgegroei. Sy ma is van 'n borskwaal oorlede, toe 't Aan Mary 't ve hom ingevat'.* (My mother [Aunty Gwen] and others watched him grow up. His mother died of a chest problem [the local term for tuberculosis]. Then Aunty Mary took him in.)

Everyone knew Enver and his mother, a single parent, from the day she moved into the community, 25 years ago. He was only 12 years old when she died and Aunty Mary decided to become his foster mother. She obtained a foster parent grant from the state to assist her in providing for him until he reached the age of 18 years. After that, he would be legally identified as an adult and regarded as able to earn an independent income. Within the Rio Street community, however, what mattered was that he was acknowledged as the foster son of a *moeder,* Aunty Mary, and that he was firmly anchored within a respectable household. These details defined Enver as a person in Rio Street.

Enver dropped out of high school at the age of sixteen. Since then he had been earning a small income as an itinerant assistant to the local men who worked as small-scale vegetable vendors. He still lived with Aunty Mary but was soon considered a marginal member of her household. When his foster grant ended, she asked him to move into the backyard shack. She also began providing him with meals on a more sporadic basis, indicating that she could not afford to do so on a daily basis any longer. His status in the community and his claim to the women's support had decreased significantly until other *moeders* like Aunty Gwen and Aunty Frances stepped into the breach. They provided him with his daily meals, allowed him to use their bathrooms or provided him with linen and a few odds and ends for his room. They provided him with assistance very discreetly, so that he was able to retain his dignity in the community. In return, he ran errands for them on a daily basis, purchasing electricity or groceries at the local mall, Nyanga Junction.

During my discussions with other young men, Enver hovered on the outskirts of our circle and appeared tentative, almost shy. He was hesitant during group conversations, rarely offering his opinion on the topic at hand. During the times when he ventured to voice his opinion or disagreed with the young women from other households, they would register his marginal status by stating, *'Sies, djy stink! Wie wil langs jou sit!'* (Yechh, you smell! Who wants to sit next to you?). In this cruel fashion, they silenced him, their remarks reminding him that he was not a legitimate member of a household and so did not have access on a regular basis to those essential facilities needed to acquire the outward style of personhood, such as a bathroom or toiletries. However, he had enjoyed some measure of respect from the young men since he became a member of the YDB$.

On his daily round of errands, Enver usually walked to the shopping centre, which was situated about a kilometre away from Rio Street. His route took him across two gang turfs, namely the WK$ and CK$ territories. During the gang conflict, he would take me aside, out of earshot of the other youths and harangue me to run the errands in my car or to drive him to the mall. At this point in our relationship, I did not know that Enver was a member of the YDB$ and on most days I would accede to his requests. However, on one occasion I curtly asked him why he couldn't walk the route himself. He protested that the WK$ would attack him then saying that *'Ma as ek met Elaine is, sal hulle niks maak'ie.*[9] (But if I'm with Elaine, they [referring to members of the opposing gangs] won't touch me.)

'*Waarom nie?*' (Why not?), I asked.

'*Want Elaine is 'n vroumens. Hulle los die vroumense allien. En ons ry*' (Because Elaine is a woman and they usually leave the women alone And, besides, we're driving), he replied.

'*Ma hoe gat hulle wiet djy's 'n Dixie?*' (How would they know that you were a member of the Dixies?), I persisted.

'*Want ek dra die tjappie. Hulle gaan ve my laat uittrek, dan sien hulle mos my tjappie*' (Because I wear the tattoo. They'll force me to undress, and then they'll see my tattoo), he shot back.

'*Was'sit? Wys ve my*' (Where is it? Show it to me), I said.

He proceeded to unbutton his shirt and revealed a tattoo on his shoulder blade, consisting of two bells and the letters YDB$ below. I struggled to reconcile the popular image of the terrifying gangster with the harmless, self-effacing figure that Enver cut in the Rio Street context. The adult women like Vonna and Aunty Gwen only spoke of him in sympathetic tones. None of the women had ever referred to the active presence of the YDB$ in Rio Street, or to the fact that some of the young adult men whom I had befriended were members of the gang. Now, in the context of a violent gang conflict, their membership of the local gang became clear. Men like Enver could not operate across the boundaries that marked the WK$ or the HL$ turf. It was as though invisible borders had been drawn between Rio Street and Grande Walk and had become impermeable and threatening to men like Enver. For the most part, these boundaries were only considered to be marginally significant during peaceful periods and he was able to navigate his way safely across these areas, except for the occasional hand sign from a member of another gang, to indicate turf possession. During the gang warfare that erupted in February 1998, however, these boundaries became highly meaningful and his identity as a male resident in YDB$ territory and therefore as a gang member was primary. His errand run had become dangerous.

---

[9] The use of the third person to denote respect to an adult during conversation is common practice in the township.

Enver had had his YDB$ tattoo done on a part of his body that was usually concealed by his apparel. Ordinarily, in the context of the Rio Street community, the tattoo remained hidden. It was only revealed in the context of the other members and reflected Enver's identity as a member of the local group of *Ouens,* streetwise men. He obtained some respect from his peers and from other men for enduring the painful rite of passage, in which he was made an *Ou* or a streetwise man. Most *moeders* feigned ignorance about Enver's and the other local young men's membership in the gang. However, on occasion, when pushed, they reluctantly admitted to knowing about the YDB$, claiming that they were harmless. Aunty Gwen only spoke dismissively of the *'jongens wat stout is'* (the streetwise men who are mischievous).

The adolescent women, in contrast, feared the YDB$, and spoke admiringly, though fearfully, of the members for stoically enduring the gangs' rite of passage into manhood, which, as I illustrate below, is marked by physical brutality. Enver had demonstrated that he had acquired the necessary toughness, the quintessential quality of manhood and that he could now be regarded as an *ou.* However, in the geographic and social context of Rio Walk, the territory of the WK$, the tattoo marked him as a *skollie* (gangster or a thug), a stranger, and a threat to the local residents. Through the act of exposing his tattoo in the context of Rio Walk, antagonists would reveal his body as belonging to an antagonistic group of men, as one out of place, the body of a stranger. Enver had looked to me, an adult woman like others in the Rio Street, to mediate his presence and to attest to his identity as a person in the context of another community. The tattoo that Enver had acquired during his rite of passage into manhood had also become the sign that marked him as a threat to men in other communities. The significance of Enver's tattoo, as the sign of local social and geographical boundaries, was operationalized by the context in which it was exposed.

Gang warfare such as that which occurred between the WK$ and the HL$ precipitates a crisis which brings the Janus-faced contradictory quality of young men's personhood as *Ouens* and as *goeie seuns* into sharp relief. During such periods, men like Enver are made aware of the different contexts, namely the moral community and the enemy gang turf, in which the different aspects of their masculine personhood are operationalized, and also of the importance of policing the boundaries between these two contexts. Enver's status as an orphan meant that his claim to the *moeders'* protection and their willingness to assert his identity as a good son was precarious. He could not risk being regarded as a *skollie* or a ruffian – someone who placed the safety of his community at risk. As he attempted to negotiate his way across the context of the moral community and the enemy gang turf, he implicitly recognized the interaction of the diverse persons, namely the young women, the *moeders*, and the enemy gangsters within these contexts, and the implications these held for his own personhood.

In the Rio Street community, like other local communities in Manenberg, young adult men are not recognized as men merely through the natural process of physical maturation. They have to be made into a particular type of man, the *Ou*, the man who polices the boundaries of the local social and moral community. The rite of passage whereby they are made into *Ouens* is widely accepted as being secret, even though local residents who are pressed for information reluctantly admit that they know about the details of this rite of passage. In the next section, I indicate that gang practices are initiated in the rite of passage into manhood for young men who, like Enver, find themselves in a liminal state, between the local markers of childhood and adulthood. These men are usually high-school dropouts, having rejected the dependency status that is associated with the role of a student, but who are still childless and without the resources such as jobs that, within the dominant ideology of masculinity, would define them as men. In addition, they lack the necessary history or life experience that, in the local, alternative ideology of masculinity demonstrates their ability to endure the toughening processes life serves to men over time.

E. Making *'n Ou*: Gangs' rites of passage

Once Enver had told me about the *tjappie* (the tattoo) that marked gang membership, I asked the other young men about their tattoos and how they had acquired them. However, when I did so, during my usual afternoon visit in March 1998, Zahir, Ziempie and the other young men met my request with smirks and expressions of outright contempt. '*Nie, o's ka' mossie ve Elaine sê nie. Elaine issie 'n Dixie nie*' (No, we can't tell Elaine. Elaine's not a member of the Dixies), Ziempie growled. Clearly, only the exclusive group of gang members, the brotherhood, in Pinnock's (1984) eloquent phrase, could have rightful access to this exclusive knowledge. I felt peeved that I could not obtain any forthright answers. Knowledge meant for the exclusive group of men, the initiated gang members, and secrecy were the hallmarks of the brotherhood. I had to look elsewhere for an explanation.

At the time a fellow researcher, William Ellis, and I were also attending counselling sessions for adolescents at the Community Counseling and Training Centre (CCATC) nearby. The group of seven adolescents consisted of both genders, although young men constituted the majority of the membership. Their schoolteachers and parents had referred them to the counsellor as a last attempt to save them from expulsion from school. These youths were considered to be at risk of joining local gangs and dropping out of the education system. During these counselling sessions, Geraldine, the counsellor, would begin by sketching a scenario that incorporated all the elements of the dilemmas that these young people faced on a daily basis in the township. The group members would then express their own opinions about the situation and the choices that the protagonists made. At this particular time, the group discussion focused on the current gang conflict.

It was during one such session that we befriended 17-year-old Ashley, who had been a member of the JFK$. That day, Geraldine had told the group of a case where a young man had been shot and killed by a rival gang. His teenaged friend had discovered his body and was faced with the dilemma of avenging his friend's death by taking the life of one of the rival gang's members, or reporting the murder to the police and letting justice take its course. Most of the young men argued vociferously for avenging the death, whilst a minority, which included a few males and all the women, argued that the matter should be left to the police and the justice system. The debate became quite heated, and Ashley, in particular, angrily led the case for vengeance. As the noise level rose, and the debate became disorderly, he stood up and repeated the phrase

'Is sy bloed broer! Hy moet sterk biene het! Is sy plig, hy moet sy broer bystaan!'
(That is his brother! He has to [show that] he has strong bones! It is his duty; he must stand by his brother!)

179

At this point, he defiantly rolled up his sleeve and displayed a tattoo on his biceps. His tattoo was of a different design to the one Enver displayed. Later, we asked him about the tattoo. He became defensive and told us that his mother had warned him constantly about the dangers of gang membership.

In 1998 he had entered his first year at the local high school, where he had befriended the members of the Junky Funky Kids. They had enthralled him with tales of their gang activities and then invited him to join them. When he agreed, he was invited to meet all the members at The Greens, the only soccer field in Manenberg, one Sunday evening, where he would be initiated into the gang. At this time the field would be deserted and they would not be disturbed as they carried out the initiation ceremony. He said that the members were armed with leather belts, wooden clubs and planks. They stood in two parallel lines, facing each other. The leader then instructed him to run through the gauntlet of gang members, who beat him with their assorted weapons. 'Why?' I asked. He looked at me in amazement for a moment. His face took on an expression that suggested that my question was almost preposterous. Then he replied,

'Om te wys dat djy sterk biene het. Djy moet wys dat djy jou man kan bystaan. Want as jou broer in die moeilikheid is, moet djy ve hom kan uithelp.' (You must demonstrate that you have strong bones. You have to display your ability to stand by your man. When your brother is in trouble [in a gang war] you must be able to assist him.)

After the beating, the gang leader tattooed the gang's insignia onto his body, using a needle and ink made from hot, melted rubber. Ashley said that he was expected to endure the tattooing process without flinching. After his initiation, he and the gang would confront commuters at the Athlone train station and demand their wallets and jewellery. They would also harass young women outside their gang turf. 'Ons'it nooit mense van Manenberg gerob nie' (We never robbed the people from Manenberg), he said.

He quit school and began hanging out in the *hok* (the cage) that the JFK$ frequented. The school authorities informed his parents of his absence from school. His mother then confronted him about his activities and demanded that he undress so that she could inspect his body for the telltale tattoo. When her fears were confirmed, she demanded that he leave the gang or leave home. His mother demanded that he accompany her to school to meet with the school principal. The principal indicated that he would allow Ashley back to school if he agreed to attend the counselling sessions at CATCC.

William and I later met with Ashley's mother, Aunty Charlotte. We informed her of our discussion with Ashley and asked her about her opinion about Ashley's actions. She spoke about her fear that Ashley's gang membership would lead him to prison:

> *'Ek wiet dat hulle ma' net stout is, en baie kere wat die mense sê van die jongens is nie waar nie. Ma' die prinsipaal het toe ve my gebel van sy wegblyery van die skool af. Ek moes, as ma saam met hom skool toe gegaan het om met die prinsipaal ontmoet. Ek 'it ve hom gesê Ashley kom uit 'n goeie huis, en as ma wou ek nie hê hy moet in die moeilikheid kom nie.'*
>
> (I know that they [the young men] are mischievous. Often the rumours that people spread about them are not true. When the school principal called me about his absence from school, as a mother, I had to accompany him to the school to meet with the authorities. I told the principal that Ashley comes from a good home and that I did not want him to find himself in trouble.)

The making of men in the township through gangs' rites of passage, like rites of passage elsewhere, is a process that marks the start of the journey into the wider world of gendered adulthood. As in other rites of passage, men are encouraged to take on the values and responsibilities that signify manhood within their communities. As boys are made into men, their relationship to the *moeders* takes on a different quality. They are expected to show less obvious emotional reliance or dependence on their own and the other *moeders*. In turn, they are expected to openly display their increased preference for and emotional reliance on their male cohort for affirmation. Through this process, the young men begin to struggle for and insist upon being acknowledged as the *moeders'* allies in reproducing the community, as they demarcate and police its geographic boundaries. This struggle is manifest in women's attempts to erase the gang's *tjappies* from their sons' bodies as well as in their attempts to draw in the state authorities to assist them in asserting their authority over their sons. However, in the final analysis, the *moeders* protect and defend their sons' reputations as *goeie seuns* or good sons, just as sons affirm and acknowledge the *moeders'* central nurturing roles in the moral community. In Manenberg, toughness and display of loyalty to local men and the *moeders* first, and then to other members of the local community, are among the quintessential values of masculinity.

Individuals who want to be recognized as men are expected to display their ability to withstand emotional and physical privation that will mark their lives, to the audience of local men. More than that, they have to display their potential loyalty to the gang, measured in their ability to withstand the severe beating and the painful tattooing. This initial display of endurance demonstrates the young man's enormous courage and the future potential to defend his brother's life even under the most difficult circumstances. The process of making a gangster reflects not only a local rite of passage into manhood but also signifies these men's embodiment of their identities as strangers within other local communities.

Men's identification as persons within the community is defined in opposition to the male non-persons, the strangers who exist outside its boundaries and who have no ties to the adult women within the local community. While men are identified as persons, and affirmed by and through their connectedness to the *ordentlike moeders*, they are identified as strangers by men located within another geographic and moral community. The *skollie* or ruffian identity is equated with the non-person, the stranger who exists beyond the boundaries of the local community. The Afrikaans term *skollie* is derived from the Old Dutch term *schoelje*, meaning 'scavenger'. 'Dutch sailors shouted *schoelje* at seagulls which snatched ships' offal from the waters of Table Bay. Later the word was used to describe vagrants who survived from pickings off dumpsites or from begging on the streets' (Pinnock 1984: 24). In the contemporary use of the term, *skollie* refers to a man without pride, a ruffian or a thug, who feeds off the resources of the community, threatening its moral integrity without providing protection for its members. Such men are unlike the *Ouens* who have earned the right to openly display their pride because they protect and police the geographic boundaries of the community. *Skollies* cannot earn the respect of other men or women and are considered to be social strangers who threaten local men's ties to the women. They signify a drain on the moral and material resources. In addition, they are also identified as men who place economic gain over and above the survival of the community, who act out of self-interest and who commit immoral, shameful acts in the eyes of the local residents. They bring shame to their own mothers and to their households and cannot be acknowledged as *goeie seuns* or good sons.

During gang warfare gangsters could only cross local boundaries if they were accompanied by a *moeder*. These women's presence as *moeders* affirms the young men's identities as *goeie seuns* in a situation where they might otherwise be identified as *skollies*. The presence of the adult woman attests to his identity as a person, someone of moral worth, who does not present a threat to the local residents. The presence of the adult woman supersedes the significance of the tattoo, in the context of another community.

Local residents such as the *moeders* also have to possess tacit knowledge about the gangs' secret activities, their aesthetics and practices through which the gang members police local boundaries, in order to assess when to accompany men across geographic boundaries. The gang's activities carried out in the context of the local community and with the knowledge of the local residents, especially the older *moeders*, give legitimacy to these practices and affirm the men who engage in them. Within the boundaries of Rio Street, gangsters become the *Ouens*, the men who are affirmed as persons. At the same time, they could also lapse into the *skollie* identity. In Rio Street, as in other local communities, *Ouens* are distinguished from *skollies* through their ability to act in the interest of the community and its residents. *Skollies*, in contrast, act only in their own self-interest and present a potential risk to the long-term interests and safety of the local residents.

F. *Ouens en Skollies*: Respectable men and thugs

Paul is the leader of the Young Dixie Boys, the gang located in Rio Street. While other young men were curious about me and willingly shared their conversations with me, Paul kept a respectful distance. When I arrived in the community, in late 1997, I would spy him standing at the top floor window of the first-floor apartment he shared with his aged mother, Aunt Gwen, and the extended family, or squatting on his haunches at the end of the staircase. He would merely nod in acknowledgement to the rather overenthusiastic greeting I shouted up to him. I first befriended the younger members of the Young Dixie Boys as discrete individuals: Ziempie, Enver, Loppa, Lippe, Zahir and Markie, a group of adolescents who had dropped out of school and who were constantly hustling for informal jobs. They often hung out in Morieda's postage-stamp size front yard between jobs, talking, or sharing a cigarette. They appeared to be caught somewhere between the innocent activities of adolescent boyhood and the style of tough young manhood. During my first visits, these adolescents were on the margins of my circle of acquaintances in Rio Street. I was interested in befriending the adolescent girls, intent on discovering their world and the issues that were important to them. These issues turned out to be some of their relationships with the very adolescent men whom I initially regarded as peripheral to my inquiry.

One afternoon, whilst we were seated on rocks on the edge of the street, in idle conversation, the girls spoke of the current conflict between the local gang, the Young Dixie Boys, and the Naughty Boys, the gang which was located at the court in the adjacent road. The Naughty Boys had accused Zahir, a Young Dixie Boy, of stealing wheels from a car that belonged to one of their members. The Naughty Boys had vowed that they would exact revenge for the theft. That very afternoon, an ominous group of young men sauntered down the road and congregated in front of Paul's house. The girls whispered *'hie kom hulle, hie kom hulle'* (here they come) under their breath as they glared at the approaching group with lowered eyes. One of the men ascended the concrete stairs to Aunty Gwen's flat, knocked on the door and was admitted into the apartment. As we waited with bated breath, Zellie, one of the young men, pointed out that most of these men stood with one hand thrust down the front of their trousers. This was a sure sign that they were each armed, clutching a weapon concealed in the crotch. They all wore baseball caps and dark glasses, through which it seemed they surveyed everyone balefully.

The lackadaisical atmosphere of the afternoon had changed to one pregnant with ominous apprehension. Even the afternoon sunlight that seemed soothingly warm now appeared to sting my skin. *'Hie kom Oom*

Booi en Aan' Dopie-hulle nou' (Uncle Booi and Aunty Dopie have come), Nadia said with relief. By now, a number of older *moeders* and a few men had approached the group, all wearing determined faces. Uncle Booi was part of this group too. He was known to be fearless, having spent two *Blou Baadjie* (Blue jacket) terms in prison for theft. During his imprisonment he was a member of the Twenty Eights, a gang that was notorious for being extremely violent, and who raped their fellow inmates as a means of asserting power over them. Before that he was a member of the Mongrels gang in Hanover Park, an adjoining township.

'*Gat binne, Elaine'* (Go indoors), Aunt Mary said to me meaningfully, as she descended the stairs to join the group. Her tone made it clear that this was no place for me or for any other younger people. All the other girls had disappeared into Morieda's living room by this time. I ascended the stairs obediently though reluctantly, torn between curiosity about the discussion that was now taking place below and concern for my safety. I chose to take up a position in Aunt Mary's doorway, where I could still survey the proceedings in the street below yet access the sanctuary of the living room if any trouble occurred. About ten minutes later the leader of the strange group reappeared and descended the stairs to the street, now followed by Paul. He was clutching his four-month-old son in his arms, wrapped in a cotton blanket. At first, this gesture seemed incomprehensible. But, even as I shook my head at his apparent lack of concern for the safety of his little son, Kyle, I was overawed by his determined display of caring, loving fatherhood. He lovingly embraced the little infant's body, apparently communicating to all that watched from the street below, through cracked doorways or apartment windows, that fatherhood took primacy over all else.

As he approached the menacing group, the older women residents and the few men surrounded him in tight, protective formation. Soon everyone was gesticulating and talking very earnestly. Fingers and hands rose and fell in concert with voices and taut facial expressions. Fragmented bits of conversation drifted up to me like verbal shrapnel. The harsh though muted voices kept me rooted in the doorway and I remained where I stood, even though I was increasingly frustrated at not being able to hear what was being said. The steely voices and the memory of Aunt Mary's command prevented me from descending the stairs. After a long while, their bodies relaxed and the talking hands and fingers now hung quietly by their sides. Faces regained composure and voices became more fluid. Soon the circle loosened: the group of strangers separated themselves from the residents and moved away from Paul. The leader shook his hand and they all turned and walked away, their lengthening shadows retreating after them. It was clear that they had reached an agreement that was acceptable to all parties.

Aunt Mary ascended the stairs and I stepped aside for her to enter, waiting eagerly to hear about the discussion. '*Wat'it toe gebeur, Aan' Mary?*' (What happened?), I asked, unable to contain my curiosity. She pointedly ignored my question, bustled through the door and loudly demanded of us to '*Sit'ie TV aan! Sit'ie TV aan, is tyd ve Bold. En Marlene maak ve ons tie asseblief*' (Turn on the TV, its time for 'Bold.' Marlene, make some tea please), silencing any further inquiries about the averted crisis. As Chantal hurried to turn on the TV, Aunt Mary sat down on the nearest couch with grace and ease and was rapidly engrossed in the images that flickered across the screen. She had just assisted in defusing a menacing gang conflict and prevented a chain of retributive violence that could have stretched over a few weeks, traumatizing every resident. Yet she did not appear to be drained by the effort. I was awestruck by Aunt Mary's ability to orchestrate the day's activities back into the routine pattern almost seamlessly, thereby actively shutting out the young men's chaos that threatened to disrupt everyone's lives in a bloody war.

It was six o'clock in the evening; a time when everyone would be watching the American soap opera, 'The Bold and the Beautiful', sipping restorative cups of tea before preparing the main meal of the day. A palpable calm reigned over the small living room, as we were rapidly absorbed in the soap opera characters' endless struggle for true love. As I watched, I realized that I would have to wait until the next day, when one of the adolescent girls who was able to eavesdrop on the adults' conversation in an overcrowded bedroom overnight would tell me what had ensued in the street below. For now, I had nothing else to do but watch and wait.

The next afternoon I returned to Rio Street, and encountered a despondent group of young men leaning against the corrugated iron fence that separated Morieda's front yard from that of her neighbours. Their eyes wore the hooded look that I had rapidly learned to associate with repressed anger. Some mumbled a greeting; others ignored me and stared moodily onto the street. I entered Morieda's house and slumped down into a chair. It seemed as though the angry, hostile faces I encountered in the yard had dissipated my initial eagerness to see the residents in Rio Street. I berated myself for only wanting to satisfy my curiosity about yesterday's events. The angry faces outside spoke volumes about an unpleasant solution that had been reached after my departure. However, the solution had angered the young men, even though it had warded off a potentially ugly gang conflict. Zellie and Nadia were watching *Simunye*'s youth program on TV. They too seemed subdued.

I had brought along some soda, bread, and cold cuts (meat) for the little group. Nadia made some sandwiches, poured the soda and offered some to the young men outside. Soon everyone was in a more relaxed mood and began chatting idly about the TV program. Conversation began to flow more easily as we ate the sandwiches. As I watched and listened, Zahir winced visibly, holding his torso. He appeared to be in pain.

'Wat gat aan mit jou?' (What's happened to you?), I asked. Suddenly a wary silence descended on the room as everyone looked at Zahir.
'Nik'sie, Elaine' (Nothing, Elaine), he mumbled with downcast eyes.
'Hy's ma' net seer, Elaine' (He's just a little sore, Elaine), Zellie said cagily.

I had unwittingly touched upon an issue that had made everyone wary. He rose to leave the room, but held the right side of his torso as he rose, his face contorted with pain.

'Ma' waarom loep djy soe skief?' (Why are you walking crookedly?), I persisted.
'Hulle't hom geslaat, want hy't by die Naughty Boyse kar ingebriek. Sê julle!' (They've beaten him up because he burgled a car belonging to the Naughty Boys gang. Speak up, you lot!), Nadia said. She looked at the others defiantly, apparently daring them to ostracize her for breaking a community code of silence.

'Wie't hom geslaat?' (Who hit him?), I persisted.

'Paul-hulle en 'ie anner Dixies. Gister' (Paul and the other Dixies. Yesterday), Claudette softly responded.

They were soon telling me about the events that had followed the tense meeting in the road. After the standoff between the Dixies and the Naughty Boys had occurred, Paul and the senior members of the Young Dixie Boys gang had questioned the younger members to establish who had participated in the burglary. All the other members had then punished the guilty party, Zahir. I was dumbfounded.

'Waarom sal julle julle eie broer soe slaat en nou sit julle hie asof niks gebeur'it ie?' (Why would you beat up your brother and then sit here and pretend it was nothing?), I demanded of the other young men.

Loppa smirked and then said laconically *'Elaine sall'ie verstaan nie.'* (Elaine would not understand). At that, the young men all walked out into the backyard.

'Hulle moes 'it doen' (They had to do it), Nadia explained. *'Paul is hulle leier en wat hy sê is wet'*. (Paul is their leader and what he says is the law.)

'Ma' waarom moes hulle ve hom soe slat?' (But why did they have to beat him up so badly?), I asked. *'Hy is dan hulle broer.'* (He is their brother.)

Nadia moved slowly in her chair, as she sought a more comfortable position. It was as if she was preparing herself to provide a long, patient explanation to me, the naïve newcomer, who knew little about tough discipline in the township.

'Ma' hy wiet, mens moetie van jou eie steel nie. Die Naughty Boys moet revenge vat as Paul nie ve hom self laat slat'it 'ie. Toe hy 'n Dixie geword'it toe wiet hy hy moet sterk biene het. Hy moet sy pak vat soes 'n man.' (Yes, but he knows that you don't steal from your own people. The Naughty Boys would be forced to take revenge if Paul did not punish Zahir himself. When he [Zahir] became a member of the Dixies, he knew that he would have to have tough bones. He must take his punishment like a man.)

I tried to make sense of my initial perception of Paul, Aunty Frances' 28-year-old son, against the one that was now emerging. He seemed to possess a quiet disposition and could be seen squatting on his haunches by himself at the end of the concrete staircase, scrunching his eyes against the harsh sunlight as he surveyed the action on the street. Now he seemed to be an implacable *Ou*, a streetwise man, who was clearly capable of carrying out severe physical assault. I laughed inwardly at my own naïveté and my benign reading of character. I was dismayed by the severe punishment meted out to Zahir, even while I understood the reasons for doing so. There seemed to be an unspoken consensus that he had to be disciplined for his actions. He had put the lives of his brothers as well as those of the other residents at risk and nearly caused a gang war through his rash actions. However, I was dismayed at the severity of the punishment that was meted out. He was 17 years old, a mere adolescent. Yet his brothers had beat him quite mercilessly. In the local context,'*Ouens*' or streetwise men like Paul were expected to mete out a form of street justice if the individual man's actions were serious enough to raise the ire of the *moeders* and threaten the safety of the local residents. The *moeders* were involved in resolving the crisis, implicitly insisting that a solution is found by the persons within the community. In this manner, the moral character of the community is protected while the opposing gang's desire for revenge is assuaged. If the police were called in to find a solution, the community's fragile image as one of moral integrity would be threatened and the stereotype of a community of social chaos and shame would be reinforced. Paul had behaved correctly by asserting his authority over one of his gang members, Zahir, and disciplining him.

The local police force remains the symbol of oppression for the Manenberg population. Historically, Manenberg residents have regarded the police with fear and barely concealed contempt. Like most Black South Africans, these residents have associated the police with their forced eviction from their old neighbourhoods, and with daily humiliation they suffered when legislation such as racial segregation was enforced on the transport system. They rarely report crimes such as burglary or rape to the local police, even in the current context, despite the post-apartheid state's efforts to transform the police force into an institution committed to civilian policing. In Rio Street, rumours abounded about police collusion with the more powerful gangs such as the Hard Livings, and local residents would not expect any justice from them. Residents trusted the historic local means of policing through the gang structure. This form of street justice existed in areas such as District Six, and was the impetus for the founding of the notorious Globe gang (Pinnock 1984). The tradition had travelled to areas of relocation such as Manenberg, and was used to implement community law and order in this context.

Paul had displayed the leadership expected of a male gang leader when he exercised his authority over the younger gang members. He and the gang had punished Zahir with the consent of the *moeders*. They had carried out the punishment by beating him up in the nearby soccer field at night, out of sight of other residents. At the same time, through his actions, Paul had indicated to the Naughty Boys that he was in control of his turf, but that he would appease their call for revenge. In doing so he had averted a gang war. Furthermore, he had informed the younger men and the other gang members that he would not tolerate any brash actions that could endanger other Rio Grande residents. In the process, Paul had reaffirmed the local moral rules on petty crime. Most residents acknowledged that theft was unpleasant but necessary for survival. Theft committed against strangers who lived in the wealthier areas of the city was an act that was tolerated. These victims were not part of the moral community, and by virtue of their class, they could afford the loss of their possessions. Theft committed against another, impoverished Manenberg resident was quite another. It would be tolerated only if it did not put local residents at risk. Paul was teaching the younger men the painful lessons of wisdom and tact – key skills needed to survive in an impoverished township such as Manenberg.

In contrast, I was blundering my way through the unspoken, subtle web of protocol expected during situations like these, and learning difficult, though necessary lessons along the way. *'Kom'*, I said to Zahir. *'Ek vat jou nou Jooste toe.'* (Come, I'm taking you to Jooste.) 'Jooste' was the shortened term commonly used to refer to the G.F. Jooste Hospital, located on the outskirts of the township. *'Ek gat saam'* (I'm going along), Markie, another Dixie piped up, eager, I supposed, for a break in the monotony of his day. *'Ja, ek oek'* (me too), Lippe said. Soon I found my little car filled with the younger members of the Young Dixie Boys, their lanky, bony limbs stretched into all available space.

'Wa 'ntoe gat Elaine nou mit daai klomp?' (Where are you going with that lot?), Aunty Gwen screeched from her perch at the apartment window on the second floor.

'Ek vat Zahir hospitaal toe' (I'm taking Zahir to the hospital), I shouted back.

She shook her head grimly, and replied *'Djy mors jou tyd, hy 's 'n skollie. Hys 'ie die moeite werd nie. Hy 't sy pakslae verdien'.* (You're wasting your time, he's not worth it, he's just a skollie.) Then she looked into the distance, ignoring me. She had deliberately used the informal address *'djy'* instead of the usual formal third person form of address that connotes the local form of respect the women show to each other. Moreover, she had defined Zahir as a *skollie*, a worthless thug. In doing so, Aunty Gwen had communicated her strong disapproval of his and my actions. I was assisting someone who had broken the cardinal rules of the local community, by stealing from a local resident. Through his actions, he had defined himself as worthless. I drove off, angry at myself for breaking ranks with many other residents who felt that Zahir had deserved his punishment and deserved no sympathy. In addition, I had forgotten that in order to reach the hospital I had to drive through Naughty Boy turf. Paul had appeased the Naughty Boys by punishing Zahir, and the *moeders* like Aunty Gwen temporarily negated his status as a person by actively condemning him as a *skollie*. In contrast, I appeared to be approving of his actions by seeking medical assistance for his injuries. In addition, I was endangering the others and myself by driving through enemy territory.

The local notions of masculinity begin with, are anchored in, and are marked by, men's actions as *Ouens* or streetwise men. They personify and define the socio-spatial boundaries that frame the local community. While the ideology of *ordentlikheid*, embodied through the actions of women as *moeders*, operates across all local communities in Manenberg, it is only from within the confines of the specific local community, such as Rio Street, in which young men's individual histories and their links to specific adult women are known publicly, that they can freely go about their daily rounds, be recognized as, and perform their responsibilities as individual men. For this reason, the young men have to demarcate and safeguard the boundaries of the local community, in which they are recognized as persons. At the same time, they also have to ensure that the next generation of potential *moeders* remains anchored in the local community. The older *moeders* are recognized as persons across the local boundaries and are able to move across the divides between the local communities fearlessly, extending their protection to the men accompanying them. In contrast to the *moeders*, men perceive single young women's movements across the boundaries of the local community as a threat to the ongoing recognition of their personhood. These women may form relationships with young men from outside the community, thereby threatening the young men's progression to, or their tenuous hold on, the next stage of manhood, namely fatherhood. The young, single women's presence within any local community personifies its actual or potential social and cultural capital and ensures young men's progress to the next stage of personhood in the lifecycle, fatherhood. Young men can form relationships with and marry young women from other communities. However, their own histories would be connected to *moeders* elsewhere and their willingness to protect and police the geographic boundaries of the community they have married into would remain suspect.

Men's dependence on these women differs across the generations. The young adult men or older adolescents who have dropped out of school and who are economically marginal still have to establish their reputation as men in the community. They are most dependent upon the *moeders* to assert their personhood as *goeie seuns* or good sons. Later, after young men have established their reputations as *Ouens*, and as they mature through the lifecycle, they acquire other identities as fathers, toughened ex-prisoners or, less frequently, permanently employed breadwinners and committed members of the Christian or Muslim faiths. As these men mature and acquire these diverse identities they rely less upon the *moeders* to assert their identities as persons in the local context. Within this set of possible, local masculine identities, fatherhood is identified as the primary identity through which men begin to display their personhood independently of adult women, and through which they are able to demonstrate their ability to nurture and sustain others emotionally and materially. However, their ability to sustain partners and children falls short of the expectation that young women have of them as husbands and fathers, namely to provide steady financial support for their families. Their identities as fathers are inherently fraught with, and fractured across the fault lines of their sporadic access to material resources.

Consequently, while older women as *moeders* can and do assert men's personhood, particularly during early adulthood, men are unable to fulfil one of the young adult women's most cherished desires and a key feature of their own respectability, namely a monogamous relationship and a stable, nuclear family. Even as the older *moeders* and the young men form an alliance, young adult men's inability to fulfil young women's expectations of a loyal monogamous relationship generates tension between the two genders within the same generation. Adult women enjoy the benefits of local boundary demarcation and the affirmation of their status as *ordentlike moeders* at a price to the younger women. Young men assert control over the young women's local community membership, first through physical violence, then through fatherhood. In short, they attempt to ensure that these young women remain permanently within the local community through the latent threat of violence and then through childbirth, embedding them further in the dense web of kin relations in the local context. The young men's relationships with young women define an alternative pathway to masculine personhood, namely fatherhood. In the following section, I examine how this pathway unfolds through young men's relationships with young women.

G. Claiming women, making fathers.

During June 1998, Zahir began dating 16-year-old Nadia. Some months later, her mother, 36-year-old Morieda, began complaining to me that Zahir was beating up her daughter. *'Ek 'it 'n restraining order op hom gekry. Ma' sy willie weg van hom bly nie. Hy bly ve ha' hie by my huis kô kuier as ek by die werk is'* (I've obtained a legal restraining order against him, but she won't stay away from him and he will not leave her. He visits her regularly here at my home, when I'm away from work), she said. Morieda had a reputation for being progressive, and for utilizing the state institutions such as the police services when she needed to, rather than calling upon the community forms of justice delivered by Paul and the Young Dixie Boys. The *moeders* disapproved of her 'modern' attitude, and spoke disparagingly of her decision to take her two daughters to the local clinic so that they could be put on a birth control regime. They regarded her with ambivalence because she refused to adhere to the local code of conduct that emanated from their authority and from the ideology of *ordentlikheid*.

Morieda did not approve of Nadia's relationship with Zahir because she feared that the young man would trap her daughter in the cycle of early pregnancy. The young man lived with his father, his stepmother and his grandparents in their extended family. Ever since his parents' divorce, he had shuttled between his mother's house in Woodstock and his father's in Rio Street. For the past two years, he had lived in Rio Street, attending the local high school until he dropped out when the school principal reprimanded him publicly for not wearing regulation school shoes. He could not live down the public castigation he received and the personal embarrassment he had suffered. He had asked his parents to buy the school shoes, but at the time neither could afford to do so. Since then, he could be seen hanging out with his friends, sometimes accompanying his father to work, where he assisted him in return for a small payment. The recent beating that he had received from the YDB$ confirmed Morieda's suspicions that he was a member of the local gang.

Soon after my encounter with Morieda, I was able to talk to Nadia about her relationship with Zahir. *'Waarom bly djy mit hom as hy ve jou soe slaat?'* (Why do you stay with him if he hits you so?), I asked.

> *'Hy willie he sy moet hie by Colleen Court uithou nie. Hy's bang een van die Naughty Boys gat mit ha uit'* (He doesn't want her to hang out with her friends at Colleen Court. He fears that she'll go out with one of the Naughty Boys), her sister, Nazli replied.
>
> Nadia smiled shyly and protested at my inquiry, simply stating that *'Dis hoe dit moet wies.'* (That's how it should be.)
>
> *'Waarom?'* (Why?), I asked.
>
> *'Hy wys dat hy ve my omgie, Elaine. Hy slat die liefde in.'* (He's demonstrating that he cares about me, Elaine. He's beating in his care and love.)
>
> *'Ma' ek slat hom 't'rug. Ek sal nog altyd by die Colleen Court uithou'* (But I beat him too. I'll continue to hang out at Colleen Court), she said defiantly.
>
> *'Soe sal hy aanhou, totdat djy sy kind kry, of djy net hie innie hys of innie Riostraat bly. Dan sal hy ophou ve jou slaf'* (He'll continue to do that, until you have his

child or until you agree to remain home or in Rio Street. Then he'll stop beating you up), her older sister replied.

She had experienced the same level of abuse from her partner, Ziempie, another member of the YDB$. These episodes only occurred when he would come to visit her and did not find her home. Later that week I walked into Morieda's house unannounced, and came upon a weeping Nadia. Her cheekbone was badly bruised, the skin radiating shades of yellow, purple and blue. She walked away to the bathroom where she washed her face and then returned looking more composed.

'Is Zahir wat ve my geslat 'it omdat ek gister weg was innie Mitchell's Plain, by my aantie' (Zahir beat me because I was away yesterday visiting my aunt in Mitchell's Plain), she mumbled in reply to my expression of dismay and surprise. Her sister and I assembled a cold compress for her from some ice we found in the refrigerator. However, when I offered to take her to the local police station to report the incident, she quietly shook her head in refusal. I stalked off angrily in search of Zahir. I found him in the little *hok* that served as the YDB$ hangout at the corner of Rio Street, along with Enver and two other YDB$ members. *'Ve wat slat djy soe ve Nadia? Wat'it sy ve jou gemaak?'* (Why did you beat Nadia up so badly? What did she do to you to deserve such as beating?), I asked him from the doorway. He looked at me with a taut face and then mumbled that *'Sy moet ve my sê wa' sy gaan. Sy kan mossie net soe stap wa sy willie, sonner dat sy vra.'* (She's got to tell me where she goes. She can't just go off where she wishes without checking with me.)

'Ma sy's mossie mit jou getroud nie!' (But she's not married to you!) I replied indignantly.

'Sy moet nog steeds vra' (She still has to ask [for my permission]), he insisted.

The stoic fatalism that the young women displayed in the face of the brutal beatings they received from their partners left me feeling overwhelmed with frustration and anger. I talked to Paul about the situation, and asked him to do something about it. He remained quiet for a while and then said,

'Elaine moet verstaan. As Nadia nou mit Zahir uitgaan, en more mit 'n Naughty Boy vannie Colleen Court, dan sit sy mos ve Zahir en allie YDB$ innie moeilikheid. Sy

wiet mos nou van al sy dinge, van sy opstaan en sy gat lê, sy wiet van al gaatjies waar hy uithou, en 'n klomp anner goed wat anners nie van hom en die Dixies wiettie. Nou as sy mit 'n outjie vannie Colleen Court uitgaan, gat sy mos ve hom sê van Zahir se dinge. Die meisies wiet, as hulle mit een van ons uitgaan, dan gat hulle mit al onse bloedbroers uit.' (Elaine, you have to understand. If Nadia dates Zahir and then decides to date a member of the Naughty Boys from Colleen Court tomorrow, then Zahir and all the members of the YDB$ are placed at risk by her actions. She knows about all his movements, from his rising in the morning to his going to bed at night, she knows about all the holes where he hangs out and about a lot of privileged information that others don't know about him and his friends. Now if she dates a guy from Colleen Court, she'll share all that she knows about Zahir with him and he'll pass it on to his friends. These girls know, if they date one of us, they date all of his blood brothers.)

A few months later, Vonna told me that people were saying that Nadia was pregnant. That same day, Morieda called me in from the street. After the usual exchange of greetings, she told me that Nadia was pregnant and that she had dropped out of school. *'Ek's baie disappointed. Al die moeite mit birth control en sy's nog steeds pregnant'* (I am very disappointed. All this effort with birth control and she still falls pregnant), she said. A few days later, Vonna told me that Zahir *'het ga't sê'* (went to tell) and that he had asked for Morieda's formal permission to visit Nadia. Morieda wasn't very happy but had acceded to his request. Morieda confirmed Vonna's story, stating that

'Hy't darem die ordentlikheid gehad om te kom sê. Ek't gesê hy kon na die huis toe kom, ma hy moet nou ophou soe op ha' slat, nou dat hy gekry het wat hy wou gehê het.' (At least he had the decency to come and tell. I said that he could come to visit her at home [i.e. gave him formal permission], but that he should stop beating her, especially now that he'd obtained what he wanted [referring to Nadia's pregnancy].)

Morieda admitted that her hopes that her two daughters would continue to remain in school were dashed, at least in the short term. She stared out into the distance, as she said bitterly

'Hulle gesien hoe't ek gesukkel mit hulle pa. Eendag gie hy support, more is daar niksie, en soe gat dit aan ve maande. Dan gat hy nog kinners by 'n anner vrou kry. Die wat ek ve hom gelos 'it. Ma' nou gat my meisies mit dieselle ou storie sit.' (They saw the struggle I had with their father. One day he'd give me [monetary] support, then tomorrow there'd be nothing. Then, to top it all, he fathered children with another woman. That's why I left him. But now my girls will sit with the same old story.)

She was quiet for a moment, then stated firmly and defiantly *'Ma' ek 'it ve Nadia gesê sy moet trug skooltoe volgende jaar. Ek sal ve haar help mit die kind.'* (But I told Nadia that she must return to school next year. I'll assist her with the child.)

During the days and the weeks that followed, we witnessed a subtle transformation in Nadia and Zahir. They could be seen spending more time together, openly displaying their affection for each other on the street. Zahir sometimes accompanied her to the health clinic for her regular prenatal examination. Every now and then, when Zahir had earned some money from some or other day job he had found, they would walk to Nyanga Junction to make small purchases for the eagerly awaited infant, such as baby oil, baby shampoo or a pack of cotton diapers. Nadia was spending more time at home, busying herself with domestic tasks. During the other young women's regular afternoon conversations in Morieda's tiny living room, they constantly bombarded Nadia with questions about the physical changes her body was undergoing, or about her latest visit to the prenatal clinic.

'Slat hy nog steeds ve jou?' (Does he still beat you up?), Marlene asked her, one day.

'Nie, hy't nou opgehou slat' (No, he's stopped beating up on me), Nadia replied shyly but proudly. *'Ek't ve jou gesê! Ek't ve jou gese!'* (I told you! I told you!), her 19-year-old sister, Nazli, followed up. *'Ek 't ve ha' gesê hy sal ophou nou dat sy sy kind verwag. Dit was soe mit Ziempie oek. Hy 't aanhou ve my geslat voor Nazir se geboorte. Ma nou gat dit bietere. Hy 't soek vir werk, en hy probeer soe ve my elke keer geld gie ve die kind, as hy werk het. Hy 't wyser geword, en hy gie om ve Nazir. Die mans is ma soe. Nadia moet ma net uithou. Sy sal sien, dinge sal bietere gaan.'* (I told her that he would stop now that she's expecting his child. It was like that with Ziempie too. He constantly beat me up before Nazir was

born. But now it's going better. He's been job hunting and he's tried to give me some money for the child when he's found some work. He's become wiser [since our child's birth] and he cares for Nazir. Men are like that. Nadia must learn to stick it out. She'll see that things will improve.)

I marvelled at her optimism, but had to admit that, given the change in Zahir's behaviour in recent weeks, she might be right. Now Nadia offered no talk about hanging out in Colleen Court. She spoke sometimes of the plans she and Zahir had of putting up a room in his grandparents' backyard, where they could live once the baby was born, or of Zahir's constant search for work so that he could provide for the baby. Even the *moeders* in the street, like Aunty Gwen, who had earlier written him off as a *skollie*, knowingly remarked that Zahir was changing. She said with some satisfaction that

'*Is reg soe, hy sal sy stoutigheid moet los. Hy sal moet opgegroei, hy's een vannie dae 'n pa. Hulle dink kinnners kry is perde koep.*' (This is correct. He'll have to end his mischievous ways. He'll have to grow up; one of these days he'll be a father. They think that having children is the same as purchasing horses.)

Nazli went into labour prematurely during the seventh month of pregnancy and gave birth to a daughter. The little girl was placed in an incubator and remained in hospital for a few weeks. When I congratulated the young couple on the birth of their infant daughter, Zahir expressed great concern for her well-being. He accompanied Nadia to the hospital as often as possible and spoke proudly of the infant's progress on his return home. As they stood around on the street, his friends listened quietly and respectfully as he described the little infant in the incubator, sometimes interrupting him to ask for greater detail about the child or the hospital. His grandmother, Aunty Dopie, gently teased him about becoming a father, and offered him advice on the infant's needs, frequently telling him what brand of baby toiletries he and Nadia should buy.

I drove them to Somerset Hospital in the city on the August day when she would be discharged. The young couple could hardly contain their nervous excitement. During the journey there, Zahir checked with Nadia every now and then about whether she had remembered to include some or other item in the brand new bulging baby bag. Once we had passed through the hospital gates, I parked the car and waited as they entered the hospital. After an hour or so, they emerged, Nadia proudly cradling the infant in her arms, wrapped in a knitted white shawl. Zahir walked alongside her, the infant gripping his forefinger tightly in her little fist. I was caught up in their obvious joy as they showed me their little girl, and the pleasure of seeing the newborn dispelled my pessimistic thoughts about the couple's lack of resources to provide for the child's needs. When they arrived home, they paid the routine visit to the neighbours' homes to show off their child. A festive atmosphere reigned in Morieda's home, as Nadia's girlfriends eagerly gathered around to witness Morieda assist her feed and bathe the little infant in the bedroom, while Zahir and his friends waited in the living room.

Despite the couple's plans to move into their own room, Nadia continued to live with her mother after the child's birth. During the first few months of little Akeela's life, Zahir and Nadia shuttled her back and forth between Aunty Dopie's and Morieda's homes. Both grandmothers provided a great deal of assistance with the child's welfare. Nadia now provided Zahir with his meals at Morieda's house, in keeping with the local expectations of a betrothed woman's duties to her partner. Zahir continued to look for work and sometimes obtained a day job on a building site or 'broking' (selling) vegetables for the local vendor at the busy intersections on Lansdowne Road. However, his hopes of obtaining a permanent labourer's job slowly receded as his constant visits to building sites, factories and to the dockyard in search of work proved futile. In the beginning, he had asked a few of the working men in Rio Street about vacancies at the various places where they were employed. They had made vague promises to him about inquiring about work on his behalf. However, these promises did not yield anything beyond the odd day job. The daily grind of searching for work was beginning to wear him down. One day when I asked about his experiences on the road looking for work he mumbled

'Is boring, soe dag in, dag uit, by 'n factoryhek staan, of oppie hoekie vannie straat sit met anners wat oek werk soek, totdat 'n bakkie miskien kom, net 'n paar van ons oplaai. Dan's die werk net ve 'n dag or twie, dan's 'it klaar.' (It's boring, day in, day out, standing at a factory gate, or sitting on a street corner, with others

who like you are also looking for work until a van comes by, picks up a few of us. Even then, the work is just for a day or two, before it ends.)

He spoke less and less about acquiring the necessary building materials to put up the one-roomed shack in his grandmother's backyard. After a few months, he began to spend more and more time hanging out with his friends on the street, and less time going out to look for work. Yet he and Nadia still continued to take pride in their healthy infant, and Zahir often took Akeela for walks down Rio Street or to visit with his friends in the local *hok*. One afternoon, he and his friends were arrested while wheeling the rusty, skeletal remains of a car to the local scrap yard. A group of police who happened by accused them of car theft and imprisoned them in Pollsmoor prison for three weeks.

Nadia was allowed to visit Zahir twice during his pre-trial imprisonment. I gave her and a few of the other men's relatives a ride to the prison each time. Each visit required a great degree of prior planning. Zahir asked to see Akeela on each visit and she needed to ensure that the child's bag and food requirements were prepared the night before. In addition, she also took Zahir a Tupperware container of homemade stew, his favourite snacks as well as some cash to pay the required bribes to the prison gangs. These payments ensured that he was allowed to watch television or buy cigarettes or just prevented him from being assaulted. Zahir's grandmother, Aunty Dopie, assisted her by accompanying her to the prison and providing him with gifts of money and food. We had to leave Rio Street at 6 A.M. to make the hour-long drive across the city, and arrive at the prison in time to avoid the long queues of people waiting patiently to enter the administrative section.

On both visits, we arrived at the prison at approximately 7 A.M., just as the sun rose and its light touched the Muizenberg Mountains in the southeast. Even so, the parking lot was filled with minibus taxis, offloading prospective visitors, who were mainly Black women. The taxi registrations indicated that they had transported these people from townships scattered across the Cape Flats. Once we entered the administrative block, Nadia and the other relatives joined another queue to register their requests to visit the respective prisoners. After that, we were assigned to wait in a whitewashed room, furnished with wooden benches, until Zahir's name and prison number were announced over a crackly intercom system. On both occasions, we waited for well over two hours before we were led away in a small group to another building containing a set of gloomy visiting booths. Here we crowded into a tiny lobby, as individual prisoners were escorted in by prison wardens and assigned to a visiting booth, where they waited for their visitors behind a grimy sheet of reinforced glass.

Each prisoner was allowed a visit of thirty minutes. A prison warden escorted Zahir into one booth and stepped back to oversee the visit. Zahir was dressed in the regulatory green prison uniform. His face lit up when he saw little Akeela, but his eyes quickly filled with tears when his daughter reached out to him from her grandmother's arms, her attempts to embrace him impeded by the glass panel. Aunty Dopie spoke with him first, as Nadia and I waited patiently in the background. The thirty minutes passed quickly, and during the final minutes, both Aunty Dopie and Nadia listened intently as Zahir passed messages to his friends and family in Rio Street, or made requests for items of clothing or food to be sent to him. Soon we were being ushered out of the building and into the parking lot. During the journey home, Aunty Dopie and Nadia shared their conversations with Zahir. Through them, I learned that other prisoners had robbed him of his denture plate, his prized Nike sneakers and his jacket while he was being transported to the prison. He and the other men were brought to trial after he had been imprisoned for three weeks. They were acquitted after the police failed to show that they had stolen the car. Zahir and the others were welcomed home to Rio Street amidst an atmosphere of celebration. When James, another young man, asked Zahir whether he had suffered in prison, he said, '*Ek'it my ouma en my huis gemis. Ma nou wiet ek van my opstaan en my ga't lê da' binne. Ek's ie meer soe bang ve tronk toe gaan nie.*' (I missed my grandmother and my home. But now I know [the routine] about my rising in the morning to my going to bed at night. I'm not so fearful of prison any longer.)

Zahir continued to hang out with his friends in the '*hok*' and on the street. Soon, however, after the relief that followed Zahir's release had passed, the young couple's poverty, their lack of resources and the pressure of providing for a young child slowly began to take their toll. Morieda complained to me regularly of the cost of providing for her two daughters and their offspring. She said that she had now stopped providing Zahir with a meal in the evening,

'want hy gie niks ve kos nie, nie eens ve die kind s'n nie. Hy't nooit geld'ie. Sy ouma stuur soe elke keer ve die kind, of gie iets ve Nadia, ma nie hy nie' (because he doesn't contribute any money to the food budget, not even that of the child. He's never got any money. His grandmother [Aunty Dopie] sends [gifts or money] for the child, or gives something [money or gifts] to Nadia, but he doesn't).

She and Nadia were quarrelling regularly about Nadia's defiance as she continued to provide Zahir with a meal, while Morieda was away at work, during the day. A year later, the *moeders* were talking openly about Zahir, who had beaten Nadia badly for daring to go off to a local dance without his permission.

'Ma hy moes ve ha' 'n pakslae gie, sy't ve dit gesoek' (But he had to give her a hiding, she looked for it), Aunty Frances said. *'Sy ka' mossie soe ve ha' soes 'n jong meisie gedra nie, sy 's nou ma van 'n kind! Lyk ve my sy soek 'n slegte naam. Hy sukkel om werk te kry. As sy nie ve werk soek'ie dan moet sy ve die kind sorre en in die huis bly. Sy 't ha' bed gemaak, nou moet sy daarop lê.'* (She can't behave like a young girl any longer, she's the mother of his child! Seems to me that she's looking for a bad name [reputation for herself.] He's struggling to find a job. If she's not seeking employment, then she should look after the child and stay home. She's made her bed, now she must lie in it.)

Zahir began beating Nadia more frequently after that for what he perceived as the slightest infraction. Nadia said that he beat her for not cooking a meal for him, or for not being at home when he came looking for her. Morieda said that she had obtained another restraining order against him, preventing him from entering her home, but that Nadia still sought him out on the sly. Tensions rose between Morieda and Zahir's grandmother Aunty Dopie after Morieda requested the older woman to talk to her grandson about his behaviour. Aunty Dopie defended Zahir's behaviour in the company of the *moeders*, stating that

'*Nadia moet haar plek ken. Sy wiet dat hy werk soek. Sy moet mos by die huis bly en ve die kind sorg. Sy kannie soe heeldag oppie straat wiessie! Morieda spoil ve haar twie meisies gevaarlik. Wat dink sy. Die lewe issie maklik nie!*' (Nadia should know her place. She knows that he's looking for work. She should stay home and care for the child. She can't be spending her day on the street. Morieda spoils her daughters too much! What did she think? Life's not easy!)

After some time, Zahir obtained work as a security guard in a little town, Saldanha Bay, about three hours away from Cape Town. He moved there, and came home every fortnight. He beat Nadia less frequently after that, and provided her with some money on a regular basis. She began spending a week or so at a time with him in Saldanha Bay. However, Morieda complained that while Zahir's behaviour improved, he sometimes beat Nadia when he arrived home from Saldanha Bay and did not find her home at the time. When I discussed this with Aunty Frances, she simply stated that Nadia should be grateful that Zahir provided some support for her and the child, and that she should spend more time at home.

During one of his visits home, I asked Zahir about his continued association with the YDB$. He replied,

'*Ek moet nou sulke dinge laat staan. Ek's nou 'n pa van 'n kind en ek moet vir haar sorg. Ma ek sien nog steeds ve my vrinne. Hulle sal altyd my vrinne bly.*' (I've got to leave those things now. I'm a father now and I have to take care of my child. But I still see my friends; they'll always remain my friends.)

His ambivalent reply suggested that while his primary concern was for the well-being of his daughter, he did not consider his contact with the YDB$ members and his continued membership of the gang to be in opposition to his new role as a father. A year later, Zahir was retrenched when the security firm that employed him shut down. He returned to Rio Street, where he joined his old friends. Soon after, he and a few of the YDB$ were arrested for a burglary. He and two of his friends, who were all members of the YDB$, were found guilty and sentenced to an effective three years imprisonment.

Zahir's transformation into fatherhood further highlights the modes of collaboration that exist between the *moeders* and the young men. The ideology of *ordentlikheid* and the *moeders'* policing practices ensure that young women learn about, and practice the appropriate behaviour of femininity. One of the key means that the *moeders* use to control and constrain the younger women's mobility is by vilifying those who dare to move outside the boundaries of the local community as *sleg*. Young men's alternative ideology and practices of masculinity not only uphold the power of the *moeders* within the local community, as the arbiters of persons but also reinforce the young women's subjection and adherence to the norms of *ordentlikheid*. Young men's punitive actions against young women such as Nadia are meant to constrain their physical movements across local boundaries and ensure that they remain within the community so that they are unable to form relationships with men beyond its borders. The young men's physical violence against the young women serves to display their emotional toughness to their male peers as well as their ability to exert their power over their partners. The physical beatings negatively reinscribe the feminine behaviours, mobility and practices expected of young women, such as confinement to the domestic space, that are also prescribed by the ideology of *ordentlikheid*. In addition, once a young woman accepts her engagement to a young man, usually, after he has acknowledged responsibility for her pregnancy, she generally provides the domestic services expected of her, such as meals, etc. He, however, may not be able to fulfil his young partner's primary expectations of fatherhood, namely financial and material support for herself and their children. In these situations, the link between the *moeders* and the young men, in their statuses as sons, prevail and assert the latters' personhood, because of the centrality of the *moeders* roles in the ideology of *ordentlikheid*. Men like Zahir are affirmed as persons, even in the face of their failure to fulfil the material responsibilities as spouses and fathers, because they are the offspring of *ordentlike moeders*, and have affirmed their mother-in-law's respectability, through the act of *ga't sê*.

After establishing their reputations as *Ouens*, fatherhood becomes the primary signifier of masculinity. Many men like Uncle Booi and Zahir attempt to fulfil their roles as the material providers for their families through criminal means such as theft. As I have argued above, this path leads mostly into the cycle of imprisonment and further toughening up through the prison gang system. However, for a few men, religious institutions and practices provide another means to acquire tough masculinity. While these religious practices and beliefs present the men with alternatives to the violent practices associated with the gangs, they enshrine an alternative toughness as the quintessential quality of masculinity, while still upholding the ideology and practices of *ordentlikheid*. Often, older, pious men initiate young men into and mentor them through the necessary religious teachings and practices, supporting and encouraging them through this alternative means to acquire the character of toughness. For these men, a religious lifestyle infuses the stringent self-discipline they exercise over themselves and their families with spiritual meaning. They are presented with many opportunities to participate in organized burglaries, drug pushing or the many other illegal means to make a living in the informal economy when formal work is scarce. They display an admirable ability to withstand these tempting offers, in the face of the hunger and general impoverishment that threaten their households. Often, they also have to stand by and watch as some *moeders* boast about their sons, the *Ouens* who have obtained money or material resources by some mysterious means to provide for their households. In addition, they attempt to guide many youth through the difficulties and the trials of a religious life, only to watch their efforts shattered as young men are recruited into the local gangs.

Most Rio Street residents admired Vonna's husband, *Broer* (Brother) Greg for being a devoted father and husband to his family. He was identified as the individual who was willing to counsel others with difficulties. Even Uncle Booi spoke about him with respect. During the time that Sharlien was experiencing problems with Spookie, she would often spend time with Greg and Vonna, sharing her pain with them. Afterwards, Greg would pray aloud for her. Greg was also the leader of a *huiskerk* or 'house church,' an informal Christian gathering, a common institution in Cape Flats townships. These churches draw on local residents for their membership, and are not affiliated to any of the large, formal Christian denominations that exist in South Africa. Individuals are only required to *bekeer* or 'be saved' in order to become members. Individuals will 'be saved' if they renounce their previous 'sinful' lives, accept Jesus Christ as their saviour, and resolve to live by the strict moral codes of the church. The church met in Vonna and Greg's living room every Sunday morning. Greg said that he had become 'saved' when he attended an evangelical meeting that was held in a tent in Bonteheuwel, the township where he grew up. At the time, he was a member of the Scorpions gang. He said that the preacher's sermon moved him to renounce his life as a gangster and to devote his life to Christ.

'Ek't oek lelike dinge gedoen, toe ek 'n Scorpion was. Ons'it vroumense verkrag, mense gerop, gegang fight. Ma' toe ek die Here ontmoet, en ek'it skaam gevoel oor al dierdie dinge. Hy't my van hierdie dinge verlos, en ve my krag gegee om weg te bly van hierdie dinge. Ek was net soes die jongens hie' buite, die wat ek ve hulle verstaan.' (I also committed vile acts when I was a member of the Scorpions. We raped women, robbed people and fought other gangs. But then I met Christ and I was ashamed of all these things. He freed me from these things and gave me strength to withstand the temptation to return to them. I was just like the streetwise men out here; that is why I understand them.)

Greg had met Vonna soon after he was 'saved' and he had convinced her to become 'saved' too. They began dating, and were married shortly after. In 1998, when I interviewed him, they had been married for eight years. At the time they met, Vonna had a daughter, Shimonelle, from a previous relationship. Shimonelle's father was married to another woman, and was in prison at the time. Greg said that he accepted Shimonelle as his stepdaughter and supported her along with their three other children. He said that he also had a son from a previous relationship. The boy lived in Bonteheuwel with his mother. Sharlien often commented on Greg's willingness to support Shimonelle and accept her as his own. She said that most men would refuse to support another man's child. Like most of the men in Rio Street, Greg worked as an unskilled labourer on building sites. At the time of our interview, he had had a continuous run of employment for the past ten or so months, and he was able to provide a steady monthly income. However, he said that before that, he was unemployed for at least a year and his household lived through a difficult period.

'Die duiwel was biesig mit my – da' was dae toe da' niks kos innie hys wassie. Ek't somtyds gevoel ek moet 'n hys gat rop. Ma' net op daai oomblik, dann'it die kerkbroers en susters, of die mense hi' innie straat iets gestuur – kos of gel' om ve ons uit te help.

Prys die Here, Hy't ve ons deur swaar tye gebring.' (The devil tempted me sorely during that time – there were days when we had no food in the house. I would feel tempted to commit a burglary then. But at those moments, then the church brothers and sisters or the residents in the street would send something, like food or money to help us out. Praise the Lord, He has brought us through difficult times.)

When Zahir, Enver and James were arrested for suspected car theft, James' mother requested Greg to pray for them. Greg and the male elders in his church organized a weekend retreat in a cave on the slopes of Table Mountain. They and a few other male members of their church spent the weekend praying and fasting for the young men, asking God

'om die deure vannie tronk toe te bind, om mit die reg te praat, sodat hulle nie ve die jong manne 'n swaar straf gie nie' (to lock the jail's doors, to talk to the judges so that they do not hand down heavy sentences to these young men).

When James, Enver and Zahir were acquitted in the trial, James thanked Greg for his prayers. Greg then invited him to join their church and to 'be saved.' James joined the church and soon he could be found participating in public evangelical meetings that were held in Nyanga Junction on Saturday mornings. These services were noisy affairs, filled with much a cappella singing, amidst loud prayers and exhortations for passing individuals 'to be saved.' James would be called upon to testify publicly about his previous life as a YDB$ member, and the secret burden of shame and guilt that he experienced about his ganging practices. He claimed that he had been relieved of this burden since he had been saved. Greg sometimes allowed James to accompany him to work, where he was sometimes hired as a casual hand. The older man also introduced him to the wider network of 'brothers', who also sought to assist the young man in his search for work. On the days that he was unable to find a casual job, James would collect funds, used clothes or canned food for the church from homes in the wealthier areas of the city. He occasionally hung out with his old friends at the *hok*, but now spent much of his time with Greg and his family.

Like Greg, his Muslim counterpart *Boeta* (Brother) Salie also cut a striking contrast to the other men on Rio Street. Salie was a devout

Muslim who helped run the *madressa*[10] for young Muslim boys at the Manenberg mosque. His wife Amina led a *madressa* for young Muslim girls in their home. He also assisted with the soup kitchen that was run by an Islamic charity, which served free, nutritious meals for the local residents on Thursday afternoons. He always wore the lace *kufiya* or skullcap and ankle-length shirt as a symbol of his religious identity and his devotion. He, too, was noted for his devotion to his wife, Amina, his children and the Rio Street community. He earned his living as a meat and vegetable vendor, travelling through the Athlone township streets, selling his produce from the back of a truck. He was renowned for selling goods to residents on credit. The *moeders* spoke of him as someone '*wie die mense se monde oophou*' (someone who fed the people). He often hired Moira's two sons to assist him on market days and during peak seasons, for example, the religious occasions such as Ramadan, Eid Al Fitr, Easter or Christmas. On occasion, they would offload produce illegally from the truck and attempt to sell them later to unsuspecting residents. The *moeders* would report these incidents to Paul, and invariably the YDB$ would punish them severely for this infraction. Salie continued to hire these two brothers, despite their reprehensible actions, saying that he had to teach them by example. During the winter of 1998, Salie was held up, robbed and fatally shot by two armed men in Manenberg Avenue. Hundreds of people from the surrounding townships and of all faiths attended his burial. The *moeders* of Rio Street mourned his death, and condemned his murderers in the strongest terms. Women like Aunty Frances wondered '*wie sal nou die mense se monde oophou?*' (who will feed the people now?)

Men like Greg and Salie attempt to follow an alternative cultural process to masculine respectability that is presented through religious faith and the associated institutions. Like the practices associated with the gangs and the ex-prisoners this process is also shot through with, and sustains, toughness as the central value of masculinity. However, here toughness is not visibly demonstrated through the men's ability to withstand physical pain. It is demonstrated through the men's exercise of spiritual, moral and emotional self-discipline, as they fight off the

---

[10] A religious school for Muslim children, where they are taught the tenets of the faith, the aesthetics of Islamic identity and Arabic literacy. Schools are separated according to gender.

temptation to earn income through illegal means, especially during prolonged periods of unemployment, while still striving to provide for families and retain some measure of respect. They also display their toughness to withstand the potential of ridicule from their male cohort as they participate in charitable actions that are customarily associated with women's work, or publicly renounce the accepted ganging practices through which local men assert their masculinity. This path to masculinity sits uneasily alongside the one advocated by the *Ouens* and the ex-prisoners, in which men acquire and display their 'strong bones'. At the same time, these men's devotion to their partners and their families does fulfil the women's desire for the ultimate respectability that is associated with monogamy and the men's commitment to them and their families. And it is the women's endorsement of these men's practices and, through their power as *moeders*, they sustain and affirm this more marginal route to masculine respect.

H. Conclusion

In this chapter I have argued that the lives of the working class coloured men of Manenberg communities like Rio Street are marked by the struggle for respect amidst the gendered and racial denigration that they experience as they attempt to breach the divide between the ideals of dominant masculinity and their lack of the cultural or material wherewithal to be recognized and respected as men. The men's crisis of masculinity reaches a peak during young adulthood or late adolescence when young men exist in the liminal state between schoolboyhood and fatherhood. One way in which they attempt to breach this divide is through the ideology, aesthetics and associated practices of the gangs. The gangs' ideology, aesthetics and practices assert toughness as the quintessential marker of masculinity in the local community. Through these practices and aesthetics, young men mark the boundaries of the local community, in which they are identified as respectable *Ouens* or streetwise men. The *Ou* identity sets them apart from the *skollie*, the male stranger or thug, whose actions emanate from self-interest and disregard for the collective welfare of the residents in the local community. While the process through which men become *Ouens* also marks them as *skollies*, these men's public biographies in the context of the local community, and their links to *ordentlike moeders* affirm and sustain their identities as respectable men in that context.

Once a young man has been made into an *Ou*, he seeks to earn further respect as a man through fatherhood. Again, while young women bear these men's children, ensuring their transition to fatherhood, the men are unable to sustain the formers' material expectations of them as fathers. Through the ganging practices and interpersonal violence, young men constrain and confine young women's movements to the local community, thereby preventing them from forming relationships with men outside these boundaries. The constraints that young men place on young women's mobility articulate with the ideology and practices of *ordentlikheid* and affirm the *moeders* power in the local context.

When young men attempt to meet the social and material expectations of fatherhood, they are faced with scarcity of work opportunities and the prolonged periods of unemployment. They often look to illegal means to acquire material resources. However, this route leads them into a cycle of prolonged periods of imprisonment, in which they are further subjected to the experiences of the prison gangs, which promotes their toughened character.

Religious practices and institutions of the Christian and Muslim faiths do present men with an alternative route to respectable masculine identity. Through these practices, toughness is acquired and displayed through men's exercise of spiritual, moral and emotional self-discipline. However, few men opt for this route to respected masculinity.

Chapter 6

Good Daughters:
Incorporating young women into respectable personhood.

Maandag het ek my ma gehelp om die vensters te was en ons het gordyne opgehang.

On Monday I helped my mother wash the windows and hang the drapes.

Fifteen-year-old Shahnaaz, diary entry, 6 April 1998.

Ek worry nie meer oor wat hulle van my te sê hettie. Die ou vrouens hie innie pad skinder heeldag van my. Hulle dink omdat ek kwaai aantrek, is ek sleg. Ma' is dies wat soe stil is, en heel dag innie hys bly, wat die dinge aanvang.

I don't care what they say about me. These old women who live in this road, gossip about me all day long. They think that because I dress so fashionably, I'm bad. But it's the ones who are so quiet and who remain indoors all day that get up to all the mischief.'

Seventeen-year-old Estelle.

Ek 'it ve ha' gesê! Is ha' eie skuld dat hulle ve ha' vekrag het. Sy wil mos da' innie shebeens in Nyanga uithou! Nou't sy skande op die hys gebring. Wat ga't die mense hie innie pad sê?!

I told her so! It's her own fault that they raped her. She insisted on hanging out in the shebeens in Nyanga. She's brought scandal to our home. What will the people in the street say?

Forty-six-year-old Monica, mother of sixteen-year-old Lindsey, who was raped while on her way home from visiting friends in Nyanga on a Saturday night.

These quotes are taken from the daily entries in the journals that I requested the young women to keep for two months. Fifteen-year-old Shanaaz's entry reflects her preoccupation with the domestic activities that the Rio Street community expects of most young women and her

211

conscientiousness as she sought to assist her mother in maintaining the outward signs of domestic order and propriety. Shanaaz's diligence in carrying out domestic tasks is an example of the adolescent women's desire to submit to their parent's authority and to assist in upholding the household's respectable reputation. However, Estelle's angry outburst indicates the enormous psychological pressure these young women experience if they dare to defy the appropriate dress codes in the face of the *moeders* intense scrutiny. Her acerbic comment pointedly identifies the limitations that inhere in the *moeders* regulatory practices of femininity, particularly feminine sexuality, as young women still find a means to maintain the outward form of feminine and sexual propriety while creatively asserting some measure of individual agency that contravenes the acceptable public presentation.

In this chapter, I explore how young women are incorporated into, and in turn incorporate, the values and practices of *ordentlikheid*, and also how they come to embody these values over time. I also examine how they negotiate their way between the outward forms and practices of local feminine propriety or *ordentlikheid* expected of them, whilst asserting some measure of agency through these practices. Through their agency, they subtly reconfigure the meanings of these practices of feminine propriety to their own ends, while still retaining its outward form.

In the previous chapters, I have indicated how the local moral economy defines a matrix of personhood in which different kinds of persons are defined specifically in relation to women as *moeders*, and also in relation to one another. I have also argued that gender and generation articulate within this matrix so that young men in their roles as *Ouen's* or streetwise men assist and reinforce adult women's roles as *moeders* or mothers, while *moeders*, in turn, assert these young men's personhood as *goeie seuns* or good sons. At the end of the last chapter, I began to show that young women are placed within this matrix in a particularly difficult, constraining position. Their development as persons emphasizes the relational quality of personhood in this community as well as the gendered and generational inequalities that inhere in young women's social location.

Each young woman is required to uphold her mother's personhood in her roles as a good daughter or *goeie dogter*. As I showed in chapter 4,

212

the *moeders* control over the young women's sexuality, as well as the young women's discipline of it, is crucial in this process. However, they are also expected to facilitate men's transformation from streetwise men or *Ouens* to fathers. Consequently, young men's transition from one type of person to another in the lifecycle is defined in relation to and through their control over the young women's sexuality. The *moeders* and the young men's struggle to control young women's sexuality places these girls in a particularly invidious position in the community. They are not only expected to uphold their own position as particular gendered persons, namely good daughters but also to buttress and partly define the personhood of the *moeders* and of the men as fathers in this community.

A. Good daughters: Incorporating adolescent women into *ordentlikheid*

The adolescent women in Rio Street are subordinate but important players in the ideology of *ordentlikheid* and ultimately in upholding the *moeders* powerful position in the community. Adolescent women's identities are primarily defined as subordinate to and supportive of their mothers' and their respective households' respectability. Residents, particularly adult women, assess the individual mother's mastery of the values and practices of *ordentlikheid* by their adolescent daughters' willingness to adhere to practices that uphold the values of domesticity, sexual modesty, obedience and respect for their mothers and their elders as well as loyalty to their own households.

Privately, individual mothers admit that their adolescent daughters are capable of making decisions independently and acting responsibly; however, they do not openly admit to their daughters' capabilities. Instead, they publicly maintain that the daughters' actions are primarily informed and driven by concern for their mothers' reputations. Similarly, young women visibly strive to adhere to the values and practices of *ordentlikheid*, affirming their own and their mothers' reputations. At the same time, they seek to realize their individual goals as best as they can, through maintaining and manipulating the outward forms of respectability. Sometimes individual goals are at odds with the processes and values of *ordentlikheid* and create enormous intergenerational tension and conflict between the young women and the older *moeders*.

Most of the young women in Rio Street express enormous respect for their individual mothers' reputations. Unsurprisingly, their respect and concern are born out of their emotional attachment to their parent. At the same time, they also benefit socially and materially when they adhere to, and seek to realize, their individual goals within the prescribed values and practices of *ordentlikheid*. The gendered quality of *ordentlikheid* is highlighted as Rio Street residents socialize their children according to strictly defined gendered roles. Young boys are automatically recognized as persons-in-the-making because they are the biological sons of an *ordentlike moeder* or members of her household. In contrast, young women have to learn the difficult lessons of respectable behaviour, which serves as a sign of both their mothers' and their households' *ordentlikheid*. *Ordentlikheid* takes on different meanings in the context of girlhood and therefore holds different implications for the personhood of girls and young women. In the following sections, I explore how young girls are initially socialized into the values and behavioural codes of *ordentlikheid* and how their persons are shaped and informed by this process.

During childhood, the values of *ordentlikheid* emphasize a girl's willingness to be subjected to the initial lessons of feminine domesticity. Young girls are first socialized into the tenets and values of *ordentlikheid* between the ages of eight to ten years when they are taught the rudimentary skills of housekeeping such as sweeping, cooking or childcare. I often overheard mothers proudly state that their daughters '*kan nou mooi eiers bak en rys kook*' (can fry eggs nicely and boil rice), or '*kan nou mooi agter die kleintjies kyk*' (take good care of the little ones [children]). Many young girls in Rio Street households are expected to assist in routine tasks such as running errands to the neighbours or watching over younger siblings indoors or as they play in the tiny front yards after school. As these young girls take responsibility for household chores, especially after school, their mobility becomes increasingly restricted to the household and its immediate vicinity. Girls who prove to be willful and less compliant are described as *stout* or naughty and are said to be behaving like *jongetjiekinders* or young boys.

The girls' mobility is further restricted within Rio Street as they are taught to regard certain spaces, such as spaces within the road and backyard spaces that are less visible from the street, and certain times of the day such as sunset and nighttime as unsafe for them to inhabit. They are often warned with injunctions such as '*As die son sak dan moet jy in die huis wees.*' (When the sun sets you must be indoors). Mothers discipline girls with physical beatings if they stray beyond the domestic space or if they are seen in the streets or outdoors at inappropriate times such as the nighttime. Young girls are often heard telling their friends that '*my ma ga't ve my slat as ek nog buite speel as dit donker is. Sesuur moet ek innie hys wies*' (my mother will beat me if I'm found playing outdoors after dark. I have to be indoors at six o' clock in the evening).

Adult women have good reason to police their young daughters' mobility, namely to ensure their physical safety after dark. In 1998, while I was working in the area, a five-year-old girl was abducted from her parents' Rio Street apartment one cold night in June. She was found dead in the undeveloped bush that bordered the area approximately four days after she disappeared. This incident generated enormous panic amongst the residents of Rio Street, and for approximately four weeks afterwards, most young girls were closely watched, were often escorted to school and kept indoors immediately after school, even during daylight hours, and were rarely seen on the street.

Girls' mobility is also restricted as part of their socialization into femininity. These girls learn early on to restrict their mobility in order to demonstrate that they are becoming the good daughters of wise, respectable heads of households, namely *ordentlike moeders*. Through this process, they are also being prepared for the greater surveillance of their persons during adolescence and early adulthood. The young girls who adhered to their older sisters' or mothers' injunctions were proudly described as '*goeie dogters, wie gehoorsaam is*' (good daughters who are obedient). In contrast, their male peers who were not yet members of the local gangs were not expected to perform any household duties, beyond running a few errands. They were allowed to play or wander freely to playing fields or parks situated beyond the bounds of Rio Street.

B. Respectable adolescent women in time and place

Rio Street adults, like most of their Manenberg peers, used various physical and social markers as a means to signal the young girls' departure from childhood. Common social markers included a young girl's entry into high school, as well as the indication that she had begun to smoke cigarettes. The obvious physical changes she experienced such as breast growth and acne were imbued with greater social significance as major signs that she was leaving childhood. Adult women remarked humorously to each other about these physical changes and double entendres such as '*sy kry mos ook nou puisies*' (she's sprouting zits too), which referred to the appearance of acne and of breasts. These comments were intended to communicate to all who heard them that the adult women were monitoring a young girl's imminent entry into full-blown adolescence closely. However, menarche was widely accepted as the most important sign that a young girl had entered adolescence.

The adult women began policing a young woman's behaviour earnestly once it was known that she had had 'her periods' – the phrase that was commonly used to refer to menstruation. Many adolescent girls told me that once they had begun menstruating, their mothers warned them '*om nie ve 'n man toe te laat om my op my lyf te vat nie, anners gat ek pregnant raak*' (not to allow men to touch my body or I could fall pregnant). These euphemisms served as warnings to the young women that their bodies, indeed their very being, had taken on primary sexual significance for adult men and women. However, they also communicated an individual mother's admission that a process had begun in which she was relinquishing direct control over the younger woman's sexuality. The young women were left in no doubt that they had entered into a period in their lifecycle that was highly charged and filled with the imminent threat of social and physical danger. If they were able to negotiate this period of their lives carefully and adhere to the tenets of *ordentlikheid* they would emerge with their reputations as *goeie dogters* (good daughters) intact. For these young women, *ordentlikheid* had expanded from the initial focus on obedience, constrained mobility and willingness to learn the rudimentary skills of domesticity to a focus on sexual self-discipline. A young woman's ability to exercise control over her sexuality was displayed by her willingness to adhere to a predictable daily routine and

216

to take on greater responsibility for household chores, and through her modest dress. The key means that adult women relied upon to police adolescent women's self-control over sexuality was strict surveillance of their movements and of their dress.

As the young girls entered adolescence, the adult women subjected their activities and their movements to even greater scrutiny. The places that young women were expected to frequent at set times during their daily round of life became the signifiers of the discipline they now exercised over their sexuality and therefore their respectability, as well as their maturing sense of responsibility within the household. Adolescent girls' ability to maintain their reputations as *skoon meisies* (clean girls, i.e. virgins) and their ability to discipline their sexuality became paramount. *Ordentlike* or respectable young women were expected to maintain a predictable daily routine, knowable to most residents, especially the adult women. This routine commonly incorporated school, home and the odd errand to a neighbour or a store. Like their younger counterparts, they were expected to restrict their movements on the street to daytime hours only and were expected to be indoors, especially after dark. Most adolescent women were expected to be attending school for most of the day or to be busying themselves with domestic chores at home. Most young women in Rio Street attended the local high school, Manenberg High School, which was located approximately 15 minutes' walk away, while a minority were still completing their primary education at a junior school nearby. Most weekday mornings these young women were seen walking to school dressed in identical school uniforms. Some accompanied very young siblings to the junior school before finding their way to the high school. The Rio Street community, like most residents in Manenberg, valued girls' education. However, given the extent of domestic tasks within these poor households, young women's commitment to this work was considered primary and took precedence over schoolwork. Good daughters were primarily defined in terms of their willingness to assist mothers in accomplishing the myriad repetitive domestic tasks that distinguished respectable households and not in terms of their diligence at schoolwork.

The Rio Street community used life-experience rather than chronological age to distinguish between two social categories of young women. Adolescent women who had dropped out of school or who had become mothers were generally perceived to be more senior and therefore more mature than their school-going counterparts, even though they were of the same chronological age. Generally, school was associated with the relatively carefree period of childhood and immaturity. Adolescent women who still attended school were expected to display more immature behaviour than their peers who had dropped out, who were employed or who were mothers. The *moeders*, therefore, watched the young school-going women more closely than the other young women, whom they defined as being socially more mature and more responsible.

The *moeders* increased their surveillance of the young women's behaviour and dress during adolescence, often commenting disapprovingly if a young woman's clothes were too risqué or if she was seen out on the street during school hours or late at night. These comments were often made in the presence of the errant adolescent's mother, communicating to her that her daughter needed to be disciplined. The mother rarely challenged these comments publicly. However, on numerous occasions, I was expected to listen sympathetically to an angry woman who defended her daughter's actions privately and commented fiercely upon her peers' hypocrisy. Clearly, these comments provoked a great deal of anxiety amongst the individual mothers, thereby illustrating that their own individual reputations as *ordentlike moeders* in the community were entwined with their adolescent daughters' ability to adhere to the values and behaviours of *ordentlikheid*. The individual mother's perception of unfairness also revealed that whilst ideally all *moeders* were expected to watch one another's daughters to the same extent, not all adult women were able to do so.

Whilst unemployed women and housewives were often able to spend a fair amount of time watching the street, and monitoring their own daughters closely, employed women found it exceedingly difficult to monitor their daughters' dress or mobility during working hours. They had to rely on the kindly advice of friends to inform them about these matters; they also had to trust that their daughters would adhere to the expected codes of respectable dress and behaviour. Consequently, Morieda, a single working mother, frequently warned her two teenaged daughters to guard their reputations, often repeating to them, *'om liewerste in die huis te bly todat ek terug kom van die werk, want julle weet die mense in die straat kan baie te sê het'* (to stay indoors [literally, in the house] instead, until I return home from work, because you know that the people in the street have a lot to say).

Adolescent girls were expected to shoulder enormous responsibility for most of the childcare and the domestic tasks, after school and over weekends. The young women rapidly developed acute skills of discernment and decision making as they decided when and how to expend precious household resources such as food, electricity or even social reputation. They had to decide how to share meagre food resources amongst hungry younger siblings; they had to decide where the younger children could play; they decided how long the television or radio could remain on and when to begin cooking the evening meal so that precious electrical power was not exhausted. They also had to decide which friends could be allowed to spend time indoors with them during their mother's absence, thereby guarding the household's respectable reputation.

The degree to which adolescent girls experienced the burdensome nature of these responsibilities varied in relation to whether they were school students or mothers who had dropped out of school, their position within the household, the presence or absence of a senior woman, and also the household's developmental cycle. As the following diary entries indicate, these differences within and between households often spelt the difference between a young woman completing domestic tasks effortlessly, or being overwhelmed by them.

Fourteen-year-old Claudette was the youngest daughter in a three-member household, comprising herself, her 22-year-old brother and her single working mother, fifty-year-old Audie. Claudette's parents were divorced when she was an infant and the family has had no contact with the father. Claudette was a school student at one of the local high schools, while her mother Audie and her brother were both employed and provided the main source of income in the household. Claudette was expected to clean the apartment and assist with the laundry over weekends and cook the main evening meal on weekdays. Claudette's diary entry for a weekday dated 25 March 1998 read, 'Today as soon as I arrived home from school, I boiled rice and lentils for supper. I then watched TV for most of the afternoon. Later I visited Nadia and watched her baby for her. I sat and talked with some friends at Nadia's house while she did the housework. I went home when my mother returned from work. We had supper. I watched TV and then I went to bed.'

Claudette's round of daily household chores is compared to that of her friend, Nadia, who described her activities on the same day in the diary entry given below.

Sixteen-year-old Nadia was the eldest daughter in a six-member household. Her 36-year-old mother Morieda was a single woman and the only breadwinner. The other members included 14-year-old Nazli, ten-year-old Mohammed, seven-year-old Naziem and Nadia's infant daughter, Akeela. Morieda was employed as a domestic worker in a wealthy Muslim household in Rylands, an adjoining suburb. Nadia had dropped out of school early in 1997 when she discovered that she was pregnant by her partner Nazir. Since then she had remained at home and assumed the primary responsibility for running Morieda's household whilst she was away at work. Nadia revealed the extent of her domestic duties in her diary entry, also dated 25 March 1998:

'Today I want to tell you what I did. Early this morning I took Akeela, my daughter, to the clinic because she was very ill. There were many mothers and their babies waiting to see the nurse and we had to wait for at least two hours before she was able to see us. When I returned from the clinic, I walked to Nyanga Junction (the local shopping mall) to buy toiletries for my daughter and electricity for my mother. When I returned home my brothers and sister had arrived home from school and I had to assist Nazli as she made sandwiches for them to eat. James, one of my friends also demanded a sandwich from me, but I couldn't give him one because there was just enough bread to make sandwiches for Nazli, my brothers and me. Nazli watched over Akeela while I washed her diapers by hand. My brothers were really irritating because they insisted on playing indoors while Akeela was asleep. They dirtied the kitchen and I had to shoo them into the front yard. Claudette came over to visit and we sat and talked and smoked a while. When Akeela awoke, Claudette watched her for me. It was 5.30 P.M. and I had to begin cooking the evening meal for my mother. I boiled rice and made a tomato stew. I watched the soapie 'Days of Our

Lives' with Claudette and Nazli at the same time as I watched the pots on the stove. I am expecting my mother to return from work soon. I will be pleased to see her. At this time of the day, I feel exhausted from doing all the housework.'

Claudette's chores appear to have been light and easily manageable in comparison to Nadia's tremendous responsibilities. Claudette's domestic load was influenced not only by the relatively small size of her household but also by its character as a relatively mature household, with mainly adult members. Her location as the youngest household member and its only dependent also implied that, unlike Nadia, she was not burdened with the care of younger siblings. Claudette and her sibling had both reached a stage where they were economically and socially independent or fast becoming so. In contrast, Nadia was the eldest daughter in a young household with a number of minor dependents, including her own infant daughter. She was overburdened with the responsibility of caring for four younger dependents and managing most of the everyday household tasks. In addition, adolescent mothers like her are expected to be more responsible and shoulder more responsibilities than their school-going peers.

However, even when the young women like Claudette and Nadia were freed from their domestic duties, they still found themselves hemmed in by the expectation that respectable daughters spent their free time indoors in their own homes or in those of their friends. Both young women's diaries were filled with daily entries in which they complained of free time that weighed them down with the prospect of nothing but hours spent watching TV or sitting around chatting with a friend.

In the entry dated Saturday, 28 March 1998, Nadia wrote, '*Vandag is ek alweer by die huis. Sit heeldag voor televisie en kyk stukke. Is baie boring hier.*' (Today, like every other day, I am home, doing nothing but watching TV programs. It is extremely boring here.) Similarly, Claudette's entry for the same day read '*Is baie vervelig vandag. Ons het net so by my huis gesit, gepraat en gerook.*' (It was boring today. We sat around at my house and chatted and smoked all day long.)

Most of the young women complained of the monotony of their daily routines, of having nothing exciting to do and nowhere to go. In most households, little or no money was available for leisure activities such as going to the cinema or shopping. The few spaces of affordable leisure in Rio Street were provided by the shebeens-cum-discos that were located in a number of *hokke*. Yet despite their sense of overwhelming boredom, these young women were very wary of being seen to frequent these more exciting places. They indicated that if they were seen in the *hokke*, they would be considered to be *in die verkeerde plek* (in the wrong place) – that is, they were perceived to be young women 'out of place'. Another young woman, 19-year-old Patricia, explained that while she often wished to go to the *hok* nearby her house, she did not go *'want die vrouens in die straat sal praat, dan sê hulle ek kom uit 'n slegte huis en dat my ma my nie reg opgebring het nie.'* (The women in the street would talk. They would say that I come from a bad home and that my mother had not raised me properly.) Adolescent women like Patricia displayed a keen awareness of how their individual reputations as good daughters were intertwined with different spaces in the community and, ultimately with their mothers' reputations as respectable or *ordentlike moeders*. Their commitment and loyalty to their mothers' and their household's reputation did, however, reap social benefits for these young women, when they sought assistance in negotiating the world beyond school or home.

Young women who adhered to the precepts and practices of *ordentlikheid* were also further incorporated into the social network of women who provided them with the precious cultural knowledge required to negotiate their lives within the community. Once a young woman expressed the desire to seek employment or assistance for a child, her mother ushered her into an expanding network of adult women that stretched across different social fields such as the workplace or state institutions. In this manner, these young women acquired the necessary social links that enabled them to traverse these seemingly intimidating institutions with greater facility. The young women became embedded in the network of adult women in earnest through two key processes, namely the search for employment after they had left school, and through childbearing and childrearing.

C. Becoming a working woman

Eighteen-year-old Zellie lived with her grandmother and her maternal uncle in an apartment on the first floor. She was her mother's *voorkind* (a woman's firstborn, usually from a relationship that precedes the primary partnership or marriage) and had been raised by her mother and grandmother since birth. A few years after she was born, her mother married a man from Laingsburg, a little town in the Karoo, and moved there permanently. Zellie remained in Rio Street with her grandmother, Aunty Lenie, and her maternal uncle, Japie. In early 1998, Zellie was attending the local high school, Manenberg High School, where she was enrolled in the tenth grade. She was becoming increasingly bored with school and often expressed a desire to drop out and look for a job instead. Zellie was an attractive young woman who enjoyed playing netball for her school team. Lately, however, she spoke despairingly of a male teacher who pestered her constantly for sexual favours, under the guise of supporting the school team and providing her with a ride to and from scheduled netball games. This situation filled her with some anxiety, enormous contempt and anger, and robbed her of the opportunity to play the sport, the one pleasure she enjoyed at school. In addition, she was also quite concerned about the anxiety that her grandmother expressed about paying her tuition and stationery fees. She frequently skipped school on Mondays or Fridays, choosing to assist her ageing grandmother at home instead.

In June 1998, Zellie began putting plans in place to find a job. Despite her obvious youth and inexperience, this search did not appear to be such a daunting task. First, she had to obtain her grandmother's consent for her to leave school. This was not difficult, especially since her decision would alleviate the constant worry about funds to pay for school tuition, uniforms and stationery. Also, if she found a job then she would provide an extra source of income for the household. She also had to enlist her grandmother's assistance in negotiating access to the existing network of working women. This did not present an obstacle either. Aunty Lenie was widely respected in Rio Street and its neighbouring communities. People spoke of her as a religious woman who never turned away anyone who sought assistance from her. She was part of a wide network of women and so could call on a number of them to assist Zellie by 'bringing her into' a job. Aunty Rashieda, who lived a short distance away in Rio Street, was one of the first women whom Zellie and her grandmother decided to ask for assistance. Aunty Rashieda worked as a machinist at the T-shirt factory in Athlone Industria, and Zellie hoped that Rashieda would talk to the supervisor about the possibilities of finding a job for her. First Zellie had to visit Aunty Rashieda to inform her about her grandmother's impending visit. *'Aan' Rashieda, my ouma wil graag ve Aan' Rashieda kô sien.'* (Aunty Rashieda, my grandmother would like to pay you a visit.) Zellie's initial visit was important for both women. First, it informed Aunty Rashieda that Aunty Lenie's request to call on her was no ordinary, everyday visit, but one in which she would be requesting some form of assistance, or lodging a serious complaint. It also served to remind Aunty Rashieda that Aunty Lenie might be calling in the assistance that the latter had provided to her in the past. Finally, it also forewarned Aunty Rashieda that she had to alert her family about the visit so that the guests could be ensured of some privacy during the visit. In the overcrowded domestic spaces of Rio Street, privacy was a precious resource and, if the older woman was making a request, she wanted to do so in private, so that her dignity was preserved even if her appeal was not met. One evening, soon after Zellie had informed Aunty Rashieda of the impending visit, she and her grandmother paid the expected visit. Zellie, who was modestly dressed in a long skirt, accompanied her aged grandmother as the latter walked slowly and with some difficulty down the road. When they arrived at Rasheida's house, they were welcomed in and made to sit in the spotless living room. After the customary offer of tea, the conversation began with lengthy, reciprocal inquiries after each woman's well-being and the well-being of her household. After a brief pause in the conversation, Aunty Lenie informed Aunty Rashieda that Zellie had dropped out of school and was looking for work. She then asked Rashieda if she could inquire about the possibility *'om ve Zellie in te bring'* (bringing Zellie into) a job at the factory. Rashieda responded as follows:

> *'Ek wiet nie op die oomblik 'ie. Ma' ek sal die supervisor vra, dan sal ek ve Aan Lenie laat wiet.'* (I don't know at the moment. But I will ask the supervisor, and then I will let Aunty Lenie know.)

Zellie sat quietly throughout the conversation, as a sign of respect to the older women and as an indication that she willingly entrusted the discussion of her future plans entirely to them. The older women did not include her in the conversation at all, except once when Aunty Rashieda asked Zellie how old she was. After Aunty Rashieda had agreed to assist Zellie, the women began to talk about less pressing issues for a while, until finally, Aunty Lenie rose, signalling that her visit was over. Zellie rose too and followed her grandmother to the door. Rashieda assured Aunty Lenie that she would begin inquiring about jobs from the factory supervisor in the morning and would send word as soon as she was able. Zellie and her grandmother said goodbye to Rashieda and proceeded home. Approximately one month later, Aunty Rashieda's daughter stopped by at Aunty Lenie's house to inform them that Zellie should accompany Aunty Rashieda to the factory the next day. Rashieda's daughter delivered the message in the customary singsong voice and phrasing that all minors used in Manenberg as a sign of deference to the age and seniority of the sender and the recipient:

'Aunty Lenie my ma sê dat Aunty Lenie moet ve Zellie sê dat sy môre oggend half-pas' *six na ons huis toe kô, sodat sy saamit my ma môre werktoe kan gaan.'* (Aunty Lenie, my mother said that Aunty Lenie should tell Zellie that she should be at our house at half-past six tomorrow morning so that she can accompany my mother to work.)

The young women's or girls' customary style of message delivery not only conveys respect for the adult recipient but also signifies that they are dutifully performing errands for the senior women.

The next morning Zellie arrived at Aunty Rashieda's house as instructed. She then accompanied the older woman to the taxi rank, where they boarded the crowded minibus taxi to the factory in Athlone Industria. Aunty Rashieda greeted a few women cheerily as she boarded the taxi, and introduced Zellie to them. Once they arrived at the factory, Aunty Rashieda introduced Zellie to the supervisor, who then escorted her to a little office in the corner of the factory floor, where she completed some paperwork. Zellie was offered a short-term work contract for two months as a casual worker. During the lunch break, Aunty Rashieda introduced Zellie to her group of friends. These women proceeded to share their lunch with their new colleague while asking her questions about herself. In the abrupt, reprimanding style of conversation that older women use on the Cape Flats to teach the youth, they proceeded to educate her about the social relations on the floor, telling her which women to avoid and which women she could ask for assistance. They also identified the men on the floor who were most likely to pester her for sexual favours and instructed her on how to avoid being harassed by them. At the end of the day, she walked to the taxi rank in the company of Aunty Rashieda and a few women who commuted home on the same route.

For most of her first day at work, and indeed for most of the time thereafter, Zellie was being embedded in a supportive web of women workers, who assisted her in learning the various aspects of the workplace, and accompanied her as she used the public transportation service to traverse the space between work and Rio Street. Zellie's initiation and progressive insertion into this group of working women were by no means gentle or easy. The women used a rough, castigating tone of voice when they educated her about the expectations at work. Often her co-worker or the supervisor, who checked on the quality of her work, would grab a garment from her, exclaiming impatiently, '*Kyk wat het djy nou hier aangevang. Djy's darem onnosel*' (Look at what you've just done. You are really so stupid!)

The other women, who were able to overhear these remarks, sniggered as the young woman was being castigated. She remained silent, no doubt cognizant of the punitive isolation that followed any *terugpraatery* or insolent 'backchat.' At the same time, the woman who had just delivered the scolding rectified the error and then taught her how to do the stitching in the correct manner. This relationship mirrored the interactions that mothers had with their daughters in the home as they taught them specific domestic skills. Very soon Zellie felt at ease at her job.

She still joined the other young women in the evening as they gathered in Morieda's living room to watch the daily episode of the soap operas, 'The Bold and the Beautiful' or 'Backstage.' During the breaks, she spoke to them enthusiastically about her work and the new peer group of adult working women into which she had been initiated.

'Die werk is hard, en djy moet kan byhou daar. Hulle't ie tyd ve jou as djy stadig werk'ie! Ma' die anners help ve my lekker uit. En Aantie Rashieda kyk uit ve my. Sy sê sommer ve die outjies hulle moettie mit my lol nie, of hulle't mit ha' te doene!' (The work is hard and you have to keep up. They don't tolerate slow workers! But the others help me out. And Aunty Rashieda looks out for me. She tells the guys not to pester me, or they'll have some explaining to do to her!)

The other girls listened to her with a mixture of admiration, envy and uncertainty. They knew that work in the textile factories was long and exhausting, having witnessed their mothers or neighbours return home from work exhausted at the end of the day. *'Ja, my ma sê is harde werk'* (yes, my mother says that it's hard work), Claudette said, confirming Zellie's opinion. Yet Zellie also spoke of the hard work with pride and now that she was employed there, and as she talked to them about her new experiences, it did not seem that bad after all. She complained about the size of the household electricity bill that she was now responsible for paying. However, we all recognized this as a veiled indication that she had been assigned a new, more adult role within the household and that she was now able to assist her grandmother to pay the household bills. In addition, now that she earned her own money, she was able to buy her own cigarettes, toiletries and other personal necessities, to the envy and admiration of the other girls. It was clear that since Zellie had begun working, her status had changed subtly but irrevocably in relation to her peers. She had become a part of the world of employed women, a world to which they did not yet belong.

Young women like Zellie journeyed away from the relative dependence of adolescence and school when they made the decision to leave school and then to find a job. In order to do so, these girls had to enlist their parents' (most often their mothers') approval and rely on these senior women's networks to gain entry to the world of work. In order to facilitate their access to the network, these young women had to demonstrate that they had carefully adhered to the values and practices of *ordentlikheid*. In addition, the younger women also had to trust the network of senior women to negotiate their access to the world of work. Through their display of trust and respect for these *moeders*, the young women were freed from the dependency and strictures of school and introduced to the cultural and financial possibilities of the workplace. For the moment, as these young initiates first entered the world of work, they were too overwhelmed by their newfound independence and their acceptance into a circle of respected adult women to be weighed down by the repetitiveness and low pay of factory work. Zellie and her school-going peers realized that, as young women learn to negotiate their way in the adult women's working world, their lives were being textured with the qualitatively different colours of adulthood. The only issue that filled Zellie with trepidation was that she was being hired as a casual worker. She was retrenched after two months, but she was told to contact the supervisor after a month. She was hopeful that now that she had established a relationship with the factory hierarchy she would be hired again.

The *moeders* incorporated these young women into their local network of support through a systematic process in which they introduced them individually to an expanding circle of 'mothers' who lived their lives across different social fields, such as the community, the workplace or the various state institutions. The individual members' links within the network were solidified and strengthened over a number of years, through their daily round of interaction with each other within the shared social contexts such as the Rio Street community, the daily bus or taxi to work and the work environment. These social bonds were reinforced with the daily accretions of shared triumphs, joys, or troubles, and also provided a valuable bank of cultural knowledge about the processes and individuals one negotiated to find employment, and access valuable welfare, educational or other social resources.

An *ordentlike moeder* ensured that she introduced her daughter as well as other younger women from her community to this support network of *moeders*, so that they were gradually embedded within it and acquired the necessary knowledge they needed to find a job, and to negotiate the subtler, less visible practices in the workplace, such as interpersonal relations with figures of authority or with co-workers. More importantly, through conversations with, and observation of their older colleagues, the young women learned how to traverse the more difficult, grey terrain of sexuality in the workplace fairly adeptly, especially when male co-workers made sexual advances. Finally, the older women also taught them how to traverse the diverse cultural and physical spaces between home and workplace or state institution, and the necessary social skills and attitude to negotiate with bureaucrats at work or in local government. Through this process, these young women were progressively embedded into the network of adult women who would initiate them into the wider world of work, and who would provide them with assistance during the inevitable household crises. The young women acquired the new cultural knowledge and gained access to other social fields while still firmly cushioned within the comfort of local *moeders'* networks that now expanded and extended beyond the realm of Rio Street. When a young woman's decision to drop out of school and to work was considered from the vantage of her location within an assuring network of moeders, then it lost its seemingly disastrous quality. After all, these *moeders* had also entered early adulthood by the very same route and had gained independence within the framework of *ordentlikheid*.

Earlier, in chapter 4, I indicated that mothers interpreted their daughters' early childbearing as a temporary affront to their respectability, and to their power as older women in the community and within the household. Yet, as I show in the following vignette, childbearing was another means by which young women were able to accrue some authority in relation to their peers and receive respect from the adult women, while still remaining within the bounds of *ordentlikheid*. While the adult women recognized that the young women had become mothers, this did not necessarily imply that these young women had gained a greater level of maturity than their childless peers. The older women could discriminate between the different levels of maturity that these young mothers possessed by assessing them in terms of the spectrum of mothering skills. They judged the younger mothers' maturity in terms of the care they demonstrated towards their infants as reflected in the latters' appearance, how frequently the young mothers were seen in public with their infants and the amount of time that they were known to *gaan uit* (go out) and enjoy leisure activities. The *moeders* believed that the energy and time that young mothers devoted to leisure activities were an accurate indication of their ability to spend their time and resources judiciously. As I indicate in discussing the next case, young mothers who took good care of their infants were judged to be young women *met meer verstand* (with more wisdom) or more maturity. These young women were assumed to balance their time carefully between leisure and childcare.

I met Janap, an 18-year-old single mother, in Rukiya's living room. On that hot February afternoon in 1998, she was seated on a couch, leaning towards the open doorway. Her one-year-old son, Moegsien, was crawling at her feet. Her position gave her a wide vista of the street. I had come to look for Amina, but Janap said that she had left to take her child to the clinic. I began explaining my research to Janap and asked her if she would allow me to interview her about her experiences as a young mother. As I spoke, some adolescent women entered the living room and began to listen to me attentively. Janap began telling me about her personal history. She, like most of her peers, was born in Manenberg. She had attended school until the eighth grade. During that year, she had met Moeneeb, Moegsien's father, whom she began to date. A few months later, she discovered that she was pregnant and dropped out of school. At that point, she was sixteen years old. During the short time that we spoke, she interrupted our conversation constantly to shout some command or other at the young women present. At one point, she said to sixteen-year-old Lindsey in an authoritative tone, *'Ga' koep gou entjies ve ons by die hok'* (Go buy us some cigarettes at the cage). She reached into the hidden recesses of her brassiere and extricated some coins, which she gave to the young woman. Lindsey looked slightly resentful, possibly at being ordered out on an errand at a time when she was more interested in listening to our conversation. She hesitated, then took the money and left. We continued to talk about Janap's life. She said that she lived with her mother and her two younger siblings in a ground floor apartment in Rio Street. Soon after she told Moeneeb about her pregnancy, he had *ga't sê*. She said that she stayed home to look after Moegsien. Moeneeb worked as a packer at the local Pick'n' Pay grocery chain store. They planned to buy a Wendy House as soon as they had saved enough money. At this point, Lindsey returned with the cigarettes.

Janap again assumed an authoritative tone with the other young women. *'Gie Lindsey lat ek gou aantstiek. Hoe ve Moegsien, Claudette'* (Give [me the cigarettes] Lindsey, so I can light up. Hold Moegsien, Claudette), she said as she passed her young son to the girl sitting next to her. She lit up the cigarette and drew deeply on it once or twice, before passing it around to the other young women. At this point, Loppa and James entered the house. *'Gat uit die huis uit! Julle wiet Rukiya issie hier nie! Wat soek julle hier? Loppa, maak toe die deur!'* (Go outside! You know that Rukiya isn't home. What do you want here? Loppa shut the door!)

'Ons wil oek hie kom sit! Janap moenie soe wiesie!' (We also want to join in! Janap, don't be mean!), Loppa protested, but he and James returned to the little front yard, both still grumbling *sotto voce* as they went. By this time I was looking at Janap with newfound admiration. Janap was the same age as some of the women in the room, but they had acquiesced to her demands, while the young men had implicitly recognized her authority.

It was clear that Janap was recognized as the undisputed leader in this little group of adolescents. One afternoon, as we stood around chatting idly on the sidewalk just outside her apartment, I asked Rukiya why she was willing to entrust the care of her house to Janap.

'Elaine wiet, sy't meer verstand as my meisies en die ander klomp vriende wat heeldag ve hulle kô besoek. Sy's meer volwasse as die res van hulle. Al het Amina al 'n kind, sy't noggie Janap se verstand nie. Mens kan sien hoe sy haar kind behandel. Ha' kind is mooi groot al, en sy kyk mooi na hom. Sy laat'ie die klomp sommer so oor ha' loop nie. Die wat ek op ha' kan depend om na my huis te kyk as ek by die werk is.'

(Elaine, you know, she has more maturity than my own daughters and the rest of the friends who come by to visit them every day. She's more adult than the rest of them. Even though Amina has borne a child, she does not have Janap's maturity. One can tell from the way she copes with her child. Her child has grown beautifully and she takes good care of him. She doesn't allow the rest of them to walk all over her. That is why I can depend upon her to watch over my home while I am away at work.)

Young women like Janap embodied a crucial generational bridge between the older *moeders* and the young women. She was certainly a young woman *met verstand* (with maturity) because she was able to discriminate the extent to which her young peers could indulge in illicit practices such as smoking behind closed doors while maintaining the boundaries of *ordentlikheid* set by the *moeders*. She did not allow the young men to remain indoors along with the young women, for fear that their presence would be read as a deliberate infringement of the bounds of sexual propriety in Rukiya's absence. Her ability to distinguish the degree of autonomy that she and her peers could exercise whilst still remaining within the realm of *ordentlikheid* set her apart as the informal leader among the young women.

D. Beyond the errand run and behind closed doors: Agency through the values and practices of respectability

However, some young women were frequently able to renovate the seemingly rigid prescriptions of behaviour and dress associated with *ordentlikheid* to realize their own goals. They were able to transform domestic space, schoolyards or seemingly innocuous friendly meetings in the street into places of vicarious leisure, whilst still remaining within the spatial bounds of respectability or *ordentlikheid*. At such moments they were able to participate in illicit beer-drinking sessions, engage in imaginary flights of romantic fantasy while listening to popular music, or participate in secret romantic liaisons with young men.

Domestic or household spaces were considered to be the key spaces associated with young women's respectability. Consequently, these locations also became the primary places in which the adolescent women could freely exercise a considerable degree of agency while still upholding their respectable reputations. Households that were headed by single, employed mothers and left in the sole care of an adolescent daughter during working hours presented the young women with some opportunities to enjoy moments of illicit leisure such as alcohol consumption or romantic liaisons with young men. On rare occasions, the group of young women was able to engage in such activities due to a serendipitous coincidence of events, such as the immediate availability of beer in the household during their visits there. However, usually, these activities required careful planning.

The young women usually planned such events secretly during social interactions at school or indoors after school. First, the adolescent woman in charge of the household during her mother's absence had to agree to the household being used for the occasion. A group of friends then pooled their financial resources and enlisted the assistance of an adult who was marginal to the community to purchase a quart or two of beer or a bottle of wine. Usually, the local drunk was persuaded to purchase the alcohol and smuggle it indoors, with the promise that he would receive a drink himself. The beer was consumed very quickly in an atmosphere of nervous excitement, much giggling and teasing, while lit cigarettes were passed around, one at a time, as one of the group watched furtively for approaching adults. Usually, the radio was tuned in to a favourite music station as some young women began dancing, helping to sustain the cheery atmosphere. However, the young host would frequently turn down the radio, while entreating the group to be less noisy so that the suspicions of the neighbours in the adjoining apartments were not aroused. Usually, the amount of alcohol that was consumed was too small and shared amongst too many to produce visible intoxication. The young women always ended these sessions with a mixed sense of secretive triumph and relief that they had participated in a taboo activity within the sanctity of the household, without apparently being discovered. On occasion, however, when it seemed as though these young women's parties were occurring too frequently, threatening a household's and a mother's reputation, some of the adult *moeders* intervened by making oblique comments to the young women, in which they hinted that they knew about their illicit activities. Such comments were rapidly passed on to the other adolescent women through their conversation networks and were enough to end the parties for a while.

Young women's friendly school-yard conversations or chance encounters with young men whilst on an errand run provided them with numerous opportunities to initiate friendships and romantic relationships beyond the boundaries of Rio Street while remaining within the social boundaries of *ordentlikheid*. Likewise, the schoolyard provided most adolescent women with a certain measure of freedom, where they were able to engage in conversations with young men or share an illicit cigarette away from the prying eyes of watchful *moeders* and even teachers. The school's empty classrooms, stairwells and building walls provided numerous private spaces where young people could interact during recess, and flirt openly or continue more serious romantic relationships. The young women were able to manipulate the principles and practices of *ordentlikheid* while experimenting with their sexuality. They still occupied the spaces of *ordentlikheid* and adhered to their predictable daily routine but, as I illustrate in the case below, were able to give a different meaning to these precepts to suit their own ends. In this fashion, they were able to pass from adolescence into adult motherhood, while still being regarded as good daughters.

Nadia had confided to me that her first serious romantic relationship had developed into a sexual relationship after she had been dating the same young man for more than a year. They were able to engage in sexual intercourse in her home or that of a close friend during school hours when adult members were away at work. Sexual liaisons like that between Nadia and her partner were planned in the schoolyard or when young women encountered young men hanging out in the street as they ran household errands or accompanied a friend on errands.

Morieda confided to me that she could predict that Nadia would become pregnant, because she had begun to break with her predictable pattern of movement, and cut school to return home early. Yet when the ever-vigilant adult *moeders* inquired about her presence on the streets during school hours, Nadia was easily able to claim that she was required at home to complete an urgent domestic task. Her apparent willingness to prioritize the needs of the household over the requirement to remain at school silenced any further inquiries about her actions. She had adequately demonstrated her acquiescence to the values and practices of *ordentlikheid*. Yet Morieda claimed that there was nothing she could do to prevent the pregnancy from occurring. She felt that she had to prevent alienating her daughter at all costs, and so she merely spoke with Nadia about being careful about her actions *'want die mense praat hier'* (because people talk here). Single mothers like Morieda who were the sole adults in their households were caught in a cultural dilemma. Their portrayal as *ordentlike moeders* within the community was also informed by their offsprings' actions. These adult women, therefore, felt compelled to defend their daughters' behaviour to their senior peers because what they most wanted was to be perceived as *ordentlike moeders* who managed respectable households. At the same time, they were left anxious about the reasons why their daughters had cut school and were home alone. These mothers were left with no other alternative other than confronting their daughters about their actions in the privacy of their homes.

In households with at least two generations of adult women, disagreements with adolescent daughters were often resolved quickly as mothers reclaimed their authority over their errant offspring, supported by the other adults in the household. However, quarrels like these were especially threatening in households where a single woman was the only adult present. If these quarrels flourished into a full-blown angry confrontation, then these mothers risked alienating the only individuals on whom they could rely to assist them in running the household. In Nadia's case, it seemed that her pregnancy was not as catastrophic as one might have expected. Morieda said that Nadia's pregnancy served as an indication that she had remained a good daughter because she was willing to pay the price for her 'mistake'. Paradoxically her pregnancy had, in fact, proved her *ordentlikheid*. It indicated that she lacked any knowledge about birth control because she was not smart enough about sexual matters to prevent the pregnancy. Consequently, her pregnancy was perceived as a 'mistake' rather than a sign of her sexual promiscuity. Nadia had also been willing to bear the responsibility of raising a child – a further indication of her incipient adulthood. When I asked most of the *moeders* about Nadia's pregnancy, initially they had criticized her for being foolish and indulging in sex without a thought for the consequences. However, they then spoke approvingly of Nadia's willingness to bear responsibility for the pregnancy, thereby illustrating that she was maturing into adulthood. Most said that '*sy was gewillig om op die bed te lê wat sy gemaak het*' (she was willing to lie on the bed that she had made).

Girls like Nadia were able to manipulate the precepts and practices of *ordentlikheid* and pass from immature school-going adolescents to maturing motherhood with their reputations as good daughters restored. Other young women were not as discreet or as astute about manipulating the principles and practices of *ordentlikheid* as an agentive means of realizing their own goals. Rio Street residents, especially the *moeders*, were extremely contemptuous of these young women when they were in trouble. The *moeders* insisted that these young women were to blame for their own problems because they had utterly transgressed the bounds of *ordentlikheid* and did not attempt to work within the limits of its principles and practices. The *moeders* unsympathetic, even cruel, responses to these women's plight only served to isolate them from the community for a time.

E. *Onnosel en onbeskof:* Young rebels challenging the boundaries of *ordentlikheid*

Young women who pushed the envelope of *ordentlikheid*, and deliberately transgressed its norms rather discreetly manipulating them, were contemptuously regarded as *onnosel* or foolish. If these young rebels experienced any problems, they were perceived as having created these obstacles themselves because they deliberately chose to challenge the norms of *ordentlikheid*. As Lindsey's case illustrates below, the *moeders* and the young women who desired to be seen as being *goeie dogters* or good girls shamed these unfortunate young offenders by gossiping about them and dissociating from them for a time.

Sixteen-year-old Lindsey was cast out from the circle of friends in Rio Street in this fashion after she was raped while she was returning home from Nyanga one Saturday evening after she had visited some friends. Lindsey lived with her mother, forty-six-year-old Monica, and her infant brother in a second-floor apartment, located above the unit occupied by Morieda and her family. Monica was the second wife of a Xhosa-speaking man, known as 'Huisbaas' (Household Head), who ran the local shebeen. Unlike most Rio Street and Manenberg residents, Monica and Lindsey were trilingual and able to converse in English, Afrikaans and isiXhosa. However, they rarely took pride in this ability, choosing to conceal this unique skill instead, as they feared the questions it would raise about their diverse ethnic origins. Monica feared and resented the malicious gossip about her Xhosa ancestry. In order to mitigate the street gossip and to prove her own and her household's respectability, she regulated Lindsey's behaviour very severely. While Lindsey's peers were given some freedom to explore spaces such as the *hok* in Rio Street during the day, she was forbidden to hang out with them there. She was expected to spend most of her free time indoors, assisting her mother to care for her baby brother and with assorted household chores. When she was allowed outdoors, she had to provide Monica with a detailed plan of where and how she would spend her time. Monica gained a reputation among Lindsey's peers for being an unduly severe parent who restrained Lindsey's mobility severely. They rarely invited Lindsey to accompany them on errands to Nyanga Junction or on visits to friends who lived in other local communities within

Manenberg. When Lindsey implored her friends to request Monica to allow her to accompany them beyond the bounds of Rio Street, even bold young women like Janap refused, claiming that *'jou ma is te streng. Sy skel sommer 'n mens verniet. Sy sal net nee sê'* (your mother is too strict. She scolds one without any reason to do so. She'll only refuse.)

Lindsey often found herself on the outskirts of her peer group, frequently unable to participate in conversations about a recent afternoon spent dancing in the *hok*, listening to music, or the last netball game that the Rio Rangers had played on the nearby netball field. As a result, she appeared diffident and unsure of her status in the group.

At school, however, she was a popular friend amongst the Xhosa-speaking girls who were newcomers to the previously coloureds-only school. They were relieved to find a handful of coloured girls like Lindsey who were capable of crossing linguistic boundaries with ease, who befriended them and who helped them settle into the new school environment. One of these young women, Xoliswa, had invited Lindsey to visit her at her home in Nyanga. When Lindsey confided in me about being raped, she said that she knew that Monica would not permit her to visit Xoliswa. So on the first few visits, Lindsey told her mother that she was going to spend the afternoon with Nazli and Nadia in their home. She was able to visit Xoliswa on a few occasions in this fashion without being detected. On the fateful Saturday, she had spent that afternoon walking with Xoliswa in Nyanga and then at her house, chatting with some friends. When it grew dark, Xoliswa and another friend accompanied Lindsey to the pedestrian bridge at Nyanga Junction, which linked Nyanga and Manenberg across busy Duinefontein road. She said that they did not realize that they were being followed by three men until they were halfway across the pedestrian bridge, which by this time of the evening was quite deserted by the usual stream of busy shoppers. She said that she and her friends became extremely fearful and increased their pace, as they glanced over their shoulders frequently to assess whether they were gaining ground against their pursuers. At that moment the men ran after them and held onto Lindsey and Xoliswa by their shirts, while they struggled to break free. Their friend Zola was able to run away and call for help, while Xoliswa bit her attacker so severely on the hand that he let her go. She too ran off to find help. By this time the enraged men turned on the still-captive

Lindsey and dragged her to a deserted spot at the end of the bridge. There they brutally raped her. They were disturbed by Xoliswa and Zola, who had returned with a few police officers. The rapists escaped, leaving a severely traumatized Lindsey lying half-naked in the dark. The police officers assisted her home to inform her mother. They then drove the weeping girl, her friends and her mother to the police station, where they took a statement from the young victims in turn. They told Lindsey not to wash herself until she had visited a district surgeon, who would remove any semen samples from her as evidence. After they had questioned the girls and taken their statements they accompanied them home. Lindsey said that it was not easy for her to provide the police officers with a statement because her mother constantly intervened, scolding her and reminding her about the numerous times she had been told not to leave the confines of Rio Street. She said that she felt ashamed because her mother repeatedly asked her,

'*Wat ga't die mense nou van my sê? Djy luister nie ve my nie. Nou sien djy wat kom van jou eie ongehoorsaamheid!*' (What will the people say about me now? You don't listen to me! Now look what has come of your own disobedience!)

Lindsey confided in me at least three days after the rape had occurred. Her mother did not own a car and so they were unable to go to the district surgeon so that she could be examined. Lindsey said that she couldn't tolerate going unwashed for a prolonged length of time, and so she had taken a bath. She went to the local clinic to be examined because she feared that she would contract HIV. The nurses there had conducted a cervical examination and had then given her a number of plastic sachets, each containing different coloured tablets that they said would prevent HIV. However, they were overwhelmed by the great number of people awaiting assistance at the clinic and so they could not counsel her about HIV or identify the drugs for her. A professional physician friend who happened to be visiting Cape Town at the time agreed to counsel Lindsey about HIV. Lindsey's mother Monica welcomed us into her home that afternoon and showed us to the only two chairs in the room. She called Lindsey, who she said spent most of her time in her bedroom. Lindsey entered the room with downcast eyes. I introduced Monica and Lindsey to Anne and told them that she had agreed to talk to Lindsey about HIV and AIDS. Monica then began telling us how the rape occurred. As she spoke, she began weeping, repeating that

'Ek't ve ha' bly gesê sy moet nie in die Nyanga gaan nie. Sy ken nie die plek nie en die mense da ken nie ve ha' nie. Nou wat gat die mense hie van my en van ha' sê? Is ha' skuld dat die ding met ha' gebeur het.' (I told her repeatedly that she shouldn't go Nyanga. She doesn't know the place and the people there don't know her. Now, what will people here say about me and about her? She's brought this thing upon herself.)

She said that the police took their statements but that they did not search the bushes at the spot where the rape occurred for clues. She also said that they did not question Lindsey or her friends about the men who assaulted them. Lindsey stood against the wall silently, nervously twisting her fingers. I tried telling Monica that Lindsey should not be blamed for the rape, but she shook her head despairingly at me. She repeated adamantly that Lindsey had not obeyed her warnings and so she was to blame for her plight. Anne and I left the despairing mother and daughter, feeling helpless about offering further advice.

Monica's concern about what the people in Rio Street would say was not unfounded. A few days later, I met Aunty Aïsha sitting in her usual spot outside her gate on her upturned milk crate. After the usual exchange of greetings, we began talking about the young people in the road. This issue preoccupied most of the older people at the time because two youths had been at the root of recent crises in the street. In the first incident, Zahir had stolen a radio from a car in Colleen Court, which was located in the Naughty Boys' gang turf. In doing so, he had broken the unspoken rule that one did not steal from the Manenberg residents. His actions could initiate a gang war unless he was punished by his own 'brothers' or by the Naughty Boys gang as an act of retributive justice. The second incident concerned Lindsey's visit to Nyanga and the rape that had ensued. Aunty Aïsha then said contemptuously,

'Deesdae maak hulle net wat hulle wil. Hulle't geen respek meer nie. Ma as hulle innie moeilikheid is, dan wil hulle huil. Die Lindsey van Monica … sy 't Nyanga toe gegaan

om da' man te gaan soek, nou sê sy sy's verkrag. Dink sy ons is onnosel?' (These days they do as they please. They have no respect any longer. But when they find themselves in trouble then they want to cry. This Lindsey of Monica's – she went to Nyanga looking for a man, and now she claims that she's been raped. Does she think that we're all so stupid?)

Aunty Aïsha's acerbic comments were embedded with the *moeders'* disquiet about recent incidents in Rio Street. An event such as Lindsey's visit to Nyanga, beyond the boundaries of her own community, signalled that the unquestioned authority of the *moeders* over the younger women was unravelling. Aunty Aïsha's suggestion that Lindsey had deliberately set out to visit Nyanga 'to look for a man' expressed the older woman's recognition that her young counterpart had exercised agency outside the precepts and practices of *ordentlikheid* and explored a new space without the *moeders* mediatory guidance; it also expressed her anger at this. Like Lindsey's mother, Monica, she reached for the established, dominant moral economy of *ordentlikheid* to explain why the rape had occurred. Both women claimed that Lindsey was ultimately responsible for the rape because she had not relied upon the *moeders* to mediate a different social and physical space on her behalf. Instead, she had usurped agency illegally from the mothers, relying upon an alternative social and cultural asset to navigate the social and physical space on her own.

Lindsey's mastery over an apparent cultural liability in the local context, namely her fluency in isiXhosa, had been transformed into a cultural asset. This skill enabled her to explore the social and physical worlds beyond the boundaries of Rio Street and indeed Manenberg. Her exploration and the unfortunate rape that ensued exposed the limits of the older women's powers to oversee the young women's activities, to mediate between the comfortable world of the local Rio Street community and the wider world on their behalf, and to protect them from assaults beyond the bounds of the local community. If Lindsey had been raped within Rio Street or in the other communities of Manenberg, the *moeders* and the young men would have sought restitution through the institutionalized processes described in chapter 4. She had pushed the envelope of the local boundaries and expanded the limits of her social world beyond the parochial, restrictive world of Rio Street and of Manenberg's myriad local communities. By the same token, she now had to seek restitution for the assault committed against her from an institution, the national police service, whose powers were mutually recognized across local boundaries and who were invested with greater credibility than the local network of *moeders* and their customary allies, the local gang. The crisis precipitated by Lindsey's rape had revealed the processual disentanglement of the young women's lifecycle from that of the older *moeders* in Rio Street. Through her anger, Aunty Aïsha registered her own and the other *moeders'* anxiety about their waning power over young adventurers such as Lindsey. More significantly, she revealed her own growing awareness of changing structural factors that allowed Lindsey to gain access to and to navigate a social world on her own beyond Rio Street, and that set in place the inevitable erosion of the *moeders'* power and their inability to halt it.

F. Conclusion

Young women in Rio street are located in a particular structural position within the local moral economy so that their personhood is more starkly and contradictorily textured by generational and gendered differences as they pass from girlhood into young womanhood. The moeders in particular attempt to minimize the contradictory demands on young women's sexuality as they socialize girls early on into the constraining femininity that is considered appropriate in this context. The precepts and practices of *ordentlike* or respectable femininity for young girls are distinguished from that expected of adolescent women. During childhood, the values of *ordentlikheid* emphasize a girl's willingness to be subjected to the initial lessons of feminine domesticity. When young girls reach the age of 8 to 12 years, the adult moeders increasingly draw them into household chores such as cleaning, childcare or cooking. The foundations for young womanhood are also prepared during girlhood. Girls lives' are increasingly marked by constrained mobility that is informed by the moral signification of social space, and of temporality. They grow acutely aware of the gendered meanings of different places within the community and the importance of the domestic space to feminine identity. They are also made conscious of the morality and the dangers of uncontrollable sexuality that is associated with darkness.

As these girls develop into young women they learn to accept the moeders' and, to a lesser extent, the young men's increasing surveillance of their movements. The extent of the surveillance is revealed when young women complain of the tedious hours of boredom spent indoors, completing domestic chores or just sitting around. Later on, their perseverance is rewarded as the young women's conduct as *goeie dogters* or good daughters is rewarded when they seek increasing employment and with it increasing independence through the network of moeders. Initially, the moeders and the young men's interests in surveilling and controlling the young women are mutually reinforcing as they both seek to uphold the respectable identities of the adult women. As young men gain recognition as *Ouens* in the community and now desire to become fathers, their interest in the young women is increasingly at odds with that of the moeders. The young men seek to make the young women sexually active, while the moeders attempt to preserve their sexuality for as long as possible. Moeders are unable to surveil their daughters to the same extent. Young women who are members of households headed by a single employed mother are often perceived to be at greatest risk of becoming *sleg* or losing their respectability. Their households, unlike multigenerational households, do not possess an adequate number of adult *moeders* to assist in surveilling the young women. Ultimately young women are able to explore their sexuality in the very spaces of respectable femininity such as the home or the schoolyard even as they visibly adhere to the behavioural regime expected of good daughters. When a young woman becomes pregnant, the conflicting interests of the other persons in her sexuality surfaces. A crisis ensues that is only resolved once the young father acknowledges his paternity and the *moeders* acknowledges the young woman's willingness to accept responsibility for her actions by acknowledging her pregnancy and bearing the child. These young mothers are able to recuperate their good standing in the community as they distinguish themselves as more mature and responsible than their childless peers. This they do by exhibiting their growing repertoire of parenting skills and as they assist the older women in policing and protecting the economic interests and social respectability of their households.

Young women who pushed the envelope of *ordentlikheid*, and deliberately transgressed its norms rather discreetly manipulating them, were contemptuously regarded as *onnosel* or foolish. The young women who are disparaged as foolish often insist on exploring friendship networks beyond the boundaries of their own community. They tend to be members of households that are perceived to be on the cultural periphery of the community because their social practices, ethnic or linguistic origins are questioned. If these young rebels experience any problems, they are perceived as having created these obstacles themselves because they are perceived as deliberately challenging the norms of *ordentlikheid*. These rebels are marginalized by the community of young women and the *moeders*. However as I indicate in the final chapter, the power of the mothers to surveil the young women and to determine who is defined as respectable persons within Rio street is waning as the socio-economic structural factors buttressing the local moral economy is changing.

Chapter 7

Conclusion

A. Taxi queens and glamorous gangsters: Emerging changes in Rio Street

Ek's nie bang ve die goed nie. Hulle gaan skool toe gedurende die dag, en dan as hulle huis toe kom, dan's hulle gangsters. Hulle'tie sterk biene nie. Hulle stiek weg agter geboue en dan skiet hulle. Die bullets travel op hulle eie. Hulle het hulle eie lewe.

I'm not afraid of this lot. They attend school during the day and then when they go home, they become gangsters. They don't have strong bones. They hide behind buildings and then they shoot. These bullets travel by themselves. They have their own life.

Fifty-six-year-old Uncle Booi, commenting on youthful gangsters.

Ek verstaan nie die klomp jong meisies nie. Hulle sal hulle maens pla vir Nikes tekkies en Pepe jeanse. En al moet daai ma kosgeld gebruik ve die klere, solank soos hulle sharp lyk op die straat. En dan koep die maens die goed.

I don't understand these young girls. They nag their mothers for Nikes sneakers and Pepe jeans. Even if their mothers use the food money to obtain those items, as long as they can look smart in the street. And yet their mothers will buy them these items.

Twenty-five-year-old Charlene, mother of two daughters.

Dit is hoe 'n outjie vir 'n meisie moet treat. Nie soes die outjies hier in Manenberg'ie. Nie soes die outjie wat ek nou mee uitgaan, wat ve 'n mens slaat en klap nie.

That's how a guy should treat a girl. Not like the guys here in Manenberg. Not like the one I'm dating now who beats me and slaps me around.

Sixteen-year-old Rozelda, commenting after watching an episode of the soap opera, 'Buzz.'

245

Uncle Booi's complaint about male students, who transformed into gun-toting gangsters with false bravado after school is out, reflected his concern that the social pathway to masculine personhood and its core value, toughness, were under threat. Similarly, Charlene's objections to adolescent women who prioritized their individual desire for brand-name items, even at the expense of the household's food budget, mirror her concern about a fundamental change in the values and practices of feminine personhood. She perceives the younger women's demand for brand-name clothing even at the expense of the household food budget as a challenge to the sacrosanct practice of femininity, namely nurturing and sustaining household needs above all else. Rozelda's comments, in the meanwhile, indicate that through the narrative of a popular television soap opera she has become increasingly aware of the possibility that young women can aspire to healthy dating relationships in which they are treated with respect. Uncle Booi's, Charlene's and Roselda's divergent responses all reflect their own experiences and perceptions of change in Rio Street. Their comments also reflect their awareness of the new technologies of violence, such as guns, the new cultural values of personhood such as consumerism and respect for younger women, as well as the new modes of socialization, such as TV soap operas, that are assisting this process of change. Clearly, these perceptions are shot through with gendered and generational differences. Their responses to the social changes that they perceived within the community are due to the generational differences between them, and the location of their individual life histories within different historical contexts. Uncle Booi's sour remarks about the adolescent men reflect an ageing ex-gangster's growing impotence in a male world where he was once respected and feared. Similarly, Charlene's response mirrors some envy towards the adolescent women, whom she perceives to be free of the worries about raising dependent children. Rozelda's remarks also reflect youthful dissatisfaction with the slow pace of change and the narrow choice of partners available in Rio Street. More importantly, all their comments emerge from their common observation of the subtle shifts in the construction of personhood and agency in Rio Street.

In this final chapter, I argue that these different commentaries originate from an awareness that a fundamental seismic shift is occurring in the structure of the moral economy and with it, a shift in the power of the *ordentlike moeders* to assert their authority within the Rio Street community.

During the early years of the new millennium, it became increasingly clear to the local residents that the adult women's ability to define respectable persons was anchored within a shifting political and economic context as the South African transition to a non-racial democracy took firm hold. As I show, later on, these changes brought in their wake changing bureaucratic policies and economic strategies that effectively dislocated coloureds', and specifically adult coloured women's, relatively privileged location within the hierarchy of deprivation. The effects of these emergent structural changes were progressively being felt in Manenberg and manifested in small but significant ways in Rio Street during the last few months of my research there. Comments made by individuals such as Uncle Booi and Charlene collectively reflected their perception of change in the ideology of *ordentlikheid*, and the implicit power of the *ordentlike moeders* to remain the bedrock of this belief system that recuperated their personhood and dignity.

Uncle Booi's remarks implied that a change in the practices and aesthetics of ganging had blurred the boundaries between the previously distinctive cultural phases that marked the male life cycle. The immature student who previously had no agency was becoming indistinguishable from the male gangster. The gangster was no longer required to 'have strong bones,' the quintessential aspect of young adult male agency. Instead, the increasing availability of guns in the area enabled these male youth to hide behind buildings and fire, because 'bullets have a life of their own.' These weapons did not require these young men's courage and wisdom to be tested. In Booi's day, their use of bricks, wooden *knobkieries* (cudgels) and knives during gang fights required them to come into close physical contact with their opponents to inflict injury. According to Booi, this contact was the ultimate test of a man's wisdom and courage. He said that '*Daai tyd moet djy wysheid gehad het om te wiet om iemand se lewe te neem het of nie*' (Then you had to have wisdom to know whether to take someone's life or not). Now the male youth behaved like cowards, exposing innocent residents to the dangers of gang cross-fire. Similarly, Charlene's complaint stems from her observation that the cultural values which sustain a household's vital economic strategies are under threat. She ascribes this primarily to the shift in the meanings of adolescent womanhood and of respectable motherhood (*ordentlike moederskap*). *Goeie dogters* are no longer being nurtured and trained to valorize and uphold a key ideological tenet of *ordentlikheid*, namely to sacrifice one's individual desire to meet the reproductive needs of the household. The *ordentlike moeders* felt compelled to provide their daughters with the items of clothing that, it seemed, were swiftly redefining the style and the agency of *goeie dogters* in the street.

Their comments also mirrored their concern about the subtle new practices that are infiltrating quotidian life, and that they observe are reshaping or blurring the boundaries between persons who inhabit the everyday world of Rio Street. They hint at the potential innovations of and shifts in agency that were now being realized across gender and through the generations in the local context of Rio Street. Young male school students can easily become gangsters. In the process they remove the cultural boundary between the *Ou* and the *skollie,* contaminating a respected masculine ideal as they threaten the safety of the local community. Young women do not subjugate their needs and desires to those of their mothers and ultimately those of the household. Instead, their mothers are pressured to meet their daughters' needs as the external world of fashion and consumerism increasingly dictates the meanings of femininity. In contrast to these pessimistic perceptions, Roselda's remarks reflect her vision of a more optimistic world in which young women are not dependent upon older women or men to be identified as persons. In this new world, the young women are identified as persons in their own right who deserve to be treated with respect and for whom healthy, non-violent love relationships are possible. Through the medium of the television soap opera she has become increasingly aware of an alternative set of gender relations that are non-violent and in which young women may demand and receive respect. The changes in personhood and agency that these three individuals remark upon are intertwined with, and reshape, the changes in the old racial order, the changing notions of personhood within the national context, together with the laws and policies that hinged upon it. The systematic erosion of this racial system holds implications for the moral economy of personhood in Manenberg that hinges upon it.

Changes in the post-apartheid context are currently unravelling the racial political economy, as well as the local moral economy and its associated gendered notions of personhood which were anchored in and yet resistant to it. I argue that these structural changes articulated unevenly with the local moral economy and the associated constructions of personhood in the post-apartheid context. This uneven articulation exposed the limitations of the *moeders* power more starkly, rendering it less permanent and ultimately less certain. The changing political economy also sustained the subtle, often subversive reconfigured meanings that the young women introduced to the outward forms of *ordentlikheid*, providing a cultural public space in which these meanings were emergent. At the same time, these emergent cultural and social gaps also defined a new moral web of power in the local context of Rio Street. This new moral web of power provided the young men and women with some room to explore the social worlds and spaces that existed beyond the boundaries of Rio Street. Through these exploratory practices, these youth acquired new values and social skills, while still maintaining a foothold in the local moral economy. Through their acts of cautious exploration and local negotiation, they were actively transforming the gendered meanings of personhood in Rio Street. Sometimes, however, through their explorations, the more courageous men and women pushed the envelope of individual agency and engaged in activities that knit them into new, emergent configurations of morality, power and personhood.

B. Unravelling the economic scaffolding of local personhood

In chapter 3, I argued that the local moral economy of *ordentlikheid* in Rio Street relied upon, and articulated with, a racially based political economy that favoured coloured women's statuses as mothers and workers. However, the racial hierarchy of deprivation has been done away with, and with it, coloured women's privileged access to the child welfare grants. The grants' monetary value was sharply reduced by national welfare budget cuts and also the state's attempts to spread welfare expenditure more evenly throughout the population. At the same time, the textile and canning industries in the Western Cape were been downsized due to the effects of trade liberalization (International

Labour Resources and Information Centre 2002). Approximately 30 000 people, most of them coloured women, lost their jobs in the textile industry during the 1990s (SAIRR 2000). These women's status as mothers and their hold over economic and moral power that ensured the physical survival of their communities waned. This uncertainty undermined the senior adult women's power to define the features of the moral economy and of local personhood. Community members' adherence to the dictates of this ideology no longer automatically guaranteed economic and material survival or, for some, even respect. Accordingly, the moral economy's purchase over residents in Manenberg was slipping, together with its notion of personhood and the associated modes of behaviour and dress styles. At the same time, this delinkage created a space for the renovation or the transformation of personhood in the local context. The renovation of personhood in Manenberg communities such as Rio Street is being expressed increasingly in the lives of the youth who are coming into adulthood in the current post-apartheid context.

The old, exclusively white spaces and institutions, having been better resourced in the past, became the sought-after spaces to occupy, work or reside in, among South Africans of all races. These spaces took on new meaning as the national cosmopolitan spaces of cultural, racial, and ethnic diversity as an increasing number of South Africans from diverse backgrounds occupied them. The youth from contexts like Rio Street also desired to inhabit these spaces, where they could learn the norms, practices and codes of the new South Africans. However, access to these spaces was only made available to those with the requisite economic resources and came at a price. Housing prices and schools fees in these areas increased enormously shortly after the Group Areas and Separate Amenities Acts were rescinded in the early 1990s, both as a means to restrict access to those who were economically well-off and as a reflection of the increased demand for these residences and services. For those who continued to live in the poorer, racially homogeneous townships like Manenberg, the media, such as television or radio, and public transportation became alternative means to access these cosmopolitan spaces, albeit through vicarious consumption of soap operas and popular music, or brief visits to popular city nightspots.

As the young men and women in Rio Street accessed these cosmopolitan spaces through the media, their social imagination, or actual, albeit infrequent, visits to popular nightspots or malls, they transgressed the locally imposed social and physical boundaries and reinvented the meaning of local public and private spaces. Through their transgressive and transformative practices, they were acquiring the cultural capital that facilitated their ability to occupy or imagine themselves as part of, the new national cosmopolitan spaces of cultural, racial and ethnic diversity. In doing so, they actively destabilized their own racial and gendered identities, prising them apart from the apartheid-imposed socioeconomic, spatial, moral or linguistic markers of gender, class and race. Their increased ability to transcend the racial, linguistic and spatial limits imposed by the old apartheid policies and their growing familiarity with the wide range of cosmopolitan South African styles, languages, spaces and social customs were the defining characteristics of a newly emerging personhood in the local context. This emergent personhood challenged the mothers' ability to produce and nurture social persons within the bounded local contexts as the central aspect of identity. Television proved to be one of the most powerful media through which the young women could challenge the adult *moeders* control over their identities as *goeie dogters*.

C. Television programs: Remaking race, remaking the nation

Since the introduction of television to South Africa in January 1976, the content of entertainment and news programs and the bodies that inhabit this virtual world have reflected national political policies and trends. Accordingly, during the apartheid era television programs broadcast on the single TV channel reflected apartheid racial policies and the belief that white culture, and specifically Afrikaner nationalist culture, were superior to the other cultures in the country. Until the late 1970s, TV broadcasters and news anchors were exclusively white. Later, more TV channels were introduced to broadcast programs that were geared to support the Bantustan[11] policy and its associated cultural

---

[11] According to this policy, each of the nine ethnic groups that constituted the African population was an emerging nation, with its own territory, language and culture. According to Afrikaner nationalists, the Afrikaners, the most advanced nation,

essentialism. After the broadcasting services were restructured in 1993, the three South African Broadcasting Corporation channels broadcast in all official languages (although English dominates), while news anchors and TV presenters represented the racial, ethnic and gender diversity of the population (Barnes in Zaleza 2003).

TV channels such as '*Simunye*' or Channel One were popular among the young women in Rio Street for good reason. This particular channel targets young viewers and its programs were devoted to popular music videos, fashion or game shows. These young women were able to watch their favourite youth programs in the afternoons and early evenings from their living rooms, while still remaining within the quintessential feminine domestic spaces. However, the messages that these programs conveyed about romance, sexuality and heterosexual relations, as well as the young women's discussions about these issues, transformed these domestic locales into transgressive spaces from which the ideas and practices of divergent, new feminine identities emerged.

Two of the most popular shows among the Rio Street women were the locally produced dating game show 'Buzz,' broadcast on Channel One, and the soap opera 'Backstage,' screened on e-TV, the independently owned station. The imagery, as well as the dialogue contained in these two programs, conveyed different notions of romance, femininity and masculinity to those which existed in Manenberg, generating a creative dissonance for, and producing intense discussion among, these adolescent viewers on these issues. 'Buzz' was a popular TV dating game show for teenagers, whilst 'Backstage' was a locally produced soap opera about youthful students who attend a media and drama school.

'Buzz' was presented by a fashionably thin, well-dressed young woman. In this popular dating game show, adolescents had to select a prospective date and then, together with their new partner, compete with another couple for a night on the town in a chauffeured limousine

---

had to nurture these nations into independence. The Bantustan Act of 1970 provided the legislation for the creation of independent Bantustans. The Transkei, the Xhosa 'homeland' was the first Bantustan to be given 'independence,' in 1975. Bophuthatswana followed shortly after, in 1977, as the 'independent' Bantustan for the Tswana-speaking people. These Bantustans deprived millions of Black South Africans of their rights to South African citizenship (see W. Beinart and C. Murray [1980], *The Southern Sotho- and Tswana-Speaking Peoples of the South African Highveld.*)

and new designer-label clothes. Youthful competitors were shielded behind a screen so that they remained invisible to their prospective dating partners. Each competitor then marketed him or herself to the prospective partner in the hope that s/he would be selected as the desired date. The individual had to select the partner who s/he thought was most compatible. In the final contest for the grand prize, the two remaining couples were tested on the degree of compatibility between the partners, in a range of areas such as TV viewing choices, food tastes, etc. The two partners who proved to possess the greatest degree of compatibility were selected as the ultimate winners.

In shows such as 'Buzz,' individual image and the ability to market oneself were the only qualities that mattered. In this show, one's physical or social roots were not traceable except by accent and language. One was able to select one's partner freely and market oneself as the most desirable partner, free from the gaze of adult women, the local notions of morality and the gossip that distinguished the *goeie dogter/ seun* (good daughter or son) from the *slegte dogter* (bad daughter) or the gangster in the local context.

One evening after I had watched 'Buzz' with a few of the Rio Street girls, we entered into a discussion about the gendered expectations in relationships. Sixteen-year-old Rozelda commented on the fact that the winning couple deserved to win because the young man proved that he could treat a young woman with respect.

'*Dit is hoe 'n outjie vir 'n meisie moet treat. Nie soes die outjies hier in Manenberg'ie. Nie soes die outjie wat ek nou mee uitgaan, wat ve 'n mens slat en klap nie*' (That's how a guy should treat a girl. Not like the guys here in Manenberg. Not like this guy I'm seeing now, who beat or slaps me), she said.

'*Hoe wiet djy dat die ou in die stuk nie oek sy meisie rondklap nie?*' (How can you tell that the young man in the show would not beat up his partner?) I asked.

'*Want hy't die meisie gesê hoe sexy sy lyk in haar rok, en hy't haar laat eerste praat toe hulle gevra was watter restaurant hulle verkies het. Hy'tie eerste gepraat en sommer vir haar oek gekies'het nie. Daai's hoe'n meisie getreat moet word – met respek, nie rondgeklap word nie Dis hoe ek wil getreat word*' (Because he paid a compliment to the girl about her sexy dress, and he let the girl speak first

253

when they were asked what restaurant they preferred. He didn't reply first and make a choice on her behalf. That's the way a girl should be treated – with respect, not being slapped around, the way my boyfriend does. That's the way I want to be treated), she replied.

'Ja, is reg so' (That's right), Nazli echoed, as the other young women nodded in agreement.

Earlier, Rozelda had told us about her partner, 22-year-old Nazir, who had punched and slapped her when he discovered that she had spent the weekend in Mitchell's Plain, another township, to visit her cousin, without his permission.

'Hy't gedink dat ek 'n anner outjie da' ontmoet het, toe slat hy ve my. Waarom kan ek nie gaan waar ek wil sonder dat ek altyd ve hom moet sê nie!' (He thought that I had met another guy there, and so he beat me. Why can't I go where I want, without having to tell him?) she said in frustration.

Her critical comments had resonated with the others' concern about the high levels of interpersonal gender-based violence amongst the youth in their community. Through this TV program, they were able to envision an alternative image of dating relationships that allowed young women to express their opinions without the fear of incurring their partner's wrath. Their comments challenged the local notions of gender roles in heterosexual relations, in which physical violence went unnoticed and was often tolerated. Ultimately, however, the young women did not comment on the fact that none of the players selected partners of another race group or that, for the most part, the show's participants reinforced rather than challenged the dominant gender stereotypes about dating behaviour.

In the other popular soap opera, 'Backstage,' the storyline revolved around a group of young adults who attended a local college of performing arts and who hoped to become radio deejays, beauty queens, jazz musicians, *kwaito*[12] artists or R'n'B singers with recording contracts. The protagonists, who were drawn from diverse ethnic or racial

---

[12] *Kwaito* is a popular South African music genre that originated in the Black townships in the 1990s. It incorporates African-American rap styles with indigenous urban slang, to produce a unique musical form.

backgrounds, lived in a commune and appeared to have the available economic resources to lead independent lifestyles away from parents, parochial local communities or other family members. During their free time, they frequented a small nightclub where fashionable dress, anxious conversation about winning a recording contract or a beauty contest and cellular telephones were *de rigueur*. The characters in 'Backstage' prized apart the old notions that South Africans should live and mix only within racially homogenous communities or that Blackness automatically signifies poverty. However, the show still reinforced South African gender stereotypes quite powerfully.

The young female characters were portrayed as modern, fashionably thin, feminine yet independent career women. However, this modern, gendered stereotype was a veneer which coated the age-old, dualistic archetype of the virtuous, self-sacrificial woman and the egotistical, gold-digging harridan that ultimately informed the protagonists' central struggles. Male characters, in contrast, were portrayed either as ambitious young performing artists or streetwise rogues, looking for easy, often illegal means to enrich themselves. Like the women in the show, all embodied the height of fashionable style. All the men actively attempted to woo over partners by classical romantic means, such as extravagant attention or gifts of flowers. While this show reinforced gender stereotypes, it portrayed young men and women sharing friendships and dating across the colour line.

Interracial dating was also discussed intensely among the young women viewers in Rio Street. In another discussion that followed after we had watched the latest episode of Backstage, 16-year-old Nazli expressed distaste for dating men who were not 'coloured.' *'Ek het gehoor dat die swart outjies gewoonlik meer as een vrou wil trou'* (I've heard that these African guys usually want to marry more than one woman), she said, expressing a racial stereotype of African men commonly held in Manenberg, namely that all African men are practising polygamists.

'Wel ek sal met 'n swart outjie uitgaan of ene trou, as hy kwaai aantrek en ve my 'n goeie huis kan gie en ve my kinders sorg. Dis nie watter kleur die ou issie, ma of hy ve jou kan sorg en jou mit respek behandel!' (Well, I would date or marry an African guy, if he was smartly dressed and could provide me with a good home and provide for my children. The point is not what colour the guy

is, but whether he can provide for you and treat you with respect!), Tessa responded hotly. Nazli looked at Tessa uncertainly, but then agreed, stating, '*Ja, as hy ve jou kan sorg en nie rondmors nie, dan mak dit nie saak watter kleur hy issie.*' ('Yes, if he can provide for you and remain loyal, then colour wouldn't matter'.)

Through these discussions about the protagonists in shows like 'Backstage,' the young women were slowly chipping away at the entrenched racial boundaries in the local context, and, in so doing, were imagining gender relationships beyond the narrow choices that their mothers set out for them. At the same time, they were also writing themselves into a national, racially diverse community beyond the boundaries of Rio Street.

In programs such as 'Buzz' or 'Backstage,' adolescents were portrayed as individuals who were able to exercise choice about dress, partners, careers and sex without being influenced by the members of the local community, especially the *ordentlike moeders*. Here the most important audience for these actors was their peers who were imagined to be located everywhere, unmarked by the signifiers of economic, social or moral status except the dress styles that were associated with an imagined cosmopolitan South African youth culture. In these shows, the old sexual, moral, spatial and economic signifiers of race were being undone. Indeed race was generally represented as a free-floating, empty category in these programs, whose meanings were recreated through the individual's actions. Reconfigurations of gender, however, remained unexplored and TV characters adhered to the rigidly prescribed gender stereotypes that renovated, rather than transformed, Rio Street adolescents' ideas of appropriate gender roles. For the youthful viewers in Manenberg, the physical, economic and social spaces that separated them from the *Buzz* or *Backstage* characters were erased though televised transmission. During this time, the mothers who customarily judged personhood in the local context faded into insignificance, together with their lessons about modest, domesticated adolescent femininity, tough, nurturing motherhood or aggressive masculinity.

Access to new cultural capital through television programs freed the young women, at least temporarily, from the stifling constraints of the local social and moral norms.

These Rio Street adolescents' transformation and renovation of the local domestic and public spaces through their consumption of TV programs and popular music often inspired the more adventurous few to find their way across the city to the cosmopolitan nightclubs or trendy beachfront neighbourhoods. However, their physical and social journey into these spaces was bedevilled by the gap between their know-how of the South African cosmopolitan style and spaces and their lack of the material resources that they required actually to inhabit this world. These Rio Street adolescents often lacked the necessary economic resources to purchase expensive designer items, and sometimes their attempts to move into the trendy new spaces set them up against the constraints of personhood in the local context.

D. Imagining the new femininity

Young women in Rio Street focused mainly on the consumption of dress styles, body image and trendy spaces in the city as an indirect means to reflect their knowledge about 'modern' sexuality. However, like their male counterparts, they still had to remain cognizant of their reputations in the local context. Consequently, they invented creative means to negotiate their way between maintaining their reputations as *goeie dogters* or good daughters and exploring the styles and spaces of the new South African woman.

During my last year of research in Manenberg, I was often called upon by the young women and their parents to act as an adult chaperone to the adolescents on their visits to the beach, the local mall in Kenilworth, or to the Waterfront at night. During these visits, the young women would be transformed from modestly dressed girls with headscarves, into fashionable sophisticates, wearing the latest name-brand jeans, athletic shoes and body-hugging sweaters. Their transformation illustrated their familiarity with the cultural and sexual grammar of these cosmopolitan spaces. There they were judged individually in terms of dress and physical attributes and not as a collective member whose reputation was assessed in terms of their mother's or their household's moral reputations. Yet they disciplined their own and each other's actions in these spaces, by interacting with others as a group. A girl who transgressed this rule, by striking up

257

conversations or going off with young men on her own, faced a barrage of verbal rebukes upon her return to the group. One of the strongest rebukes she could receive was: '*Hulle sal dink djy's 'n taxi queen.*' (They'll think that you're a taxi queen.) In the local context, it was widely rumoured that the taxi queen was the young woman who obtained free transport to the trendy city nightspots from local mini-bus taxi drivers in return for sexual favours. She had broken away from all local forms of moral and sexual restraint and displayed apparent unconcern for her own moral reputation. Ultimately, she represented the extreme cost of utter moral and sexual degeneration, because she used her sexuality for individualistic, selfish motives. The courageous young women who wished to push the envelope of locally imposed norms of femininity still remained fearful of being labelled taxi queens, and the implications of this label for their individual reputations in Rio Street. This identity embodied the intergenerational tension that emerged from the contestation about gendered personhood, femininity and modesty. Unsurprisingly, young women who were labelled taxi queens were often evicted from their parental households.

I met 17-year-old Chantal about a week after she returned home to Rio Street. She had been living in Sea Point, a trendy neighbourhood on the Atlantic seaboard, for the past five months. When I met her, she was dressed in tight-fitting black jeans, a figure-hugging black sweater and a pair of high-heeled, open-backed mules. Her peroxide blonde hair was cut extremely short in the style that was fashionable among Black female kwaito stars, and she sported a set of perfectly manicured fingernails. Her sister, 19-year-old Patricia, appeared childlike and quite plain in comparison, in her loose-fitting sweatpants and plain white T-shirt. We were seated in their living room, watching Patricia feed her four-month-old son. '*Almal het gedink dat ek die een sou wies wat pregnant word*' (Everyone expected me to be the one to fall pregnant), Chantal said.

> '*Elke ou vrou in die pad het baie te sê gehad oor hoe ek aantrek, en hulle't baie te sê gehad omdat ek klubs toe gegaan het in die Kaap, mit Gavin wat die taxi ry. Ma' kyk nou wie die baba huistoe gebring het. Patricia, die stil ene, wat gemaak het soos sy gesê is, en wat heeldag in die huis gebly het. Nie ekke nie – die een wat hulle mos sê is 'n Taxi Queen. Hulle gedink dat ek dit doen met al die mans. Ek't ma net 'n lekker tyd gehad en ek het al die interessante mense van orals ontmoet.*' (Every old woman

in this road gossiped about the way I dressed and they had a fat lot to say about me going to the clubs in the city with Gavin, the taxi driver. And look who brought the baby home – Patricia, the quiet one, who did as she was told, and spent all her time indoors. Not me, the one they called the Taxi Queen. They think because I went to the clubs, I was doing it [having sex] with all the men. I was just having fun, meeting all these interesting people from everywhere.)

Patricia listened quietly to her sister's tirade. Chantal said that her father, who had ruled their home with an iron hand since their mother's death, had banned them from going out after sunset. He also refused to provide them with any pocket money for outings or for new clothes. She said that a friend took her to the clubs in Long Street and that she had a great time. After that, she stole out from home each Friday night and attended the clubs regularly. She claimed that since she had befriended Gavin he had given her a ride to the city. But she said bitterly that

'Hulle dink ek slap met Gavin sodat hy my Kaaptoe kan ry. Hulle kan nie dink dat ons net vriende issie.' (They think that I sleep with Gavin so that he will drive me to the city. They can't imagine that we're just friends.)

Chantal's father had evicted her after he had learned that she was hitching rides to the city from the local minibus taxi drivers. Gavin, the taxi driver, had offered to help her and took her to the house in Sea Point. She soon discovered that the house was owned by Rashied, the leader of the HL$ gang and that he ran an illicit drug trade from there. She said that a few other teenagers from Manenberg lived there too. An older woman in her thirties ran the house. The teenagers were expected to cut blocks of crack into smaller pieces of 'rock' for sale on the street. In return, they were given free accommodation and R800 (US$80) per week to spend. Chantal said that they enjoyed shopping for clothes at the stores in the popular Victoria and Alfred Waterfront. She said that she had learned to dress in a more fashionable manner from Mina, the housekeeper, and from watching the other young women in the club. Mina had also taught her about contraception and that's why she would never be in Patricia's situation. She had befriended some of the young white women she had met at the clubs and had learned that they too used contraceptives.

'*Hulle's nie sleg nie, alhoewel ek wiet dat al die ou vrouens hier sal dink dat hulle sleg is*' (They're not bad, even though I know that the old women here would think that they had loose morals), she said, as she remarked on the general perception of young women who dressed fashionably and attended the clubs in the city centre.

The police raided the house in Sea Point one evening. Fortunately, that day the group of teenagers had not cut up any crack and so they were all watching a video when the police arrived. All the young people were legal minors and so they were given a severe warning and escorted to their homes in Manenberg. Chantal said that her father had given her a severe beating. She said grimly, '*Ma' ek sal weer my way terug vind as alles oor is. Hy kan nie vir my hier hou nie.*' (But I'll find my way back there once the heat has died down. He can't keep me, prisoner, here.)

In order to market themselves individually, unmarked by their place of origin in Manenberg, these young men and women needed access to resources such as the expensive name-brand clothes or the cosmopolitan, hybrid spaces that enabled them to break out from the socio-economic and physical constraints of the township. In the context of a depressed national economy, young women like Chantal could only access these items or places through the friendships they formed with relatively better-off taxi drivers or powerful gangsters. While these friendships provided them with individual agency and the possibility of carving a different life-path for themselves beyond Manenberg's boundaries, they also presented them with new constraints.

Like the young Berber women in Abu-Lughod's study (1990) who desired Western-style negligees and lingerie, adolescents like Chantal were written into new, gendered and economic relations of power that subjugated them in novel ways. These relations opened up new, diverse vistas of existence that they too could desire or attain, and that would have freed them from local generational and gendered constraints. And for a very few, the meaningful and lasting friendships or relationships that they developed with young, better-off men whom they met in these nightspots may have meant the difference between a life of poverty in Manenberg and a qualitatively better one in the city's middle-class suburbs. However, these successful relationships were the exception rather than the rule. Often the young women's ability to break free permanently from the impoverished lifestyle in Manenberg was based increasingly on their educational training, their adeptness at switching linguistic codes, and their acquisition of the necessary social skills and personal style associated with their better-off peers.

More often the girls' relations with the taxi drivers and the gangsters from similar socio-economic backgrounds implicated them in activities that pushed them back into the very impoverishment they sought to escape, or new relations of gender subordination that were possibly life-threatening. They were also publicly renounced by their local peers – and sometimes found themselves outside the very networks that they had to rely on in the local context for their future material and social well-being.

E. Reconfiguring the masculine meanings of space in the local context

Like the young women who have reconfigured the meanings of domestic, living-room spaces as they consume soap operas, some adolescent men have carved out an alternative public space for themselves, in the form of the *hok* or cage, where they too are able to engage in activities and conversation beyond the reaches of the older generation. According to the local residents, *hokke* were first constructed in Manenberg in the late 1980s as some men sought to create self-employment opportunities and meet the local demand for housing. During the late 1990s, some of the large *hokke* were transformed into glamorous multi-roomed sites that usually served as local nightclubs and discotheques. They also served as the headquarters for the powerful gangs and were used as meeting-places where gang activities were discussed. In contrast, smaller *hokke* were humbler, one-roomed spaces that doubled as corner shops and as the meeting places for the smaller, less powerful gangs.

The *hok* or shack in Rio Street fell into the latter category. It was a lean-to, constructed out of a few corrugated iron sheets secured against the side-wall of the apartment block. The owner operated a small shop from a little apartment window which opened onto the *hok*. A small speaker suspended from the roof with wires connected to a radio somewhere in the apartment belted out the latest tunes on Radio Good Hope, the station that was popular for playing the latest local and international R'n'B and rap artists. The music was interspersed with deejay chatter about popular Cape Town clubs such as Dockside and the Galaxy. Since 1994, local radio stations have broadcast more news and discussions about local events on the Cape Flats and provided detailed reports about gang practices and attacks during periods of local unrest. In this way, gang activities that had been shrouded in secrecy in the past or that had gone unreported became public knowledge and gangs acquired greater notoriety.

A few arcade game machines filled the small space and appeared to be constantly occupied by young men engrossed in the flashing images on the small screens. Other young men hung out in conversational groups, sharing a cigarette or taking a swig from an illicit bottle of cheap wine. During February 1998 at the height of the gang war between the Hard Livings (HL$) and the Clever Kid$, these young men discussed the most notorious gang, the HL$ and their activities intensely, often expressing admiration for the gang's defiance and its members' ability to avoid arrest. The TV music videos and radio broadcasts of African American rap artists such as Tupac Shakur and Dr D.R.E. were extremely popular in the *hokke* of Manenberg in 1998. Tupac's lyrics about Black men's ganging practices in American inner-city neighbourhoods resonated with these young men's experiences. Invariably someone would play a tape recording of his music in the Rio Street *hok*, and everyone would sing along. Tupac's song 'Strictly for my N.I.G.G.A.Z.' was by far the most popular. The lyrics described his defiant, macho stance in the face of an unnamed opponent, a situation that many of these local men had been in. They began to refer to each other as niggaz rather than *broer* or 'brother.' Gang members also competed with each other in taking on the hand signals, gold jewellery and phrases associated with these performers. The HL$ had renamed their turf 'East Side' and painted a huge mural of Tupac Shakur on a building wall, thereby appropriating this powerful cultural image to assert their own dominance in the area, and to gain the respect of the smaller, less powerful gangs like the Young Dixie Boys of Rio Street.

The *hok*'s dual function as corner shop and as a male hang-out where gang activities were openly discussed provided a visible masculine place within the local public space. The young men's actions and conversations in this space moved the gangs' activities from the peripheries of the local community to its centre. At the same time, the gangs' secret rites of passage became a part of the public domain through the radio talk shows, and their notoriety increased, apparently with impunity. The young men of Rio Street, who had little opportunity to obtain employment, openly talked of alliances with, and membership of, the more powerful gangs as their sole means of obtaining respect in the local context. In doing so, they were relocating men's status as gangsters at the heart of masculine personhood. In the process, they challenged the senior women's power to define the public spaces as a moral sphere and destabilized their roles as the sole arbiters of personhood in the community. At the same time, they appropriated the international symbols of the rap music industry and reconstituted the gangster image to denote glamour and allure within the community rather than unfamiliarity and danger.

F. Conclusion

Throughout this book I have endeavored to show that, despite the attempts of the apartheid state to reify the meanings of colouredness through policies such as the Population Registration Act of 1959 and the Group Areas Act of 1960, coloured people situated in townships such as Manenberg, on the apartheid spatial and socio-economic periphery, created their own meanings of community and of personhood within the very social spaces and economic interstices of separation.

In the preceding chapters, I have argued that the cohesiveness of the Rio Street community, the survival of its residents and their personhood has hinged on and effloresced from the local moral economy of personhood in which the personhood of coloured adult women as *ordentlike moeders* dominated. Throughout the book, I have shown how the diverse gendered and generational modalities of being a person in this context were threaded through, entangled with and silhouetted by the ideology of respectability or *ordentlikheid* associated with the adult women's personhood as *ordentlike moeders*. I have indicated that this particular cultural ideology became dominant in the context of

Manenberg township in concert with, and partly as a result of, structural political and socio-economic factors that shaped, informed and ultimately reified the economic and spatial meanings of the racial category 'coloured' just prior to and during the apartheid era.

In chapter 2, I indicated that while the various social science discourses in conversation with the state informed the debate about the meanings of colouredness and rendered the category more fluid and indeterminate, ultimately the forced implementation of apartheid policies such as the Population Registration Act of 1959 and the Group Areas Act of 1960 set in place the processes of racial categorization and separation that reified the racial category 'coloured.' The Population Registration Act anchored colouredness within those bodies whose racial origins were ambiguous and obscure and located them politically between the racial categories white and African. The implementation of the Group Areas Act forcibly removed coloureds from the spatial core of urban power and relocated them to peripheral zones within the urban geopolitical context. Coloureds' forced removal and relocation established residential townships such as Manenberg on the inner periphery of the urban areas. As a result of these processes, coloureds were located in a subordinate racial, economic and spatial position vis-à-vis people classified as white, but held a privileged location within the hierarchy of deprivation vis-à-vis South Africans who were classified as African.

The racial reification and embodiment of the category coloured were also gendered by the Western Cape's particular location within the racialized South African political economy. South African geopolitics legislatively defined the Western Cape as a coloured labour preference area, defining coloureds as the preferred source of cheap labour within this province. The specific feminized labour needs of the Western Cape textile and canning industry economy placed coloured women in an economically powerful position within working-class communities such as Manenberg.

At the same time, the Afrikaner nationalist ideology during the apartheid era defined white masculinity as the epitome of South African personhood, thereby ideologically marginalizing coloured, African and Indian men. In addition, the coloured working class men of Manenberg were further marginalized economically by the particular gendered

264

requirements of the Western Cape economy (mentioned above) and the seasonal, impermanent nature of the manual work that was available to them. Most working-class coloured men were hired as casual employees in the construction industry or as labourers in the Cape Town docks. The decline in the South African shipping industry with the imposition of economic sanctions in the 1980s decreased labour opportunities in the docks. Similarly, unskilled and semiskilled labour opportunities in the construction industry were impermanent, increasing during the dry summer months and decreasing during the wet winter months when inclement weather conditions reduced construction. Working-class men's lack of employment opportunities resulted in a high unemployment rate amongst the men of Manenberg, and specifically Rio Street. Most men in Rio Street were permanently unemployed and unable to live up to the ideological values associated with dominant masculinity which dictated that they had to support their households economically and provide shelter for dependent women and children.

Single and unmarried men were further marginalized by the gendered biases that inhered in apartheid-era social security grants as well as public housing policy in Cape Town city. Rented accommodation for coloured households was only provided to families with mothers and dependent children. While women were provided with accommodation on the basis of motherhood, men could only obtain accommodation on the basis of marriage and not on the basis of fatherhood. Similarly, social security grants, colloquially known as child welfare grants, were provided to women as the primary, though indigent caregivers of dependent children. Social security policy considered men to be secondary to children's upbringing, rendering them ineligible to receive social security grants on their children's behalf. The public housing and social security requirements influenced household development in Manenberg, placing adult women firmly at the economic core of the household, and defining them as the key arbiters between the workplace and state institutions on the one hand and their own communities on the other. These gendered and racial outcomes of the state's population, urbanization and welfare policies together with the labour needs of the provincial economy shaped the space within which a new meaning of colouredness could emerge.

In chapter 4, I examined how Manenberg residents drew upon the above-mentioned historical and socio-economic processes to create an alternative moral universe of meaning within the everyday township spaces and quotidian social relations and discourses from which a new notion of personhood, of colouredness, emerged. By reorienting their worldview and their social interactions in relation to the alternative moral economy, buttressed by its core values of social and biological reproduction, and sustained through its associated ideology of *ordentlikheid*, Manenberg residents created and were directed toward alternative gendered lifepaths to personhood. These alternative routes to personhood recuperated a positive sense of community and mitigated the corrosive effects of the wider race-based socio-economic system in which people classified coloured were considered to be non-persons.

The alternative moral economy and its associated ideology of *ordentlikheid* or respectability hinged upon, and reverberated with, adult women's key roles as arbiters between their communities on the one hand and the workplace and the state on the other. In the context of Rio Street, this moral economy centred around the principles and practices that ensured the biological and social reproduction of households and of the community. These core principles were located in women's identities as mothers or *moeders* in the domestic sphere. The adult women reinterpreted their role as biological and social mother within their own households, reconfiguring it and renovating it with their statuses as social welfare recipients and workers to define their identities as *ordentlike moeders*. The aesthetics, practices and values of mothering effloresced outward from the domestic sphere into the township as these women performed and policed their identities of *ordentlike moeders* beyond the household. As these women performed their personhood as *ordentlike moeders*, and as they espoused and defended the values of social and biological reproduction, they actively constructed, as well as produced the ideology and discourse of *ordentlikheid*. They actively assessed, regulated and redefined township spaces and residents' personhood through the ideology and discourse of *ordentlikheid*. In this manner, the different stages of the life cycle within the local community, as well as the gendered and generational meanings that shaded these identities, were defined through and in relation to the personhood of the *ordentlike moeders*. Men were automatically defined as *goeie seuns* or good sons

266

through kinship ties to the adult women and by virtue of household membership. During adolescence and early adulthood, they were also defined as *Ouens* or streetwise men. This identity signified young men's ability to display emotional and physical toughness, as they defined and defended the geographic boundaries of their communities against the gangsters from the outside. In contrast, *ordentlike moeders* and *goeie dogters* or good daughters exhibited their personhood by their abilities to sustain their own households and the wider community through social nurturance and biological reproduction.

Women began their moral careers as *ordentlike moeders* when they bore children, ideally after they had had a *skoon troue* (a clean marriage) or more commonly when their male partners claimed responsibility for their pregnancy. The *ordentlike moeders* policed their own and the younger women's moral careers by regulating female sexuality through the moral evaluation of adolescent and adult women's dress codes, the moral codification of social space and the delimitation of female mobility within the public arena to daylight hours and thereafter primarily to the domestic space. All adolescents and adult women who wished to demonstrate their personhood as *ordentlike moeders* or *goeie dogters* were required to dress modestly and expend their energies ensuring that their households and secondly their community were socially sustained and economically supported. The adolescent women's identities as *goeie dogters* were enmeshed with and resonated with their mothers' identities as *ordentlike moeders,* as the daughters' adherence to the tenets and practices of *ordentlikheid,* in turn, demonstrated each mother's *ordentlikheid* or respectability. The cohort of *ordentlike moeders* in turn socialized the younger, adolescent women into the aesthetics, tenets and practices of respectability as they oversaw their femininity, taught them how to negotiate the bureaucratic labyrinth of the national social security system, assisted them to obtain employment in the textile industry and finally taught them how to assist other residents. As these mothers and daughters performed and demonstrated their respective *ordentlike* or respectable personhoods, the accretions of their everyday actions over time recuperated and reproduced a positive sense of community, buttressed by and anchored in the moral principle of the social and biological reproduction of persons.

In contrast to the life-giving and nurturing qualities of women's personhood, adult men's identities in Manenberg were defined by their ability to display emotional and physical toughness. Structural factors such as unemployment and legislated racial discrimination prevented these men from realizing the expected goals of dominant masculinity, namely the material ability to support a household. Instead of historical familiarity with, and experiences of, the processes of racial exclusion from the bastions of masculinity throughout coloured men's lifecycle, exposed emotional and physical toughness as the quintessential quality of masculinity. This quality was embodied in the local phrase *sterk bene* or 'strong bones' and was displayed in diverse ways in different male persons through the lifecycle.

The toughening-up process began in middle to late adolescence, as young men sought recognition as *Ouens* or streetwise men within the context of the local street gang. Usually, these young men had dropped out of school and were eager to show that they were no longer children who had no agency. These young men required the necessary emotional and physical courage and toughness to participate in the violence that was associated with the activities of the street gangs. These youth demonstrated their claims to male personhood to their fellow gang members when they first established their emotional and physical toughness as they stoically withstood the severe physical beatings meted out to them during their initiation into the gang. As they performed their identities as *Ouens*, these young men's ganging practices articulated with the *ordentlike moeders* actions in three key ways.

First, through their often violent ganging aesthetics and practices, they demarcated the physical and social boundaries of the local geographical and social community which defined the local space in which the *ordentlike moeders* authority to identify and sustain persons was recognized and respected. Secondly, the *Ouens* also ensured that their young women partners confined their mobility to the spaces within the local community, often by threatening them or physically beating them when they moved beyond its set boundaries. In this manner they limited these women's contact with men from outside, preventing them from learning about the local *Ouens* ganging activities and thereby ensuring their safety and security. Finally, these *Ouens* also ensured that the successive generation of *moeders* remained anchored within the local community, thereby securing its social, economic and physical maintenance and continuity. Their personhood, embodied in the ideal of the *Ou* or the streetwise man, also enabled them to acquire the wisdom to distinguish between men who were identified as members of the local community and those who threatened its existence. It also implied that they were able to discern young male residents' actions within the local community that exploited its resources while threatening its moral integrity. The *Ouens* together with the *moeders* identified these transgressors and defined them as *skollies* or thugs, whom the *Ouens* punished for their infractions. While men's violent actions as gangsters were necessary to demarcate the boundaries of the local community, they were also antithetical to the life-enhancing principles at the heart of the moral economy. Their ganging practices were therefore directed at other men who originated from or resided in the spaces beyond the geographic, temporal and spatial limitations of the community. The *Ouens* were only recognized or identified as gangsters by those who existed outside the ambit of the moral economy.

Once young men had established their personhood as *Ouens*, they usually progressed to the next stage of personhood in the lifecycle, namely fatherhood. During this stage in the lifecycle, men's actions temporarily came into conflict with those of the adult *moeders*. The conflict between these two close allies occurred as the young men secured access to the one central resource, namely young women's sexuality, that signified and sustained the adult women's personhood as *ordentlike moeders*.

Most young women claimed that their male partners began pressuring them for sex after they had been dating for a prolonged period of time, usually one to two years. The men's demands placed the young women in a dilemma. The young women were reluctant to use contraception because birth control was frowned upon as a sign of immorality or promiscuity and perceived as a threat to the reproductive impetus that ensured the continuity of the community. Yet these young women were also unsure about bearing children early. When a young woman's pregnancy was confirmed, her ambivalence about childbearing increased as she was filled with shame for bringing her mother's character and her household into disrepute. However, the ambivalence was quickly dispersed when the young father claimed responsibility for

269

the pregnancy, thereby rescuing the young woman's, her mother's and her household's reputation.

Once a young woman had established that she was pregnant, a young man established his transition to fatherhood by claiming responsibility for the pregnancy by paying a formal visit to her parents to *ga't sê* or go tell. During this visit, the young man apologized to the woman's parents, specifically to her mother for bringing her household into disrepute. He pledged to honour the young woman and the unborn child by promising to assume responsibility for them. Often the young man was accompanied by his mother during his visit, as a further sign of his honourable intentions. At this point in his life, the young man's identity as an *Ou* was performed alongside and in tandem with his new identity as a father, thereby enhancing his personhood as an adult man. His decision to accept the responsibilities of fatherhood served as a further indication of his increasing purchase on wisdom and his ability to make independent decisions expected of adults. Most young fathers sought to realize their pledge to provide material and emotional support to their partners and their children. However, structural factors such as the lack of employment opportunities for unskilled and semi-skilled men prevented them from accessing the resources to provide the requisite economic support on a constant basis. Consequently, fathers in Rio Street were faced with a yawning chasm between the cultural expectations of fatherhood and the economic realities of limited employment opportunities. Many sought to breach this gulf as they attempted to fulfil the dominant societal expectation, as well as their partners' fervent hopes that they provide the economic means to start independent households. However, economic reality dictated that most relationships in Rio Street during the early stages were conducted between partners who remained rooted within their natal households, while offspring were shuttled back and forth. Some relationships matured into independent or semi-independent households years later, as couples were able to move into their own backyard shacks, were assigned their own apartments or took over the primary responsibility for supporting a parent's household. However, most relationships fractured as men were unable to find the necessary employment to fulfil their desire to become permanent breadwinners or occupy their own households. For men as fathers the term 'strong bones' captured the bitter disappointment that they faced as they came to terms with the reality that they were unable to provide for their children or their partners on a constant basis through legal work, or that they faced the risk of imprisonment as they provided support through illegal means.

Some young men continued to struggle between periods of unemployment and the welcome respites of casual work while hanging onto the hope that they would obtain permanent employment eventually. However, many others also took the weighty decision to support themselves and their dependents through illegal gang activities such as theft or drug dealing even though they ran the risk of arrest and long-term imprisonment. In either case, these men were inevitably faced with the challenge of holding onto, and creating, alternative pathways to fatherhood while being unable to provide economic or, in the case of prisoners, even emotional support for their partners and their dependents. A few men sought to achieve recognition as fathers through religious faith and the associated institutions. These men demonstrated their strong bones through their exercise of spiritual, moral and emotional self-discipline as they fought off the temptation to earn income through illegal means while struggling through long periods of unemployment.

While men's personhood at the various stages in the lifecycle was shaped and formed by the values of emotional and physical toughness, girls' and young women's personhood was defined by their diligent adherence to the values and practices of *ordentlikheid*.

In chapter 6, I explored how girls and young women were incorporated into, and in turn incorporated, the values and practices of *ordentlikheid* as well as how they came to embody these values over time. I also examined how they negotiated their way between the outward forms and practices of local feminine propriety or *ordentlikheid* expected of them, whilst asserting some measure of agency through these practices. Through their individual agency, they subtly reconfigured the meanings of these practices of feminine propriety to their own ends, while still retaining its outward form.

However, since the onset of democracy in South Africa in 1994, the social and spatial landscape in South Africa has shifted and is more fluid. The old meanings of race and personhood have become unhinged, and the old racial hierarchy of Black deprivation, in which coloureds, and adult coloured women, in particular, were more favourably located has unravelled. Consequently, the very cultural, spatial and socio-economic pillars which the processes of racial separation produced and which anchored the moral economy in Rio Street are crumbling fast. The social processes through which persons such as *moeders* are identified in the moral economy are weakening. In turn, the certainty of the *moeders'* agency to identify, sustain and uphold other persons and households in the community is failing. At the same time, the spatial and social isolation of Rio Street is waning, as the younger generation of men and women are increasingly acquiring access to the more diverse, cosmopolitan spaces that exist beyond the social, economic and spatial reach of the *moeders* or the older generation.

Local meanings of personhood in Manenberg are being renovated and reconfigured by the male and female youth using the signifiers of global youth culture. Consumer culture par excellence enables youth to assert their membership of the new South African nation and to erase their apartheid township roots as well as the negative meanings attached to race. The emergent notions of personhood emphasize the individual's familiarity with the cosmopolitan styles and spaces of the new South Africans whose bodies are no longer anchored in specific racialized spaces or marked with ethnic accents and dress codes. The individual aim is to develop a consummate skill to manipulate space, linguistic codes, accents, dress style and attitude so that ultimately one is able to route and reroute one's roots, as it were, and consume the image of the new South African in the rainbow nation. In this manner, these youth appear to break free from archaic, racist apartheid notions of personhood in the national context, as well as moral notions of personhood in the local context. Yet whilst this emergent construction of personhood enables individual men and women to learn the skills, attitudes and styles that could free them from racial ghettoes, and cross boundaries of race and class with ease, freedom can only be had through ready access to material assets such as financial resources or transportation. The less-well-off male and female youth who reside in areas such as Manenberg write themselves into new configurations of gendered power relations as they form liaisons with powerful male gangsters in their struggle to obtain the material resources that allow them to break free from the social, economic and cultural constraints that are imposed in the local community.

Bibliography

Abu-Lughod, L. (1990) 'The romance of resistance. Tracing transformations of power through Bedouin women', *American Ethnologist*, Vol. 17, No. 1, pp. 41-55.

Abu-Lughod, L. (1993) *Writing Women's Worlds. Bedouin Stories*, Berkeley: University of California Press.

Alexander, N. (2002) *An Ordinary Country: Issues in the Transition from Apartheid to Democracy in South Africa*, Pietermaritzburg: University of Natal Press.

Arens, W. and Karp, I. (eds.) (1989) *Creativity of Power: Cosmology and Action in African Societies*, Washington DC: Smithsonian Institution Press.

Barnes, T. (2003) "Days and Bold' the fascination of soap operas for black students at the University of the Western Cape'. In: P. T. Zaleza and C. Veney (eds.) *Leisure in Urban Africa*, Trenton: Africa World Press, pp. 343 – 356.

Bickford-Smith, V., Van Heyningen, E. and Worden, N. (1999) *Cape Town in the Twentieth Century: An Illustrated History*, Cape Town: David Philip.

Boonzaaier, E. and Sharp, J. (eds.) (1988) *South African Keywords. The Uses and Abuses of Political Concepts*, Cape Town: David Philip.

Bourdieu, P. (1999) 'Structures, habitus, practices'. In: Elliot, A. (ed.) *Contemporary Social Theory*, Oxford: Blackwell Publishers.

Breckenridge, K. (1998) 'The allure of violence. Men, race and masculinity on South African goldmines 1900 – 1950', *Journal of Southern African Studies*, Vol. 24, No. 4, pp. 669-694.

Bundy, C. (1986) 'Remaking the Past: New Perspectives in South African History', Department of Adult Education and Extra-Mural Studies, University of Cape Town.

Cape Herald, 2 August 1969.

Cock, J. (1991) *Colonels and Cadres. War and Gender in South Africa*, Cape Town: Oxford University Press.

Coetzee, J. M. (2000) *Disgrace*, New York: Penguin Books.

Cohen, D. and Atieno Odhiambo, E.S. (1992) *Burying SM The Politics of Knowledge and the Sociology of Power in Africa*, London: Currey.

Comaroff, J. and Comaroff, J. (eds.) (1993) *Modernity and its Malcontents. Ritual and Power in Postcolonial Africa*, Chicago: University of Chicago Press.

Connell, R. W. (1987) *Gender and Power: Society, the Person, and Sexual Politics*. Palo Alto, CA: Stanford University Press.

Constant-Martin, D. (1999) *Coon Carnival. New Year in Cape Town*, Cape Town: David Philip.

Davenport, T. O. and Saunders, C. (2000) *South Africa: A Modern History*, London: Palgrave Macmillan.

Donham, D. (1999) *History Power Ideology. Central Issues in Marxism and Anthropology*, Berkeley: University of California Press.

Du Pre Roy, H. (1994) *Separate but Unequal: 'The Coloured' People of South Africa — A Political History*, Johannesburg: Jonathan Ball.

Field, S. (2001) 'Oral histories of forced removals'. In: S. Field (ed.) *Lost Communities, Living Memories. Remembering Forced Removals in Cape Town*, Cape Town: David Philip, pp. 11-14.

Fortes, M. (1993) 'The concept of the person'. In: G. Dieterlen (ed.) *La Notion de Personne en Afrique Noire*, Paris: Editions de Centre National de la Recherche Scientifique, pp. 283-319.

Gevisser, M. and Cameron, E. (eds.) *Defiant Desire. Gay and Lesbian Lives in South Africa*, Johannesburg: Ravan Press.

Giddens, A. (1984) *The Constitution of Society: Outline of the Theory of Structuration*, Berkeley: University of California Press.

Gilroy, P. (1987) *There Ain't No Black in the Union Jack: The Cultural Politics of Race and Nation*. Chicago: University of Chicago Press.

Gluckman, M. (ed.) (1972) *The Allocation of Responsibility*. Manchester: Manchester University Press.

Goldin, I. (1987) *Making Race: The Politics and Economics of Coloured Identity in South Africa*, London: Longman.

Goody, J. (1966) *The Developmental Cycle in Domestic Groups*, Cambridge: Cambridge University Press.

Gordimer, N. (1990) *My Son's Story*, Cape Town: David Philip.

Gramsci, A. (1971) *Selections from Prison Notebooks*, Q. Hoare and G. N. Smith (eds.) London: Lawrence and Wishart.

Guy, J. and Thabane, M. (1984). 'The Ma—Rashea. A Participant's Perspective', paper presented at the University of Witwatersrand History Workshop.

Harris, G. G. (1989) 'Concepts of individual, self and person in description and analysis', *American Anthropologist*, Vol. 91, No. 3, pp. 599-612.

Harvey, D. (1973) *Social Justice and the City*, London: Edward Arnold.

Heese, H. (1984) *Groep Sonder Grense: Die Rol en Status van die Gemengde Bevolking aan die Kaap 1652 — 1795*, Bellville: Instituut van Historiese Navorsing, Universiteit van Wes Kaapland.

Hendricks, C. (2001) "Ominous' liaisons. Tracing the interface between race and sex at the Cape'. In: Z. Erasmus (ed.) *Coloured by History. Shaped by Place*, Cape Town: Kwela Books, pp. 29-44.

Hobart, M. (1990) 'The patience of plants. A note on agency in Bali', *Review of Indonesian and Malaysian Affairs*, No. 24, pp. 90-135.

Hommel, M. (1981) *Capricorn Blues: The Struggle for Human Rights in South Africa*, Toronto: Culturama.

Hountondji, P. (2000) 'Tradition. Hinderance or inspiration?', *Prins Klaus Fund Journal*, No. 4, pp. 19-22.

Jeppie, S. (1990) 'Popular culture and carnival in Cape Town. The 1940s and 1950s'. In: Soudien, C. (ed.) *The Struggle for District Six. Past and Present*, Cape Town: Buchu Books, pp. 67-87.

Jeppie, S. (1990) 'The class, colour and gender of carnival: aspects of a cultural form in inner Cape Town c 1939 – 1959', University of Witwatersrand History Workshop.

Johnstone, F. (1976) *Class, Race and Gold. A Study of Class Relations and Racial Discrimination in South Africa*, Lanman, Md: University Press of America.

Karis, T. and Carter, G. (eds.) (1972) *From Protest to Challenge: A Documentary History of African Politics in South Africa 1882 — 1964*, Johannesburg: The Federation.

Karp, I. (1995) 'Agency, agency, who's got agency?', Paper presented at the meeting of the American Anthropological Association, Washington D.C., November.

Kinnes, I. (2000) *From Urban Gangs to Criminal Empires. The Changing Face of Gangs in the Western Cape.* Pretoria: Institute of Security Studies, Series 48.

Koen, C. (1997) 'A socio-demographic profile of Manenberg residents and a summary of the key problems the community face', unpublished manuscript, University of the Western Cape.

Kondo, D. K. (1990) *Crafting Selves. Power, Gender and Discourses of Identity in a Japanese Workplace*, Chicago: Chicago University Press.

Kratz, C. (1991) 'Amusement and absolution: transforming narratives during confession of social debts', *American Anthropologist*, Vol. 93, No. 4, pp. 826 — 851.

Kratz, C. (1994) *Affecting Performance Meaning, Movement and Experience in Okiek Women's Initiation*, Washington D.C.: Smithsonian Institution Press.

Kratz, C. (2000) 'Forging unions and negotiating ambivalence: personhood and complex agency in Okiek marriage arrangement'. In: I. Karp and D. A. Masolo (eds.) *African Philosophy as Critical Inquiry*, Bloomington: Indiana University Press, pp. 136-171.

La Guma, A. (1964) *And a Threefold Cord*, London: Kliptown.

Lemon, A. (1991) *Homes Apart: South Africa's Segregated Cities*, Cape Town: David Philip.

Lewis, G. (1987) *Between the Wire and the Wall. A History of South African 'Coloured' Politics*, Cape Town: David Philip.

Lewis, J. (2000) *A Normal Daughter. The Life and Times of District Six*, (Video-recording) Cape Town: Idol Pictures.

Lund, F. (1996) 'Report of the Lund Committee on Child and Family Support', Pretoria: Department of Welfare.

Macmillan, W. M. (1968) *The Cape Coloured Question: A Historical Survey*, Cape Town: A. A. Balkema.

Magona, S. (1992) *Forced to Grow*, Claremont: David Philip.

Marais, J. S. (1937) *The Cape Coloured People 1652 — 1937*, London: Longmans.

Marks, S. and Trapido, S. (eds.) (1987) *The Politics of Race, Class and Nationalism in Twentieth Century South Africa*, London: Longman.

Mattera, D. (1987) *Memory is the Weapon*, Johannesburg: Ravan Press.

Mda, Z. (2007) *The Madonna of Excelsior*, Oxford: Oxford University Press.

Morrell, R. (2001) 'The time of change: men and masculinity in South Africa'. In: Morrell, R. (ed.) *Changing Men in Southern Africa*, London: Zed Press.

Murray, C. (1981) *Families Divided. The Impact of Migrant Labour in Lesotho*, Johannesburg: Ravan Press.

Oyewumi, O. (1997) *The Invention of Women. Making African Sense of Western Gender Discourses*, Minneapolis: University of Minnesota Press.

Patterson, S. (1953) *Colour and Culture in South Africa: A Study of the Status of the Cape Coloured People within the Social Structure of the Union of South Africa*, London: Routledge Paul.

Paulse, M. (2001) "Everyone had their differences but there was always comradeship' Tramway Road Seapoint 19208 — 1961'. In: S. Field (ed.) *Lost Communities, Living Memories. Remembering Forced Removals in Cape Town*, Cape Town: David Philip, pp. 44-61.

Pickel, B. (1997) 'Coloured ethnicity and identity: a case study in the former coloured areas of the Western Cape South Africa', *Demokratie und Entwicklung*, Series No. 28.

Pinnock, D. (1984) *The Brotherhoods: Street Gangs and State Control in Cape Town*, Cape Town: David Philip.

Plaatjie, S. (1969) *Native Life in South Africa before and since the European War and the Boer Rebellion*, New York: Negro University Press.

Platzky, L. and Walker, C. (1985) *The Surplus People: Forced Removals in South Africa*, Johannesburg: Ravan Press.

Ranger, T. O. (1985) *Peasant Consciousness and Guerrilla War in Zimbabwe*, Harare: Zimbabwe Publishing House.

Rive, R. (1988) *Emergency: a Novel*, Cape Town: David Philip.

Rosaldo, R. (1980) *Ilongot Headhunting 1883 — 1974. A Study in Society and History*, Stanford: Stanford University Press.

Ross, R. (1999) *Status and Respectability in the Cape Colony 1750 — 1870. A Tragedy of Manners*, Cambridge: Cambridge University Press.

Saunders, C. (1988) *The Making of the South African Past: Major Historians on Race and Class*, Cape Town: David Philip.

Schapera, I. (1967) *Western Civilization and the Natives of South Africa. Studies in Culture Contact*, London: Routledge Kegan Paul.

Scharf, W. (1986) 'Street gangs, survival and political consciousness in the eighties', Paper presented at Western Cape Roots and Realities Conference, 16 — 18 July, University of Cape Town.

Shell, R. (1994) *Children of Bondage: A Social History of the Slave Society at the Cape of Good Hope, 1652 – 1838*, Johannesburg: Witwatersrand University Press.

Simons, J. and Alexander, R. (1983) *Class and Colour in South Africa 1850 — 1950*, Harmondsworth: Penguin.

South African Institute of Race Relations (2000). *South Africa Survey 2000*. Roosevelt Park: South African Institute of Race Relations.

Spivak, G.C. (1990) *The Post-Colonial Critic: Interviews, Strategies, Dialogues*, New York: Routledge.

Stack, C. (1997) *All Our Kin: Strategies for Survival in a Black Community*, New York: Harper and Row.

Statistics South Africa (1996). 'The People of South Africa. Census 1996', Pretoria: Statistics South Africa, *Report no. 03-01-26*.

Steinberg, J. (2005) *The Number: One Man's Search for Identity in the Cape Underworld and Prison Gangs*, New York: Jonathan Ball.

Stone, G. L. (1991) 'An ethnographic and socio-semantic analysis of lexis among working class Afrikaans—speaking coloured adolescent and young adult males in the Cape Peninsula 1963 — 1990'. M.A. Thesis, Department of Psychology, University of Cape Town.

Swanson, F. and Harries, J. (2001) "Ja, So was District Six! But it was a beautiful Place.' Oral Histories, Memory and Identity'. In: Field, S. (ed.) *Lost Communities, Living Memories. Remembering Forced Removals in Cape Town*, Claremont: David Philip, pp. 62-80.

Theron, E. (1976) 'The Theron Commission Report. A Summary of the findings and Recommendations of the Commission of Enquiry into Matters Relating to the Coloured Population Group', Johannesburg: South African Institute of Race Relations.

Tobias, P. (1961) 'The Meaning of Race', A Lecture Given to Inaugurate a Seminar on Man, Johannesburg: South African Institute of Race Relations.

Van der Ross, R. E. (1973) 'A political and social history of the Cape coloured people 1880-1970', Incomplete Thesis, University of Cape Town.

Van Onselen, C. (1985) 'Crime and total institutions in the making of modern South Africa. The life of Nongoloza Mathebula 1867 — 1948', *History Workshop Journal*, pp. 62-81.

Western, J. (1981) *Outcast Cape Town*, Cape Town: Human Rosseau.

Whyte, S.R. (1997). *Questioning Misfortune: The Pragmatics of Uncertainty in Eastern Uganda (Vol. 4)*. Cambridge: Cambridge University Press.

Wicomb, Z. (1987) *You Can't Get Lost in Cape Town*, London: Virago.

Williams, R. (1977) *Marxism and Literature*, Oxford: Oxford University Press.

Wilson, F. and Ramphele, M. (1989) *Uprooting Poverty: The South African Challenge*, Cape Town: David Philip.

Wilson, M. H. (1936) *Reaction to Conquest: Effects of the Contact with Europeans on the Pondo of South Africa*, London: Oxford University Press.

Wilson, M. H. and Thompson, L. (1969) *The Oxford History of South Africa*, Oxford: Clarendon Press.

Wolpe, H. (1988) *Race, Class and the Apartheid State*, London: James Currey.

Worden, N. (1989) 'Slavery and post-emancipation reconstruction in the Western Cape'. In W. James (ed.) *The Angry Divide. Social and Economic History of the Western Cape*, Cape Town: David Philip, pp. 31-39.

Yawitch, J. (1981) *Betterment: The Myth of Homeland Agriculture*, Johannesburg: South African Institute of Race Relations.

A Tribute:
Elaine Rosa Salo (1962-2016)

Kelly Gillespie
Department of Anthropology and Sociology,
University of the Western Cape

Elaine Rosa Salo Born: June 20, 1962 in Kimberley, South Africa. Died: August 13, 2016, in Newark, Delaware, USA, aged 54

Southern African Anthropology lost a lodestar last year. The death of Professor Elaine Rosa Salo on August 13, 2016 in Delaware, United States of America, has been met with deep mourning from scholars and activists from all over the world, and especially from across our continent. She died at 54-years old after two major battles with cancer over sixteen years. Elaine's passing resonated intensely in the communities of African feminists and Gender Studies scholars in whose company she spent most of her professional life. But while Elaine identified her work in the tradition of African and Black feminisms, it was always informed by her training in anthropology. A commitment to anthropology in method and in theme was an important part of her life's work. It is for us not only to celebrate the legacy of her ethnographic work, but also to reflect on the place of our discipline in Elaine's career, how it mattered that her thinking and action were informed by anthropology. This includes confronting the significant question as to why Elaine chose to spend so much of her working life outside of anthropology departments. In the spirit of Elaine's searing commitment to truth-telling, it is important to speak frankly and in the clearest possible terms, about her experience of South African universities, and of anthropology in particular.

Elaine was born in Kimberly in 1962, the daughter of the late Rosa and Edgar Salo. Rosa was a primary school teacher in schools in the urban and rural areas around Kimberly. Edgar earned his living as a bricklayer, but was also an outstanding musician, giving his daughter a life-long love of music, especially jazz. Elaine attended the William Pescod School in Kimberly, doing sufficiently well to gain entry into the University of Cape Town (UCT) in 1980, where she completed her undergraduate and Honours degrees in anthropology. The choice to attend UCT was not an easy one. Her elder brother, Bertram, was attending the University of the Western Cape (UWC), the historically 'Coloured' university in Cape Town, that had been opened through the apartheid state's Extension of University Education Act, Act 45 of 1959, which fortifyied racial segregation in higher education. Bertram's life at UWC was caught up in the intensity of anti-apartheid student movement politics, which at UWC in the 1970s had been given fresh impetus by the Black Consciousness Movement. It was decided that Elaine and her brother Ken would be sent to UCT for their studies, gaining entrance through the racial quota system by which historically white universities were maintained as such.

Being a young black woman 'tokenised' at the elite white university during the height of apartheid rule was a deeply alienating experience. Elaine realised at once that UCT was not remotely a place made to welcome her. This was perhaps most forcefully demonstrated by not being allowed to live at UCT's residences, which were in designated White Group Areas of Cape Town. The university did not see it fit to break this law in order to support its black students. Elaine mitigated UCT's institutional racism through her involvement in political work beyond the university. She joined the United Women's Organisation launched in the Western Cape in 1981, which joined forces with the Women's Front in 1986, to become the United Women's Congress, an important organisation in the United Democratic Front. Elaine worked in community and church-based movements on the Cape Flats. In particular she began connecting with women active in church work in Manenberg, women who were sustaining black community life in the thick of the apartheid regime's racial violence. This experience of community-based political work set the terms not only for Elaine's politics and intellectual commitments, but also for her future research site. She recognised in black working-class women a capacity for care and world-making in the face of terrible life conditions, a capacity that became both her long-term research interest and a foundational impulse towards a life-long commitment to feminism.

Elaine described how she had to resist becoming what she called a 'native informant' in the UCT anthropology department. Archie Mafeje, decades earlier in the same department, had described the same phenomenon. She learned fast the treachery of elitist academic practice through her experience of moving between activist work in township and academic life in the white suburbs. This discrepancy gave her a sharp distaste for the hallowed halls of the academy, even as she loved the ideas and the learning they offered. Anthropology, and in particular ethnographic methods, gave her some space within the academy to traverse this uncomfortable distance, but she had to invent a manner in which to conduct her research that did not trade in intellectual expropriation and the objectification of township lives she cared deeply about and felt part of. She was to find resources for this new ethnography in feminist praxis.

Elaine was particularly aggrieved by the UCT Anthropology Department when she was told by some of her lecturers that she was not of the right 'caliber' for postgraduate studies. True to spirit, Elaine went ahead and acquired scholarships to complete an MA degree in International Development at Clark University in Massachusetts, USA in 1986, and a PhD in Anthropology at Emory University in Georgia, USA in 2004. She returned to South Africa with a well-regarded dissertation, the basis of this book, titled 'Respectable mothers, tough men and good daughters: Making persons in Manenberg township, South Africa' (Salo, 2004).

Manenberg became the centre of much of Elaine's writing and thinking. She was a committed ethnographer, seeing the discipline as a way to stay close to the lives of people on the margins of Cape Town and of South African society. She cared deeply about the people with whom she conducted research, about how she represented those lives, and what became of them over almost twenty years. Her research was a way of being in the world, a willingness to become entailed in the lives of others, to share her energies and resources, and to live her life open to the pleasures and complications such an entailment obliges. She called this entailment 'co-existence with our interlocutors', insisting that we recognise a 'shared geopolitical space in which the field is home' (Salo, 2015). *The field as home.* The implications of that formulation shake the foundation of anthropology. As her colleague and friend Terri Barnes explained, 'Elaine cared so much about getting all this right that her Manenberg masterpiece was never finished' (Barnes, 2016).

But she did leave us with an archive of published writing and recordings about her Manenberg work (Salo, 2014; Salo, 2009; Salo, 2007b; Salo, 2007c; Salo, 2002; Salo, 2003; Salo and Davids 2009), as well as other feminist writings (Salo, 1999; Salo 2005; Salo, Ribas, Lopes and Zamboni, 2010; Salo and Fauke, 1998; Kemp, Madlala, Moodley, Salo, 1995), a series of editorial introductions to the journals *Feminist Africa* and *Agenda*, published interviews with African feminists (Salo, 2013b; Salo and Mama, 2001), reflections on research and writing (Salo, 2015; Salo, 2010a; Salo, 2010b; Salo, 2008; Salo, Liersch, Mohlakoana-Motopi, Maree, 2014), and a set of popular pieces on contemporary politics (Salo, 2016; Salo, 2013a; Salo, Achmat, Jacobs, 2003). In a broad review of the history of *Agenda*, the feminist journal she edited, Elaine pointed to how much of the writing on women in the apartheid system lent itself to broad theorisations of gender rather than to careful attention to the lives of the women being discussed. She writes of Hilda Bernstein's 1975 discussion of rural women in Bantustans,

> Bernstein's narrative placed the marginalisation of black women squarely at the centre of her analysis as she explained the gendered effects of the apartheid state's Bantustan policies on their lives. However, her text also rendered black, rural women's daily acts of subversion and their subjective experiences invisible…. That African women in particular were the apparently silent subjects of these analyses seemed relatively unproblematic. (Salo, 2007, p. 190)

It is to African women *in particular*, in all their complex unromantic, heroic, daily specificities, that Elaine attended. This was what brought her intersectional feminist and ethnographic practice together: an attention to the lived and composite experiences of women, and also men and queer people and old people and teenagers, living in the violent afterlife of the apartheid project. 'Ultimately,' Elaine writes, 'it is only by zooming in on the social spaces… by examining the local conceptions of personhood and morality extant in these social spaces, and how these are influenced by gender and age, that one is able to understand [them]' (Salo, 2002, p. 404). It was through the very anthropological concepts of personhood and morality that she found ways to show how life in Manenberg could never be represented with a singular subject nor a singular narrative. In Elaine's writing, Manenberg mothers could find the dignity to hold their families together in the toughest of corners, but wield that very same dignity as a means of humiliating their daughters. The intensity of relational life, always in the process of negotiation, always creative of ways of living, ways of coping, ways of generating 'alternative moral world[s]' (Salo, 2007c) and 'alternative local meaning[s] of personhood' (Salo, 2002), were what she was most compelled to examine.

Her own life experience, as well as the attention she gave to the lives of people living in some of the poorest areas of Cape Town's peripheries, kept Elaine's suspicion of the elitism of the academy very sharp indeed. She refused the kind of academic practice that exists for its own sake, that works as a means of gatekeeping and sustaining privilege. And, in so doing, she kept reminding us of the immense work still to be done to make South African universities livable for black people.

I am mindful of an email I wrote long years ago to then dean Paula Ensor, that UCT was as much a Bantustan institution as UNITRA, Turfloop and now Walter Sisulu...caught up as much in its own parochial triumphalisms of WASPish practices…. [W]e were all apparently blind to these contextual histories, aspiring only to be one of the few goldfish to be let into the fishbowl… despite Mamdani's warnings about such settler mentality and with that of course, its own mean, cruel violence against the quickly infiltrating Other and sometimes even its Own…. I recall Sam Radithlalo and I making a habit of literally yelling *Hoezits* as loudly as we possibly could across the deathly white silence that was University Avenue, and Sinfree Makoni resolutely refused to remove his township style Sporty [cap] in meetings. He wore that Sporty, just so, jauntily, defiantly at an angle on his head as if to mark himself as a body out of place. Even Francis Nyamnjoh faithfully continued to translate such unspeakable cruelty of the unseeing, deaf structure, into international journals as recently as the late 2000s. For a while, I refused to speak anything other than *Kaaps* in the corridors of the AGI [African Gender Institute], whilst recognising the anger on the faces of other colleagues who have since left, to become published renowned poets, social scientists and such in global corridors of the academy. It is as if we were not good enough, until we had 'proven ourselves' in the Civilizing North, and even then, even then, we just about managed to get our foot in the door. Thank the ancestors for the connectedness with those workers, cleaners, whose abject bodies reminded us on a daily basis of origins and of the need for dignity even to the most menial in that place (Kriger, 2017).

I heard Elaine remark once that it was trying to survive the South African university, and that it was worrying about other black women's capacity to survive it, that made her sick. After her first round of cancer treatment, I think she found a way to direct her anger into joyful, life-affirming action. She had an intense commitment to mentoring students, particularly to seeing black women through the viciousness of university life and into their own careers and writing. So many young black women have spoken of Elaine as a mentor, and told stories of how she would offer the kind of intergenerational care that would ease them through the worst moments of their degrees (Machirori, 2016). She poked fun at the ridiculous pomp, and self-aggrandising of the academy. She tried to make us laugh at ourselves – her wicked humour was infectious and shocking in its honesty. Her generosity was legendary, always opening her home, bringing an ease, a comfort, to academic spaces and relationships, and between people from very different social spaces (Jacobs, 2016). She connected people with each other. She connected people with ideas. And at the centre of that project of connection, of joyful connection, was the work of building a world in which the violence of hierarchy is dismantled. All the time she put herself forward as an example of how to live differently, how to care about the things that matter, how to show up in the project of building an alternative world.

Elaine drew much of her resources for remaining in the academy from conversations with colleagues in other parts of the continent and the global south, colleagues who had a more sophisticated understanding of the tasks of decolonising knowledge practice than existed in South African universities. From many conversations with colleagues at CODESRIA in Senegal (Salo, 2012), Mozambique and Kenya, Brazil and Peru, Elaine blended a feminist praxis with Africanist and southern theorisation and with local black thought. She was doing this well before the student movement of 2015 forced decolonisation debates onto the agenda of universities. In 2013, Elaine wrote a searing popular piece that showed her prescience in matters that the South African academy was so very slow to understand. Arguing against what she called 'scholarly parochialism', she wrote,

> The feminist tradition I was introduced to drew on the works of European feminists such as Simone De Beauvoir, Emma Goldman, Alexandra Kollontai, Virginia Wolfe and contemporary North American Cynthia Enloe, Catherine McKinnon and Mary Daly. None of these women, however, engaged with race or the intersectional identities of

women of colour. African-American feminists such as Sojourner Truth, Audre Lorde, bell hooks and Elizabeth Spelman resonated more profoundly with my own experiences as they insisted upon the recognition of racism in shaping black femininities and black women's struggles.

However, it was both personal experience in the anti-apartheid women's struggle and through reading South African women such as Olive Schreiner, Charlotte Maxeke, Fatima Meer, Emma Mashinini, Jacky Cock, Isobel Hofmeyer, Jenny Schreiner, Phyllis Ntantala, Ellen Kuzwayo, Zoe Wicomb and more recently, Mmatshilo Motsei, that I knew I had come home. I was enriched by the doyennes of a homegrown South African feminist tradition that takes account of women's race, social statuses, geographies, sexualities and personal histories.

In the anti-apartheid women's struggle I was inspired by the pragmatic maternal feminism of women such as Albertina Sisulu, the women in the Black Sash and the more radical activist feminist tradition of Elizabeth van der Westhuizen and Emma Mashinini in the educational sector and trade union tradition. I continue to draw inspiration from a veritable continent of African feminist thinkers living and writing on a continent that many South African scholars located exclusively within the Eurocentric tradition barely know of, or whom they often dismiss. They are poorer for imagining this intellectual tradition as being so shallow as to dismiss it or so primitive and backward that it had no history before the arrival of the Europeans.

The canon of African male intellectuals in the social sciences such as Franz Fanon, Amilcar Cabral, Samir Amin, Archie Mafeje, Ben Magubane, Paulin Hontoundji, Thandika Mkandiwire, Mahmoud Mamdani, Ebrima Sall, Adebayo Olukushi and Paul Zaleza would barely get a mention in many curricula, while African feminists would receive the merest whisper. Those scholars who ignore these intellectual traditions from the continent are deserving of pity because they deny themselves the joy of discovering other humanistic traditions. The scary part is that they are let loose to teach young people' (Salo, 2013a).

In truth, anthropology in South Africa was not ready for Elaine, not even by the time she died. And she was certainly not given the support to think and write us into the new directions she intuited. She should have been able to use her considerable writing skill to experiment with a kind of ethnographic writing that created vast space for new thinking on our practice, opened paths for new ways of being an anthropologist and for writing the lives of others. In her last years, the most beautiful words flew from her, many of them in extraordinary Facebook posts that spoke of a writer able to blend academic prowess and politics with astute self-awareness and deep compassion. It was a new kind of non-fiction writing that drew on the best of Elaine. That her life was cut short by cancer just as she was opening into a new phase of her writing is an awful cost to our discipline and our collective scholarship. We will not have the pleasure of responding to the moves and willful provocations (Ahmed, 2014) that Elaine would have made in her later years, the integration of the many threads of her thinking and her life's work. We are poorer for it. But, perhaps, we are now beginning to confront the kinds of questions she has been asking all along, that our discipline and our universities have been too stubborn or too scared to acknowledge.

We should reflect deeply on the fact that our departments were too stuck in old paradigms and institutional cultures to be able to hold a life and career as fierce and forward-looking as Elaine's. For so many years she brought questions and critiques that were too easily avoided, critiques that only came to find their necessary force during the recent student movement protests, which she supported even through her last cancer treatment and from so far away. We can no longer afford to avoid Elaine's questions. I hear her voice now, high and strong, full of *Kaaps*, and full of faith in the possibility of another way of learning, of knowing, of teaching, of living. I hope we can live up to that faith.

References

Ahmed, S. (2014) *Willful Subjects*, Durham: Duke University Press.

Barnes, T. (2016) 'Elaine is…'. *Mail & Guardian Thought Leader*.
http://thoughtleader.co.za/terribarnes/2016/08/22/elaine-salo-is/

Jacobs, S. (2016) 'The Year of Elaine Salo', *Africa is a Country*, December 31. http://africasacountry.com/2016/12/year-of-elaine-salo/

Kemp, A., Madlala, N., Moodley, A. and Salo, E. (1995) 'The dawn of a new day: redefining South African feminism'. In: A. Basu (ed.) *The*

Challenge of Local Feminisms: Women's Movements in Global Perspective, Boulder: Westview Press, pp. 131–162.

Kriger, R. (2017) 'Lest we Forget III — Decolonisation ... of What?', Robert Krige Facebook, April 3.
https: //www.facebook.com/robert.kriger.9/posts/1429178507134722

Lewis, D., and E. Salo. (1993) 'Birth control, contraception and women's rights in SA: A Cape Town case study', *Agenda*, No. 17, pp. 59–68.

Machirori, F. (2016) 'Rest in Love, Dear Elaine Rosa Salo', *FungaiNeni: Contemporary Thought and Analysis*.
https: //fungaineni.net/2016/08/14/rest-in-love-dear-elaine-rosa-salo/

Salo, E. (1999) 'From Woman to Women: Feminist Theory and the Diverse Identities of South African Feminists'. In: Prah, K.K. (ed.) *Knowledge in Black and White: The Impact of Apartheid on the Production and Reproduction of Knowledge*, Cape Town: Centre for Advanced Studies of African Society.

Salo, E. (2002) 'Condoms are for spares, not the besties: negotiating adolescent sexuality in post-apartheid Manenberg', *Society in Transition*, Vol. 33, No. 3, pp. 403–419.

Salo, E. (2003) 'Negotiating gender and personhood in the new South Africa: adolescent women and gangsters in Manenberg township on the Cape Flats', *European Journal of Cultural Studies*, Vol. 6, No. 3, pp. 345–365.

Salo, E. (2004) 'Respectable mothers, tough men and good daughters: producing persons in Manenberg Township, South Africa', unpublished PhD dissertation, Emory University.

Salo, E. (2005) 'Multiple targets, mixing strategies: complicating feminist analysis of contemporary South African women's movements', *Feminist Africa*, No. 4.
http: //agi.ac.za/sites/agi.ac.za/files/fa_4_ standpoint_1.pdf

Salo, E. (2007a) 'Gendered citizenship, race and women's differentiated access to power in the New South Africa', *Agenda*, No. 72, pp. 187–196.

Salo, E. (2007b) 'Mans is ma soe: ganging practices in Manenberg, South Africa, and the ideologies of masculinity, gender, and generational relations'. In: E.G. Bay, and D.L. Donham (eds.) *State of Violence:*

Politics, Youth, and Memory in Contemporary Africa, Charlottesville: University of Virginia Press, pp. 148–178.

Salo, E. (2007c) 'Social construction of masculinity on the racial and gendered margins of Cape Town'. In: T. Shefer, K. Ratele, A. Strebel, N. Shabalala, and R. Buikema (eds.) *From Boys to Men: Social Constructions of Masculinity in Contemporary Society*, Cape Town: UCT Press, pp. 160–180.

Salo, E. (2008) 'Women in the academy'. In: G. Ruiters (ed.) *Gender Activism: Perspectives on the South African Transition, Institutional Cultures and Everyday Life*, Grahamstown: Institute of Social and Economic Research, Rhodes University, pp. 202–213.

Salo, E. (2009) 'Coconuts do not live in townships: cosmopolitanism and its failures in the urban peripheries of Cape Town', *Feminist Africa*, No. 13, pp. 11–21.

Salo, E. (2010a) 'Beyond equity committees and statistics'. In: D.L. Featherman, M. Hall, and M. Krislov (eds.) *The Next Twenty-Five Years: Affirmative Action in Higher Education in the United States and South Africa*, Ann Arbor: University of Michigan Press, pp. 297–309.

Salo, E. (2010b) 'Men, women, temporality and critical ethnography in Africa — the imperative for a transdisciplinary conversation', *Anthropology Southern Africa* Vol. 33, No. 3&4, pp. 93–102.

Salo, E. (2012) 'African governance and gender: from a politics of representation to a politics of transformation', *YouTube* video, 8: 23, posted by CODESRIA, on August 1.
https://www.youtube.com/watch?v=IEByVhozVYg

Salo, E. (2013a) 'Lessons in race and African feminism', *IOL*, September 8.
http://www.iol.co.za/sundayindependent/lessons-in-race-and-african-feminism-1574641

Salo, E. (2013b) 'Sylvia Tamale Talks to Elaine Salo', *Agenda*, Vol. 27, No. 4, pp. 65–68.

Salo, E. (2014) 'Lecture by Elaine Salo at NAI', The Nordic Africa Institute.
http://nai.uu.se/news/articles/2014/06/04/160927/index.xml

Salo, E. (2015) 'Autobiography and the research context: a reflection on unbecoming the 'native' anthropologist'. In: S. van Schalkwyk and P. Gobodo-Madikizela (eds.) *A Reflexive Inquiry into Gender Research:*

Towards a New Paradigm of Knowledge Production and Exploring New Frontiers of Gender Research in Southern Africa, Newcastle-upon-Tyne: Cambridge Scholars, pp. 171–188.

Salo, E. (2016) "Caster Semenya — the ancients would have called her God': the international re-imagining and remaking of sex and the art of silence'. In: S. Montañola, and A. Olivesi (eds.) *Gender Testing in Sport: Ethics, Cases and Controversies*, New York: Routledge, pp. 150–167.

Salo, E., Achmat, Z. and Jacobs, S. (2003) 'Black gays and mugabes — a conversation', *Chimurenga*, No. 4, pp. 26–30.

Salo, E., and A. Mama. (2001) 'Talking about Feminism in Africa', *Agenda*, No. 50, pp. 58–63.

Salo, E., and B. Davids (2009) 'Glamour, glitz and girls: the meanings of femininity in high school matric ball culture in urban South Africa'. In: M.

Steyn, and M. van Zyl (eds.) *The Prize and the Price: Shaping Sexualities in South Africa*, Cape Town: HSRC Press, pp. 39-54.

Salo, E., and C. Fauke. (1998) 'Perms, patriarchy and politics: women's issues in the 1999 general elections', In: *Women and Democracy in South Africa*, Commission for Gender Equality.

Salo, E., Ribas, M., Lopes, P. and Zamboni, M. (2010) 'Living our lives on the edge: power, space and sexual orientation in Cape Town townships, South Africa', *Sexuality Research and Social Policy* Vol. 7, No. 4, pp. 298–309.

Salo, E.R., Liersch, F., Mohlakoana-Motopi, L. and Maree, M. (2014) 'Carrots or sticks? A study on incentives to attract and retain women in science, engineering and technology in South Africa' In: B. Thege, S. Popescu-Willigmann, R. Pioch, and S. Badri-Höher (eds.) *Paths to Career and Success for Women in Science: Findings from International Research*, Wiesbaden: Springer, pp. 163–191.

www.ingramcontent.com/pod-product-compliance
Lightning Source LLC
Chambersburg PA
CBHW060027030426
42334CB00019B/2214